praise for *Pig City*

'Every city needs a book like this, that gathers a couple of decades of the rock scene and places it in the town's cultural and political context. Brisbane is lucky Andrew did this and did it so well.' **Robert Forster**

'*Pig City* burst onto the literary landscape like a meteor: unexpected, urgent and HOT … Many have attempted to follow the model of academic rigour blended with lively prose and timely memoir, but few have succeeded as well as Stafford. An Australian classic.' **Clare Wright OAM**

'I read *Pig City* in 2005, as part of my induction into the musical history of Brisbane. I couldn't put it down. Any city lucky enough to be honoured with such a chronicle is a very lucky place.' **Paul Grabowsky AO**

'No one told a better history than Andrew Stafford of a time and place where everything happened at once, and when we were once all one.' **Lindy Morrison OAM**

'Brisbane was once a town that people died in but did not believe in, a place that people fled for other cities and countries to take their songs to the world. That Brisbane vanished – everything changed – and *Pig City* tells you how.' **Peter Milton Walsh (the Apartments)**

'*Pig City* had a profound impact on Violent Soho, and on all of us as individuals. It gave us a sense of pride in the musical history of our city, so much so we started putting our postcode (4122) on everything – Mansfield, Brisbane!' **James Tidswell (Violent Soho)**

Andrew Stafford is a freelance journalist and author. *Pig City*, originally published in 2004, is his first book. The second, *Something To Believe In* (2019) is a music memoir. His work has appeared in *The Guardian*, *The Age*, *Griffith Review* and, exclusively, on his Patreon page: patreon.com/andrewstafford

PIG CITY

from THE SAINTS to SAVAGE GARDEN

Andrew Stafford

UQP

First published 2004 by University of Queensland Press
PO Box 6042, St Lucia, Queensland 4067 Australia
Updated edition published 2006
Reprinted 2008
10th anniversary edition published 2014
Reprinted 2017, 2019, 2020

This edition published 2024

University of Queensland Press (UQP) acknowledges the Traditional Owners
and their custodianship of the lands on which UQP operates. We pay our respects
to their Ancestors and their descendants, who continue cultural and spiritual
connections to Country. We recognise their valuable contributions to Australian and
global society.

www.uqp.com.au
reception@uqp.com.au

Cover design by Tony Giacca
Author photograph by Richard Waugh
Typeset in Palatino by Post Pre-Press Group
Adapted by University of Queensland Press
Printed in Australia by McPherson's Printing Group

 University of Queensland Press is supported
by the Queensland Government through Arts
Queensland.

  University of Queensland Press is
assisted by the Australian
Government through Creative
Australia, its principal arts
investment and advisory body.

ISBN 978 0 7022 6879 3 (pbk)
ISBN 978 0 7022 7019 2 (epub)
ISBN 978 0 7022 7018 5 (epdf)

contents

foreword

Brisbane's a bit of a weird place. Maybe it always has been.

Summers here are relentlessly scorching, and the closest beach is nearly an hour away. As I write this, it's a 37°C afternoon in the middle of January. Already, barely three weeks into 2024, two live music venues in Fortitude Valley's nightclub precinct have shut their doors for good. Even more disappointingly, these venues were two of the only places that welcomed younger, more punk-oriented bands and audiences. While this is a blow, I'm not worried about the next generation of Brisbane bands.

I spent my teenage years desperately trying to start a band on the Sunshine Coast. In my final year of high school, it finally happened. By that time, I was catching the train down to the city, spending my afternoons and evenings at house shows and then trying my best to make the last train home. These bands made Brisbane feel like another world, geographically close but culturally miles from the relatively insular Sunshine Coast. What most of my school peers would scoff at was embraced with enthusiasm by this underground scene I'd stumbled upon. For a 16-year-old boy born in Mackay, finding my people in the Brisbane music scene cracked open a new world of possibilities.

Reading *Pig City*, I recognised parallels with my own formative experiences with music in Brisbane. Growing up in conservative Queensland, I was immediately drawn to punk in my early teens. I worshipped the Dead Kennedys, the Germs and, of course, Brisbane's Saints. I felt like I'd faced some of the same adversities described in the book in my band's early days on the coast and in the city: police/ security intimidation, indifference or flat-out disdain from peers, and shows that descended into chaos. These events defined my contradictory early days in music, filled with simultaneously the most exciting and frightening experiences – just like the bands in *Pig City*.

Though often overshadowed by Sydney and Melbourne, it's not like Brisbane's never had anything going for it. Anyone who considers themself a music fan knows the Saints and the Go-Betweens. More recently, Violent Soho put Brisbane on the alt-rock radar. But it was the more obscure bands described in Andrew Stafford's book that really captured my attention as a teenager.

I can remember when I first heard Razar's Task Force (Undercover Cops). The squealing guitars at the beginning, the sardonic tone of Marty Burke's voice and the drum roll that kicks it all off. For my money, it's one of the catchiest punk songs ever written. The lyrics are vicious, sneering and humorous – the 'oink' chants at the end are especially hard not to sing along to. The Leftovers' Cigarettes And Alcohol is another obvious highlight of Brisbane's golden punk era. The frustration, the humour and the jagged chords spoke to me like nothing else had. There is something not only uniquely Australian about these two songs, but also uniquely Brisbane. These touchstones inspired me to start writing my own songs.

A lot of that frustration was likely a result of Brisbane's political climate in the late '70s. I was shocked to learn about the Hillbilly Dictator, Joh Bjelke-Petersen, having previously not known much about him other than that he was the state's longest-serving premier. His contempt for democratic values set a precedent for some of the populist governments that have risen to power in recent years. The stories of corruption and violence at the hands of Bjelke-Petersen and Queensland police are dark shadows that cloud 20th-century Queensland's grim history.

Those days may be long gone – along with many of the bands – but the memories still linger. The community radio institution 4ZZZ is still in Fortitude Valley and has been blasting the sounds of the underground for almost 50 years now. Young singers are still emulating Chris Bailey's passionate drawl and Marty Burke's snotty shouts. House shows are still being hosted by those willing to allow fellow music lovers into the backyards of their rentals. Brisbane will always be Pig City to me.

—Eamon Sandwith
January 2024

introduction – know your product

She comes from Ireland, she's very beautiful
I come from Brisbane, and I'm quite plain
— The Go-Betweens, Lee Remick

If popular music really is a universal language, it's curious how easily a song – even a commercially obscure one – can come to symbolise a city's identity. The stories of London, Liverpool, Manchester, Dunedin, Detroit, Memphis, Nashville, New York, New Orleans, San Francisco and Seattle are inextricably entwined with the music made there. Robert Forster, however, could never have imagined that his self-deprecating paean to an actress would become so fabled in his home town.

This is understandable. Queensland's often stifling subtropical capital doesn't exactly spring to mind when discussing the world's great musical cities. Partly this comes down to Australian pop and rock's poor-relation status next to the United States and the United Kingdom. Inside Australia, too, Brisbane for decades wore a provincial reputation as a big country town, at least in the southern capitals of Sydney and Melbourne.

Of course, one of the most successful bands in recording history began life in Brisbane in the late 1950s. But the

Bee Gees didn't so much outgrow the city as outgrow Australia. Struggling for recognition, the Brothers Gibb began an exodus of musicians out of the country when they left for their native UK at the beginning of 1967, the year before a peanut farmer, Joh Bjelke-Petersen, took control of Queensland's ruling Country Party (later the National Party).

The literature on Australian pop is only beginning to accumulate, so again it is understandable that Brisbane, so far, has rated little more than a footnote. The bigger problem is that the footnote has remained the same, recycled in various contexts by various authors: that music in Brisbane – especially the punk scene of the late '70s – was overwhelmingly a reaction to the repression of the Bjelke-Petersen era.

This is partly true. Bjelke-Petersen's rule of Queensland between 1968 and 1987 was nothing if not iron-fisted. Public displays of dissent were often brutally suppressed; the rule of law was routinely bent to the will of those charged with its enforcement; minorities were treated as simply another obstacle on the path to development. To top it all off, the electoral system was hopelessly rigged in favour of the incumbents. 'Here,' writes Rod McLeod, 'in a city practically under police curfew, you fucked and fought, got stoned, got married, or got out of town.'[1]

But it makes little sense to give a politician too much credit for the creation of a music scene. Major cultural movements result from an intersection of local, national and international factors. The Saints were not so much a reaction to living in a police state as they were a response to the music of not just the Stooges and the MC5, but the Easybeats and the Missing Links. And it's doubtful the national success of a string of Brisbane acts in the '90s – from Powderfinger to George – could have happened without the nationalisation of the Triple J network.

Of course, it would be naive to suggest that growing up in a climate of fear and loathing did not heavily distort the prism through which these artists saw the world. As Saints guitarist Ed Kuepper says, 'I think the band was able to develop a more obnoxious demeanour, thanks to our surroundings, than had everyone been really nice.' In the words of Australian music historian Ian McFarlane, 'That Australia's most conservative city should give rise to such a seditious subcultural coterie is a sociological phenomenon yet to be fully explored.'[2]

This book is my attempt to document the substantial yet largely unsung contribution that Brisbane has made both to Australian popular culture and to international popular music. In doing so, I aimed to chart the shifts in musical, political and cultural consciousness that have helped shape the city's history and identity. In its broadest sense, *Pig City* is the story of how Brisbane grew up.

Pig City concentrates on the quarter-century from 1975 to 2000. It only touches on the '60s and early '70s, by way of explaining the convergence of political and cultural forces that began to exert their pull upon the city at the dawn of the punk movement.

By the 1980s National Party campaign billboards featured the benign face of the premier accompanied only by the words 'Joh' and 'Queensland', so synonymous had the two become. Thus, when the government finally fell in 1989, it marked a divorce that could only be read as a metaphor for broader changes. As novelist Andrew McGahan writes in *Last Drinks*, his fictionalised account of the Fitzgerald Inquiry into police corruption that eventually resulted in the government's downfall:

> For 30 years those in government and their friends had, in looking after their own interests, kept Brisbane frozen in time. The city was caught in the perpetual twilight of the 1950s, as though the '60s and '70s that had wrought so much havoc around the rest of the world had quietly passed Brisbane by. But it couldn't have remained frozen that way forever. Even if

the Inquiry hadn't come along and split the state apart,
something else would have given somewhere. But because it
had all been dammed up and fettered for so long, it meant that
when finally the regime did fall, decades of pent-up energy
burst forth in a fury. It wasn't simply a generational change. It
was an explosion.[3]

As it happened, the state election of 2 December 1989
coincided with the second Livid Festival. Away from the
bands, a crowd of punters gathered around a single black
and white television to watch as the results poured in. The
city's youth had always reserved a special place in their
hearts for the National Party: when it was announced from
the main stage that the government had been overthrown,
the answering roar was just about the loudest thing heard
all day.

The first Livid Festival, held on 21 January 1989, was a
circuit-breaker for Brisbane. Featuring a line-up consisting
almost entirely of expatriate Brisbane artists, it emphasised
the unusual strength of the connection between the city
and its music scene. 'We had some really great home-grown
stuff, and we wanted to bring it all back, put it together
and have a best of Brisbane,' festival producer Peter Walsh
says. Queensland is a parochial place, and not just about its
football teams.

Truly universal pop songs, though, may as well come
from outer space. Savage Garden, for example, grew up in
the city's working-class southern outskirts, something that
had no discernible impact on their sound. Yet when the pop
duo played the closing ceremony of the Olympic Games in
Sydney 2000, they were heralded as municipal ambassadors
at home. For Darren Hayes, however, playing to a worldwide
audience from the biggest stage in the world was simply the
fulfilment of a childhood ambition:

I just know that ever since I was about 12 or 13 I've had this
vision of standing on a stage in front of about 80,000 people.

I sometimes wonder if, when I get there, I'll actually like it, but it's necessary. For whatever reason, I have to follow this through to its logical conclusion. I can't see any other way.[4]

In a book of this scope, many worthy performers have inevitably fallen through the cracks. *Pig City* was never intended to be an encyclopaedia of Brisbane bands. Nevertheless I have tried to give space to those groups who, while not being afforded wider recognition, succeeded in leaving their mark. To have excluded the likes of Razar and the Parameters for the perfectly sound reason that relatively few people even inside Brisbane have ever heard of them would not only have been neglectful of their contributions, it would have been an abrogation of this book's purpose.

While history's light always shines most brightly on the successful and the influential, *Pig City* at least attempts to place their achievements within the context of their surroundings, and to provide a glimpse into the soul of a town that, for all its banality, unwittingly tilled the soil of its very own rock & roll creation.

pineapples from the dawn of time

(1971–1979)

CHAPTER ONE

a million people staying low

The fist made a sound like two footy boots smacking together and the blood spurted and the student went down, and the line of police blue seemed to smile benignly.

— Pat Burgess[1]

When the charge came, it was as unexpected as it was brutal. As the police stormed over Wickham Terrace with batons raised, protesters paused in shock, frozen for an agonised second, caught as their minds instructed their bodies to fight or flee. Many were inexperienced campaigners at their first demonstration.

Steve Gray was not one of them, though. He'd been here before, been at this very spot the previous evening, when nothing untoward had happened. Restless, he'd been cruising around the scene, cheekily pointing out the undercover officers mingling among the crowd. But now things were serious. With the screaming crowd breaking up all around him, he fled down the hill into the darkness.

Reaching the bottom of the hill, Gray paused over the steep drop as two friends rushed to join him. Some jumped heedlessly; others turned towards the rocky face and clambered down. Most just slid on their backsides. Small and agile, Gray negotiated the small cliff-face with ease, but one of his friends fell, twisting an ankle. Moving more slowly, they soldiered on towards the brightly lit Roma Street markets.

Once safely inside the maze of alleyways, the trio relaxed, and began making their way back to the safety of Toowong. Rounding a corner, they almost collided with three heavy, brown-shirted police officers. Quick as a snake, one of them grabbed Gray by the hair. Twisting its length around his wrist, he hoisted his slightly built opponent to eye level.

'Bang. Bang. Bang,' said the sergeant. 'If I ever see you at a demonstration again, I'm going to kill you.'

It's both an understatement and a cliché to say that Queensland is different. Peter Charlton wrote a book trying to explain why in 1983. He came up with two words: 'Distance. Climate.'[2] It is indeed an enormous state: from the capital, it is nearly a 24-hour drive north to Cairns, even further west to Birdsville. It's also hot: even Brisbane, in the south-east corner of the state, endures a prolonged summer in which the mercury hovers around 30°C for five months or more. Winter days, if they can be labelled as such, average around 20°C.

More to the point, as any southern visitor will moan, it's bloody humid. From September onwards, thick black thunderheads form over the MacPherson and Main Ranges to the south-west before dumping huge amounts of rainfall over the city. With the humidity comes a certain sluggishness, and it's equally a cliché to observe that isolated cities in warm climates move at a slower pace than elsewhere. While fostering a more casual attitude to clothing and a laid-back demeanour, such places also tend to be conservative, slower to warm to new ideas.

But Brisbane made an early exception for rock & roll. In February 1958 Buddy Holly played three of his six Australian shows at the Cloudland Ballroom. The same year the Bee Gees arrived in Australia from the Isle of Man and began performing anywhere they were allowed, including the television program *Brisbane Tonight*. Another teenage guest was one Little Rock Allen, later known as Billy Thorpe. After both the Bee Gees and Thorpe moved on to seek their fortunes elsewhere, the Beatles' Festival Hall show in June 1964 provided an infinitely bigger jolt to the city's youth culture.

For a few short years the doors of the city's clubs were thrown open to rock & roll bands. The best of them was, unquestionably, the Purple Hearts. Playing a brash, uncompromising brand of R&B – their name was derived not from the war medal but from the uppers favoured by English mods – the band's tough sound was easily the equal of the early Master's Apprentices and even Sydney's Missing Links, whose song Wild About You the Saints would, years later, cover on their debut album.

But with less than an album's worth of material released during their entire existence, the Purple Hearts lack the recording history of the few breakout Australian acts of the '60s. After moving to Melbourne, the band broke up in January 1967, their promise largely stillborn.

Queensland had been ruled since 1957 by Country Party leader Frank Nicklin, a farmer, teetotaller and Methodist preacher. It was a background shared by many of his colleagues and, indeed, the Labor opposition of the time. Queensland politics was peculiarly rural in outlook, with the Country Party (renamed the National Party in 1973) the dominant conservative coalition partner over the city-based Liberals. Such remains the case today; the reverse, of course, applies in all other Australian states.

The sharpest illustration of the primacy of the bush in Queensland political life was the infamous gerrymander, introduced not by the Country Party but by Ned Hanlon's Labor government in 1949. In fact, the term gerrymander was something of a misnomer. A gerrymander represents the drawing of electoral boundaries in a way that serves the

interests of the governing party. This certainly took place
in Queensland, but it was the malapportionment, which
meant that one vote in the west of the state was worth up to
three in Brisbane, that was the critical issue.

The 'malamander' was designed to prevent the
metropolitan zones, which held the largest number of voters,
from dictating political terms to those in the regions. It did
more than that: for four decades the malamander ensured
the vast, sparsely populated territory west of the Great
Dividing Range lorded it over the populous cities. Originally
the malamander had advantaged the Labor incumbents it
was meant to serve; when the disastrous Labor Party split of
1957 handed government to the Country Party, the situation
was reversed.

After further tweaking the electoral system to their own
benefit, the Country/National Party found itself able to
secure a majority of seats in parliament even if it polled the
lowest percentage of primary votes. Over time, this reduced
both the Labor and Liberal parties to virtual irrelevancy
and laughing-stock status.

Having the seat of power lying out beyond the black
stump threw up some interesting parliamentary statistics.
By the late '70s the members of the National Party cabinet
all shared very similar backgrounds. All were men, hailing
from the bush or small country towns. All had worked
in the primary industries sector before entering politics.
None had undertaken tertiary studies; many, including the
premier, had barely progressed beyond primary school. All
were married and had raised their children long before the
social challenges of the '60s and '70s.[3]

For much of the 20th century, education in Queensland
was chronically neglected. Between 1919 and 1939, the
textbooks in the small number of secondary schools remained
unchanged; between 1924 and 1952, not a single new high
school was built in Brisbane. The men ruling the state were
the products of this system and the inheritors of its failings.
As Peter Charlton observes, 'It explains much of the state's

conservatism, suspicion and resistance to change.[4] It also accounts for the nickname given to Queensland by many commentators: the Deep North.

The anti-intellectualism of the government and the poor education levels of its representatives meant Queensland, and Queenslanders, became a frequent target of ridicule and derision in the south. A former lecturer in education, Rupert Goodman, remarked in 1969:

> The rest of Australia thinks Queensland is a hillbilly state and that we're an uncultured mob. Frankly there's a lot of truth in that. You only have to look at most of our politicians and listen to them in debate. Unqualified, unskilled, untrained, and undereducated, many of them repeat themselves, have bad diction, poor language, are unable to think on their feet or get any message across simply or succinctly.[5]

For many Queensland voters, however, such bumbling was endearing. When one considers the comet-like rise and fall of Pauline Hanson, whose One Nation party achieved its most spectacular success in the Queensland state election of 1998, it still is. It means the politicians are never too far above their masters. As Andrew McGahan writes:

> Queenslanders were always wary of the more sophisticated types – they *liked* their representatives to be awkward and stumbling. They mistook it for honesty. So much so that the Queensland parliament sometimes bordered on a sideshow collection of the ugly, the misshapen and the incoherent.[6]

The New Left movement of the late '60s was galvanised in Queensland by the intertwined issues of the Vietnam War, conscription and civil liberties. Before this time, as historian Ross Fitzgerald points out, public marches were rarely used as tools of political action. After the first conscription demonstrations were held at Monash University in Melbourne in

1965, however, they were to become a regular feature of Queensland life.

Ed Kuepper (The Saints): There were other things that linked people together in those days [besides music]. Politics was an important area. Australia was still involved in the Vietnam War, so the moratorium marches were a big thing. You'd meet people – they became social events as well as being expressions of political consciousness.

But to protest in Queensland usually meant committing a crime. Under the Traffic Act, police permits were required to hold meetings, to march along any road, and to carry and display placards. (Placard permits came at the additional fee of $1.) Permits could be refused without reason, although appeals against refusal could be argued before a magistrate.

On 5 October 1966, 26 people were arrested during an anti-conscription demonstration. Marches had been held in capital cities elsewhere throughout Australia on that day without incident. This set the tone for subsequent events, conjoining the issues of the rights to free speech and free assembly with anti-Vietnam sentiment.

The radical movement found a natural haven in the sprawling, leafy surrounds of the University of Queensland in the inner western suburb of St Lucia. In 1967 two groups were formed on campus: the Civil Liberties Co-ordinating Committee and the Society for Democratic Action. From these two groups came the nucleus of students that would establish community radio station 4ZZZ in the '70s.

Alan Knight (4ZZZ): There were two things that influenced us. We were culturally influenced by the whole rock music explosion; the Beatles and things like that. But we were also to an extent influenced by the hippies. So you had this mixture of rock music, psychedelic drugs and ultra-leftist politics, which led to a lot of very strange demonstrations.

By 1966, however, the initial spark of the post-Beatles boom had faded. The biggest new band in Brisbane was Bay City Union, led by Matt Taylor, later the leader of Chain (Bay City Union also featured latter-day Master's Apprentices bass player and prominent manager Glenn Wheatley). But with only one single to their credit, Bay City Union's résumé was even thinner than that of the Purple Hearts. The band split in 1968.

Brisbane was dull. The city simply shut down on weekends. The saying used to go that on Sundays you could have fired a cannon down Queen Street in the city centre and not hit anyone or anything. For young people, the prevailing atmosphere was a fetid, fermenting mixture of enervating heat, boredom and unrelieved tension.

Two noted radicals, Mitch Thompson and Brian Laver, found a novel way of releasing the pressure, staging multimedia extravaganzas at the old Communist Party headquarters at Brisbane Trades Hall, near Central Station. These Sunday-evening speakeasies were named Foco, a Cuban–Spanish word meaning guerrilla encampment.

> **Brian Laver:** We wanted to politicise people, we weren't just about providing entertainment. But the formula worked, I think, because there was nothing to do on a Sunday night, it was boring as shit, and so people mobilised in their hundreds. I don't think there would have been a time where we had less than 500 people.

The shows were a melange of live music, theatre, film, food, poetry and debate spread among the venue's rooms, with bands sharing the main hall with theatre group Tribe, featuring a young Geoffrey Rush. But as Foco grew – to the point of regularly attracting turn-away crowds – it inevitably became a political target. When an MP claimed it was a distribution centre for illegal drugs, the end was near.

John Stanwell (4ZZZ): It became a real threat, because good middle-class kids were going to see it. So the [authorities] basically smashed it. They set it up with a drug scare on a night where we had brought up a band from Melbourne, the Wild Cherries, which was our biggest financial exposure, and it bankrupted it.

The Wild Cherries had formed in 1964 as a jazz combo, but they had been transformed into a relentless psychedelic outfit by the arrival of former Purple Hearts guitarist Lobby Loyde in 1967. Soon after, Loyde joined the Aztecs, fronted by another Brisbane expatriate, Billy Thorpe, with whom he explored a harder blues-based sound.

During the same period two of the remaining Purple Hearts returned to Brisbane, forming a new band, the Coloured Balls. The band gigged around the city until 1969 without committing anything to vinyl. It wasn't until February 1972 that Loyde, who had remained in Melbourne, took the name for a new version of the group, releasing the cult classic *Ball Power* the following year. But by then the bottom had long since fallen out of the beginnings of an original music scene in Brisbane.

Ed Kuepper: There wasn't anything happening musically to speak of. It was an incredibly dead scene. It seemed unbearable to me at the time. Bands that were working were doing covers of Deep Purple, which I found pathetic. I had nothing but total contempt for that area of musical existence. There was just nothing.

If inspiration were to be found, it would have to come from elsewhere.

Frank Nicklin retired from politics in January 1968. His long-serving deputy, Jack Pizzey, was elected unopposed as

Country Party leader and premier. The deputy leadership was contested by three men: Ron Camm, the Minister for Main Roads; Lands Minister Alan Fletcher; and the Minister for Works and Housing, 57-year-old Johannes Bjelke-Petersen.

Although little known in the wider electorate and not highly regarded either inside or outside his own party, Bjelke-Petersen was a shrewd numbers man, and he won the job, along with the additional portfolios of Aboriginal affairs and police. When Jack Pizzey dropped dead of a heart attack six months later, Bjelke-Petersen, against all expectations, was elected unopposed as premier.

Born in 1911 in New Zealand to Danish immigrants, Joh Bjelke-Petersen had a difficult early life. His family moved to Queensland three years after his birth, settling on a farm (later named Bethany) outside Kingaroy, near the Bunya Mountains north-west of Brisbane. With his father frail and his family extremely poor, farm duties were left largely to Joh.

His older brother, Christian, was studious and sensitive, with no taste for the backbreaking labour of farm work. He later died at the age of 22. Joh maintained that the stomach ulcers that cut Christian down were brought on by too much study, a telling assessment.[7] Joh was a doer, not a thinker, with no time for abstract philosophy or cultural pursuits, unless it involved spreading the good news of his strict Lutheran faith.

A bout of childhood polio briefly slowed Joh down, leaving him with one leg half an inch shorter than the other. But he was made of sterner stuff than his brother, and at 13 he left school to work the farm full-time, dreaming of lifting his family from poverty. He was convinced that his faith and, above all, hard work would reward him.

I was filled with a tremendous desire and a tremendous determination to work and to strive and to overcome the

> problems that confronted my parents and I was encouraged by
> my mother who worked long hours . . . We had extreme poverty
> but I was rich in that my parents gave me a deep understanding
> of spiritual things by their lives and their influence.[8]

This Calvinist outlook of 'hard work = money = success = salvation' accounts for Bjelke-Petersen's fanatical pursuit of state development while premier.[9] Whether it was the drilling of oil on the Great Barrier Reef or the tearing down of historic buildings, Bjelke-Petersen was not about to let arcane concerns about conservation and heritage get in the way of the more important business of wealth creation.

It also explains his passionate pursuit of unfettered free enterprise and his hatred of anything that smacked of socialism. After entering parliament in 1947 as the member for Nanango, Bjelke-Petersen's maiden speech – indeed, almost all his speeches – stressed the freedom to develop without any kind of regulation from the state. Instead he attacked the evils of drinking, gambling (including the broadcasting of horse-racing), imported films and working on the Sabbath.

After becoming premier, Bjelke-Petersen retained the police portfolio, vowing to make law and order his own personal crusade. He was less concerned about the allegations of official corruption swirling around the force. A tightly controlled Royal Commission held over the summer of 1963–64 had turned up nothing, but then, the government was in the force's pocket. Journalist Evan Whitton characterises the relationship in these terms: 'you stand for law and order; we are your loyal spear-carriers in this unending battle; an attack on the force, or individuals therein, is an attack on you and your policies'.[10] This mutual agreement would ultimately benefit both parties.

Bjelke-Petersen had been a vocal critic of the gerrymander during his time on the opposition benches. Once in power, he became its staunchest defender, further manipulating the system to his advantage. 'We believe,' he said in a statement thick with unintended irony, 'in the rights of the minority as well as the rights of the majority.'[11]

A more humorous but revealing comment on Bjelke-Petersen's attitude to democracy came from a National Party conference in July 1977. Rebuking the prime minister, Malcolm Fraser, for criticising the South African apartheid regime, Bjelke-Petersen offered the following: 'We have got to get away from talking about majority rule – it just doesn't add up.'[12]

The real genesis of this story lies not in the foundations set down by any band, but in the unlikely shape of a sporting tour by the South African rugby union team in the winter of 1971.

The Springbok tour came amid a rising tide of condemnation of South Africa's apartheid laws, and their arrival in Australia was met with fierce demonstrations, which rolled continuously as the team and their entourage were hounded from state to state. Matches in Melbourne and Sydney were interrupted as protesters invaded the pitch. Hundreds more in the stands blew whistles similar to those used by the referees, turning the games into high farce.

Bjelke-Petersen was at the low ebb of his early premiership. The previous October, he had survived a challenge from within his own ranks by a solitary vote, his own. He was perceived, even within his own party, as a wowser and a country bumpkin. Further, both he and his ministers were under pressure over conflict of interest allegations in relation to their numerous share portfolios, in particular with mining giant Comalco, and Bjelke-Petersen's defensive media handling of the issue saw him branded a weak and ineffective leader.

The Springbok tour gave the premier the law-and-order ticket he needed to banish that perception for good. His proclamation of a month-long state of emergency caused immediate uproar: the suspension of civil liberties and the granting of extraordinary (and unspecified) police powers on the pretext of protecting a visiting football team from political dissenters was unprecedented. It earned the premier the nickname Jack Boots Bjelke.

The result was predictable. Protests against the tour were further inflamed, and the government itself became the target, with 40 unions declaring an immediate 24-hour strike. With the government preparing to go to two by-elections, Bjelke-Petersen wasted no time in linking the unions (and by extension the ALP) to anarchy in the streets. No one, however, foresaw the level of force with which the protests would be crushed.

The Springboks finally arrived in Brisbane on 22 July. They were greeted outside their lodgings, the Tower Mill Motel, by about 300 demonstrators and an equivalent number of police. The standoff did not prevail long: after just 15 minutes, police charged the crowd, scattering them into Wickham Park below. Many were assaulted. But they were not easily dissuaded.

> **Alan Knight:** What you've got to understand with these demos, they didn't last for an hour or so. They went for days, in the face of this police violence. People just kept coming back. They'd get biffed or roughed up and then they'd come back later on.

Demonstrations began again the following morning, and ended in a stalemate when staff from the Holy Spirit Hospital, next door to the motel, complained to police that noise levels were disturbing patients. A silent vigil ensued and eventually the crowd dispersed peacefully, although some remained through the night. It was the next day – Saturday 24 July, the day of the Springboks' first match – that was to bring matters to a head.

The premier issued a warning. 'I would not be surprised if the demonstrators open a new line of attack. I have heard that it could be rough in the streets today.'[13]

The proclamation of the state of emergency had enabled

the government to move the match from the scheduled venue of Ballymore Oval in Herston to the Royal National Association showgrounds in Bowen Hills. Surrounded by high walls and topped with barbed wire, the fortress-like showgrounds were considered the better venue to deter protesters. Thus, instead of targeting the game, between 1500 and 2000 demonstrators assembled in Victoria Park opposite the grounds before marching slowly up to Wickham Terrace, eventually camping themselves once again at the foot of the Tower Mill in the gathering darkness of the late afternoon.

Commensurate with the Saturday crowd, the police ranks had swelled to an intimidating 500, not just uniformed and plain-clothes ranks from the city, but country 'brownshirts', bussed in as reinforcements by the police commissioner, Ray Whitrod. Among the crowd were two young law students, future Queensland premier Peter Beattie and barrister and civil libertarian Terry O'Gorman. For both, what transpired that evening proved to be a pivotal event in their lives.

> **Terry O'Gorman:** It was my involvement as a legal observer [of the demonstration] that was my introduction to the whole scene. I remember after the police charge a particular law student who was organising the legal observers came back, thoroughly traumatised by it. Prior to that I'd come from a very Catholic, Christian Brother, right-wing education and family background. So, from that point of view, it was fairly formative.

Wickham Terrace winds along the northern ridge overlooking Brisbane's central business district, lined by upmarket hotels and medical clinics. Opposite the Tower Mill lies Wickham Park. Fringed by gigantic Moreton Bay fig trees, it slopes steeply down towards Albert Street, which runs directly through the city heart, and the Roma Street markets. At the lower end of the park was a small cliff-face, now a stone wall up to four metres in height. The terrain would put the protesters at an unusual disadvantage.

At five o'clock, Whitrod gave a statement to the crowd: 'There will be no action from police as a group if you move back to the white line, except that there can be individual police action if necessary and in the event of large police action reasonable notice will be given.'[14] This pronouncement did nothing to quell the thickening knot of fear rising in the stomachs of the protesters.

Steve Gray (4ZZZ): Moving through the crowd, you could spot the plain-clothes police. The demonstrators were chanting 'Paint them black and send them back,' and this busload of coppers pulls up. And they get off the bus and start chanting back, 'Paint them red and shoot them dead.' So, not surprisingly, the tension started to rise on both sides of the street.

At 6.54pm, minutes before footage of the protest would go live around Australia courtesy of ABC news, Whitrod told his men to 'move to the other side of the road'.[15]

As commissioner, Whitrod did not enjoy the support of his rank and file. Police Minister Max Hodges had brought in the well-educated South Australian a year earlier after convincing Bjelke-Petersen that he risked being dragged under by the still-circulating rumours of official corruption. Whitrod thus had a brief to reform the force, but his prosecution of some police for malpractice earned him the enduring enmity of not only the powerful police union, but the premier as well.

Whitrod was also regarded as a soft touch on students, preferring conciliation and dialogue to force. Only the previous day the country police he had brought in for the occasion had passed a motion of no confidence in him. Thus the proposed orderly move forward – intended by Whitrod simply to move the demonstrators off the road to the opposite footpath – did not eventuate. The violence of the subsequent charge caught even seasoned protesters by surprise.

John Stanwell: These were the country cops who were

brought in, with the old [khaki] uniform. They'd been brought in especially for the football game by this new commissioner who was regarded as a pinko liberal bed-wetter, and basically they broke ranks and went berserk. We were cannon fodder.

The protesters immediately found themselves being forced down the hill into Wickham Park as baton-wielding police wrought their vengeance. More police were waiting in the park. As the panicked mob fled towards them, they sprung from the shadows of the trees, tackling and clobbering anyone within reach. Those that evaded the ambush were forced to scramble or jump down the cliff-face as the police gave chase.

Lindy Morrison (The Go-Betweens): It radicalised everybody . . . What I remember most vividly is the actual fear, of running away from police with batons, and seeing them bashing friends. Whoever stumbled and fell got heavily beaten, and all of us were too scared to stop and help.

Peter Beattie: It's one of those indelible things imprinted in my mind about oppression, about violence, about excessive power. I ran down to Trades Hall and I remember trying to do the gentlemanly thing by letting some of the women in first, and I got beaten up for my trouble.

That same day, the two by-elections were held. The government won both. One seat, Maryborough, had been a Labor stronghold for 56 years; the other, Merthyr, was situated only a few kilometres away from the violence at Tower Mill.

Bjelke-Petersen's leadership would not be challenged again for another 16 years.

CHAPTER TWO

guerrilla radio

The University of Queensland's home campus of St Lucia is one of the largest and oldest in Australia. It is also among the most traditional. On the sandstone cloisters of the Great Court a collection of historic scenes, philosophers and gargoyles are carved in self-conscious appropriation of the grandeur of its European antecedents. Inside the court, jacaranda trees advertise their presence each October in an explosion of lavender. It used to be said on campus that if you hadn't started studying by the bloom of the jacarandas, you were destined to fail.

Radiating outwards from the court in all directions is a rash of newer, ruder structures, devoid of character or consideration, mindful only of the need to accommodate an ever-growing number of students, a living metaphor for Brisbane itself: traditional and reserved at heart yet, in its conflation of progress with sophistication, unable to stop itself from trampling into vulgarity. Arguably the worst embodiment of this tendency is the Abel Smith Lecture Theatre: named after the former governor of Queensland, the squat, sunken roundhouse also goes by the unflattering nickname of the Pizza Hut.

By the late 1960s, as the centre of higher learning in a state not known for its commitment to intellectual endeavour, the university was arguably the most politically polarised in Australia. On 26 July 1971, two days after the Springbok police riot, a general university strike was declared, protesting both the ongoing state of emergency and, with particular outrage, the conduct of the police at the Tower Mill.

John Stanwell vividly recalls the impact the incident had on campus. A law student, Stanwell had earned his activist stripes in the early anti-conscription protests and was no stranger to police brutality.

> **John Stanwell:** The excesses of the police on that night was not a huge surprise to us per se – we'd seen it plenty of times, although this was on a scale and with a ferocity that we hadn't seen very often. But the real issue was that among the crowd, there were a large number of young students who were not particularly radical, who had never been involved in demonstrations before, and who had gone along to this one event and had the shit beaten out of them. And that just totally freaked them out. It radicalised the entire campus.

The problem for the students was how to make themselves heard outside the confines of the university. With no support from the mainstream press (dominated, as it is today, by the state's only broadsheet, the *Courier-Mail*), trying to present a genuine alternative viewpoint in Queensland was strictly an underground enterprise: even the distribution of political or religious leaflets without a permit was banned.

A more ambitious effort to reach a wider public had been made in 1968, with the attempted establishment of an alternative newspaper, the *Brisbane Line*. But the bravery of the exercise wasn't matched by the primitive resources available. Each issue needed to be individually typed, laid out with glue and paper and hand-stapled together. With most newsagencies refusing to stock them, the papers were distributed by anyone with sufficient nerve to risk arrest, a beating or both selling them on the street. The paper folded after three issues.

The university strike lasted all week, during which time students and staff staged an occupation of the student union headquarters. With access to a printing press (used for production of the student newspaper *Semper Floreat*), the choice of venue was as much a pragmatic decision as an expression of solidarity. But the futility of risking continual arrest for the cause of producing leaflets was becoming obvious to all concerned.

Along with Stanwell, it was a *Semper* editor, Alan Knight, who floated the idea of establishing a pirate radio station. Knight saw radio's potential to tie the multi-hued strands of Brisbane's youth culture and resistance movement together:

> **Alan Knight:** Radio allowed the whole package. It brought in music. It allowed for a certain kind of theatre. It was cheap, most radio receivers at that stage had FM on them, and it could be located somewhere relatively safe, in this case the university campus, without police interference.

A mature-age history student, Jim Beatson, was similarly attuned to the need for a more sophisticated and less labour-intensive means of information transmission. With the week's classes abandoned, he began looking more seriously into the feasibility of radio.

> **Jim Beatson:** People at progressive gatherings were very prone to saying, 'Let's set up a pirate radio station,' and I largely ignored them because I thought it would be a lot harder and more complicated. But we went to see this guy who was working in either the physics or engineering department, I can't remember which, and he told me that setting up a pirate radio station was a relatively easy thing to do. The only problem was that it was also easy to monitor illegal transmissions and then block them.

In 1968, Beatson worked as a printer in England, where he purchased an FM radio, something that had proved redundant on his return to Australia. After some tests in mono on the ABC in the early '60s, FM had already been dismissed by the conservative federal government as a passing fad, and one that would, moreover, surely come and go with rock & roll itself.[1]

AM radio reflected this complacency. Years earlier Bob Dylan's twin peaks of *Highway 61 Revisited* (released in 1965) and *Blonde On Blonde* (1966), closely followed by the Beatles' *Sgt Pepper* (1967), had given birth to album-oriented rock; by the early '70s this was accelerating towards the orchestrated mush of full-blown progressive rock. AM, however, was stuck in a rigid format of Top 40 singles, talkback and commercials, even as singles were being vastly outsold by the likes of Pink Floyd's *Dark Side Of The Moon*.

While in England, Beatson had been particularly impressed by the tones and taste of the BBC's John Peel, the doyen of British rock broadcasting. Peel's influence was reflected by the ABC's Chris Winter, then hosting a weekly program called Room To Move. With Winter playing music from successful albums that no commercial broadcasters dared touch, there was an obvious gap in the market for a well-directed youth radio station.

At 26, Beatson was slightly older than most of the other students. He was also an unusually clear thinker and a brilliant organiser.

John Stanwell: It was Jim that said, 'Let's set up a real radio station, get a real radio licence.' He was unquestionably the driving force. He understood that it was not going to be a Mickey Mouse effort; that it was about (a) getting resources, (b) building alliances, and (c) working out a way in which it could be legitimate, or at least tolerated, because it was never going to be legitimate in the conventional sense! That's quite a shift in thinking on one level, and yet if you look back

through all those things that we'd already done, it was a
logical development. Others were probably thinking along
similar lines, but Jim, unlike everybody else, actually thought
of making it a real radio station.

Perhaps Beatson's real talent, though, was his detection
of bigger changes in the wind that would, over the next four
years, turn Australian cultural and political life on its head.
Outside Queensland, the foundations were already being
laid for a series of developments that would blow the field
of communications wide open.

The ultra-conservatism of Queensland's state government
in the early '70s was not reflected nationally. After more
than 20 years of conservative Liberal–Country Party
coalition rule, the country was stagnating, out of step with
the accelerating social changes of the era. The election
of Gough Whitlam's Labor Party to national office in
December 1972 briefly captured a mood of optimism
and renewal, and precipitated a vigorous period of social
reforms.

After being quietly buried in the late '60s, the push
for the introduction of FM and public broadcasting was
regaining momentum. This was largely thanks to the
lobbying of the Music Broadcasting Society, founded in
Victoria in 1968 to agitate for the commencement of 'fine
music' broadcasting. While its aims were radically different
to those of the Queensland students (despite Beatson's
reputation as a classical buff), the overall message was the
same: communities were not being adequately serviced by
existing radio formats.

Commercial stations were adamant in their opposition to
public broadcasting, and their interests had been supported
by the federal coalition. Also standing in the way of
FM's introduction was the fact that the international FM
broadcast band (88–108 MHz) had already been given over

to Australian television, the product of an ill-judged decision to expand television broadcasting in the VHF range instead of across the internationally accepted UHF spectrum.

In 1972, prior to Whitlam's ascension, the Australian Broadcasting Control Board (ABCB) damned the potential introduction of public broadcasting licences as, in John Tebbutt's words, a 'waste of a frequency'[2] and suggested that if FM was to be introduced, it should be on the UHF band. This would doubtless have been music to the ears of radio manufacturers, as imported FM radios with standard VHF receivers would have remained useless.

Whitlam's election changed the state of play. Public broadcasting was thrust onto the national agenda, and the new government was bound to a policy of media diversification (one only tepidly supported by the responsible minister, Senator Doug McLelland – Rubber Dougie, as he was sometimes known – who had initially backed the ABCB report). In early 1973 the University of Queensland Media Committee was formed to lobby for a broadcasting licence.

Beatson virtually hand-picked a team according to individuals' skills. Stanwell's background was in event coordination and promotion. Marian Wilkinson – then a significant presence in the women's movement on campus – and Alan Knight were aspiring journalists. Stuart Matchett was an arts student and music fan who, like Beatson, had spent time in England; Ross Dannecker, an engineering student, became technical adviser. Still others, including first-year student Helen Hambling, became the announcers and volunteers of the future.

In May, Beatson flew to Canberra to discuss the possibility of being granted a licence. An offer for an educational licence similar to that already given to Adelaide University – which stipulated that music could not be played – was rejected. Fortunately by this time another senator, Jim MacLelland, had been appointed to chair a standing committee querying the wisdom of the ABCB's earlier report. Beatson, Dannecker and Matchett prepared a submission that they later presented in Sydney.

Jim Beatson: The three of us went down and everybody was talking about the need for small groups to have a say on air, that marginalised groups weren't getting a voice on the radio. And at some point I got quite agitated and made this blinder of a speech, saying that it wasn't minorities in Australia that were dissatisfied with radio in Australia, that whole majorities were dissatisfied, and as proof of that I pointed out that the biggest-selling albums of the day weren't getting any airplay at all.

MacLelland's committee issued an interim report castigating the ABCB's earlier decision. Whitlam responded swiftly, announcing an independent inquiry into public broadcasting. The inquiry, chaired by the BBC's Sir Francis McLean, delivered its report in March 1974. It recommended both the introduction of FM broadcasting and the granting of public licences, and set out a progressive plan for the removal of television from the VHF band in order to accommodate FM radio. In November the Music Broadcasting Societies of both New South Wales and Victoria were offered the first experimental FM licences.

While the fine-music broadcasters had won their battle, the public broadcasting war was far from over. Beatson's committee stepped up its campaign, lobbying various Brisbane community groups – everyone from hi-fi companies to Children By Choice – impressing upon them what they stood to gain from a new radio station. Many wrote in turn to the government expressing their support. With Whitlam's government already staggering, the committee also lobbied directly, paying a visit to Bill Hayden's electorate office in Ipswich.

Jim Beatson: Hayden at that stage was the treasurer, and we popped into his office – a number of us had known him for many years – saying, 'Bill, things aren't looking good for Labor, quick, hand out the licence before you get the arse.' We didn't think they'd get dismissed; we just thought they'd get beaten at the polls. There was no doubt that if [Sir John] Kerr hadn't sacked Whitlam, he would have gone to the next election and been savagely defeated.

The first breakthrough came in early 1975, with the university granted a trial stereo FM broadcast, coinciding with the campus' orientation week in February. Ross Dannecker (whose technical know-how had been vital in impressing MacLelland's committee) constructed a one-kilowatt transmitter and antenna, while various electronic companies loaned the necessary sound equipment. Over orientation week, the new station went to air for 20 hours, working under the call sign of 4ZZ–FM.

The experiment proved the group's capacity to run a radio station, but with Whitlam's government in terminal disarray, Canberra was in no rush to hand out broadcasting licences to universities. It was not until Whitlam replaced Doug McLelland with the left-leaning Moss Cass, backed by Whitlam confidant Jim Spiegleman as his head of department, that there were serious moves towards resolving the issue. When the government set up a committee for the establishment of public broadcasting, Beatson was invited to join.

Jim Beatson: I was rung up and asked if I was interested in being on a government committee. I said, 'Oh yeah?' and they said, 'Well, we'll fly you down and have a car pick you up, what's your home address?' And it was a chauffeur-driven white Mercedes-Benz. I was picked up and dropped on a plane and taken to one of those expensive restaurants in Sydney, and told I would be very welcome, and I thought, 'What have I done?' Of course, later on I realised that I was the token radical. I said to them, 'I only want to be on the committee if I can still wear my jeans and a denim jacket, I don't want to compromise,' and

they said, 'Oh, we only *want* you if you're going to wear denim.'
I didn't realise that that was my role, to look good to the left
while Whitlam was still there!

Anyway, I employed Helen Hambling to manage the station
project while I was in Sydney, and the first thing I did when I
arrived was I went and had a look at our file. And on the desk
was a letter that I'd written to Cass saying, in a very polite
way, get on with it and hand out the licence, please. And it just
said in the margin, 'Jim,' meaning Spiegleman, 'this group of
people seem great, why don't we get them a licence as quickly
as possible, what can you do? Moss.' So I knew then we were
certain to get a licence.

Plans were made for 4ZZ–FM to go to air permanently
on 1 December. Assisted by the student union, a 10-kilowatt
transmitter and antenna were purchased.

By this stage, of course, Whitlam was doomed. The
Malcolm Fraser-led opposition may not have been quite as
conservative as Bjelke-Petersen's state regime, but neither
was it likely to be sympathetic to a group of leftist radicals
from the Deep North, most of whom had police records. To
get the licence in time was clearly going to involve making
compromises that went beyond the merely sartorial.

John Tebbutt writes that most of the participants in the
McLean inquiry recognised the oppositional nature of
public broadcasting, and many (including Beatson) saw
the medium as an opportunity to continue the program
of social change begun in the '60s. Unexpectedly, it was
Trevor Jarvie of the New South Wales Music Broadcasting
Society who stated the case most boldly: 'I think it is plain
that we are discussing an alternative version of human
society.'

But the Department of the Media understood this in
more prosaic terms, suggesting that what the delegations
were really asking for was to be included in Australian

society, not to revolutionise it. As Tebbutt says, 'The very fact of having to negotiate with the state for acceptance demands compromise from movements aimed at securing structural change.'[3]

John Stanwell: Once you realise that you're talking about a successful, tolerated, legal medium, then you're talking about a mass minority audience. You're not talking about a megaphone; you're not talking about a worthy thing in someone's car boot that's not being distributed. You're actually talking about using the tools of the mainstream with full knowledge that that was going to lead to compromises.

But for some of the more starry-eyed on campus, any such ideological betrayal was anathema. The committee soon began to fragment into factions divided between the pragmatists, led by Beatson and Stanwell, and the more doctrinaire radicals determined not to sell out what they saw as the coming revolution.

In August a second experimental broadcast was conducted, this time from the Park Royal Motor Inn in the city, which was hosting a hi-fi show. The station was assisted by Bill Riner, an American émigré and broadcaster then working for easy-listening AM station 4KQ. Riner was at first regarded with suspicion in some quarters, coming as he did from 'the heart of the beast', as Stanwell puts it. But he quickly proved his worth.

Bill Riner: I had some skills that I thought I could help people with, so in the lead-up to the station going on air, I did some production workshops, told people how to splice and odds and ends, and how to get by with only a little bit of equipment . . . I had a burning desire to work in FM radio. Sonically, it was an amazing challenge. I was into sound as art and making radio as art, and that was another thing that was very appealing. It was really just about being a part of something, and the longer I stayed there, it was more and more apparent that I was involved in something of great significance.

With the opening date approaching, there remained the task of building a real studio within the student union offices. In a remarkable piece of DIY enterprise, this was accomplished from scratch not by contracted builders, but by staff and volunteers, led by architecture student Kevin Hayes. (This led to occasional hiccups in planning: after knocking down walls upstairs, it became apparent that the weight of equipment to be moved in posed a serious safety hazard to those below. The red-faced group asked to move down to the basement instead.) They were joined by the bearish figure of John Woods, the station's first full-time radio pro. Arriving in new clothes, Cuban heels, and nursing a bad hangover, he was pressed straight into bricklaying.

As the government lurched towards the constitutional crisis that sealed its fate, a decision was made. Whitlam announced that 12 experimental licences would be handed out to tertiary campuses, 11 of which were to be given to university administrations, the last to the University of Queensland's Student Union. In order to push the licences through, Cass had relied on the subterfuge of classifying the stations as 'educational'. But the licence, against all prior agreements, allowed for only low-power transmission. Worse, the already purchased 10-kilowatt transmitter, which was being imported from the US, had been 'lost' on a New York wharf, an event about which Beatson still harbours suspicions.

Jim Beatson: We'd sworn that we would never go to air without a full licence. But it was clear Whitlam was in deep trouble, and the government was going to come to an end one way or another very soon. And given that the transmitter was lost, we decided to go to air on low power. It was a decision that we were very reluctant to make. The licence still hadn't even been issued at the point when we announced we were going to begin broadcasting.

The story of the governor-general's dismissal of the Whitlam government on 11 November 1975 (and the significant role the Queensland premier played in engineering the coup, leading Whitlam to famously decry Bjelke-Petersen as a 'Bible-bashing bastard') has been told elsewhere. Suffice to say that with the licences signed but not yet sealed and delivered, it caused panic at the new station. The opening date was pushed back until 8 December.

Jim Beatson: The general manager of the PBAA [Public Broadcasting Association of Australia] was then working for the minister in Canberra. He rang me and said, 'Look, I've just been in the minister's office and all your group's police records are sitting on the minister's desk. I just thought I'd let you know that they're taking a very close look at you.'

For three weeks the possibility that three years' work would come to nought was very real, with the caretaker minister, Peter Nixon, threatening to scotch the licences. In an extraordinary move, Beatson and Stanwell 'sacked' themselves from their positions, with cleanskin Ross Dannecker installed as station coordinator. This was of course a ruse, but it was hoped that by appearing to purge anyone with police records from the board, the station stood a better chance of survival in the face of the new regime.

As it turned out, in the run-up to the general election called in the wake of Whitlam's sacking, the coalition proved itself open to persuasion, especially with at least two of the proposed new stations situated in marginal electorates. Realising that he couldn't very well proceed with the granting of some licences over others, Nixon indicated that Labor's decision would stand. The union's licence – for one kilowatt – was at last handed over.

A new radio station had been born. The problem now was what to do with it.

With its well-modulated tenor and rounded vowels, the voice could easily have hailed from the ABC. But the contents of its speech – betrayed by a slight but telltale quaver of nerves – spoke otherwise:

> You're listening to 4ZZ–FM in Brisbane, bringing you stereo FM rock on a frequency of 105.7 megahertz. 4ZZ–FM is Brisbane's first new radio station in over 30 years and first ever stereo FM station. 4ZZ–FM is not only Queensland's first stereo FM station, it is also a public broadcasting station, non-commercial and non-ABC, a product of the Labor Government's initiatives in the field of the media. These initiatives have created a host of new stations . . . As a result the Australian public is receiving a more diverse variety of program sources . . . To attempt to impose limitations or restrictions on public broadcasting is to seriously threaten a fundamental liberty, that of free speech. While it is easy to lapse into rhetoric in defence of free speech, we've been forced to make a stand and we intend to do so from the start. We see that freedom in danger of becoming hypothetical . . . With the time at three and a quarter minutes past 12, let's get down to some serious business. From *Who's Next*, this is the Who, and Won't Get Fooled Again.[4]

The late John Woods' opening manifesto to mark the official birth of 4ZZ, while eloquently establishing the station's raison d'être, was notable for its understatement. It resisted any temptation to make any comment on Whitlam's sacking, a topic about which all at the new station felt passionate, and made only veiled references to the role the station hoped to play in Queensland politics. With the station's position still very tenuous – the caretaker attorney-general, Ivor Greenwood, had already cast doubt on the legality of the station's licence – it was thought better to let the music make the most powerful statement.

Not all were in favour of such discretion. The tensions and contradictions inherent in a broadcaster that styled itself as a vehicle for radical change, yet relied on the goodwill of the state for its very existence, were already shaping the station in ways that would prove pivotal to its future development. From its inception, 4ZZZ/Triple Zed (as it became in February 1976, when the ABCB made the decision that all FM stations would have three-letter call signs) would explore the boundaries of public broadcasting.

Although Triple Zed began with a full-time paid workforce of 12 – all of whom received the same necessarily meagre wage – it was taken for granted that anyone who contributed to the station had the right to a say in its operations. Being dependent primarily on the generosity of subscribers and a significant amount of volunteer labour, it was fundamental to the station's ethos to operate as a collective. Thus while policy was thrashed out in often fiery collective meetings, day-to-day implementation and management of those policies was left to staff.

The staff did, however, possess a negative quorum (meaning that for any decision to stand, a majority of staff had to be involved in the vote) that provided a bulwark against any collective takeover. Although the quorum was never used, the inherent power differential between staff and volunteers helped sow the seeds for the factions developing within the station. It was inevitable that Triple Zed's founders would be protective of what they had created; equally inevitable that those desiring change would at times complain bitterly of being disadvantaged or even shut out of negotiations.

Helen Hambling: With the benefit of hindsight, because that first group worked so closely together for such a long period of time, and achieved so much – from nothing to an operating radio station – the bonds were probably very strong, and I think in retrospect that was probably a little bit exclusionary. Not that I think that was deliberate, but when you get a strong, connected group of people, it's probably more difficult to break into that than a more porous organisation.

Triple Zed had been born of two primary motivations: to provide an alternative source of information in a state poorly served by a docile media, and to cater for the large number of radio listeners equally disenfranchised by the anaemic musical fare dished up by commercial AM radio. While most of the station's founders regarded these objectives as entirely complementary, the relative proportions of airtime granted to music, news and information became the most keenly fought issue of Triple Zed's early years. In the hothouse political environment post-Whitlam, there was also the question of just how far the station could afford to go in pursuit of its objectives.

Jim Beatson: There were huge divisions within the station. Within the first 12 months there were very bitter arguments between the pragmatists, of which I was one, who argued that if we kept a low profile and pretended that they'd sacked me and the other left-wing troublemakers, then they would [leave us alone]. And on the other side there was the more militant faction, who we characterised as brainless, who said, 'Oh no, you've got to fight them openly.'

Stuart Matchett: I remember we had one meeting where Jim Beatson said that if you really thought what you were doing was being revolutionary, maybe you should think about not working on a radio station. If you thought the most important thing was the armed struggle in South Africa, maybe you should go to university and study medicine, be a doctor and go there. Doing interviews and playing music in Brisbane maybe wasn't the way you were going to achieve what you were after!

Triple Zed was the only station among Whitlam's dozen with its own news and information service, consisting of fully accredited journalists, in addition to prominent future scribes Marian Wilkinson and Steve Gray. With two experienced broadcasters in John Woods and Bill Riner, Triple Zed boasted a professional edge lacking in its interstate peers. The first issue of the station's subscriber journal *Radio Times* spelled out the newsroom's intentions:

> Have you ever noticed how identical and predictable the commercial news services are? Are you disappointed at the way existing news services shirk their responsibilities by avoiding controversy? . . . There are numerous local pressure groups in the community who receive very little coverage in the media, and that which is given trivialises the issues and distorts their position in the political spectrum. The mass media thrives on the perpetuation of myths . . . We won't be accepting press releases from political parties as documents of absolute truth, but will combine them with our own independent investigations.[5]

This spiel was backed up by items on Aboriginal land rights and East Timor, which had just been invaded by Indonesia. Triple Zed was better placed to make feature reports than hard news: working on a shoestring, the station could hardly afford access to wire services, meaning that most bulletins were compiled simply by 'borrowing' reports from other agencies. But the news team quickly became adept at twisting others' work enough to find their own angles.

Still, given the station's limited reach, tiny audience share and willingness to run with politically marginal issues, Triple Zed's newsroom was at first seen as something of a novelty in political circles. One incident was to prove otherwise. Contrary to Beatson's wish to maintain a low profile, Triple Zed was about to become arguably the closest thing Queensland had to a genuine political opposition.

* *

In the dawn of 29 August 1976, 40 Queensland police, backed by a light aircraft, a helicopter, a customs launch and two black trackers, launched a raid on a hippie commune at Cedar Bay, south of Cooktown in far north Queensland. Shots were fired and a helicopter buzzed the surrounding rainforest as police entered the commune. The state government claimed the raid was intended to catch an escaped prisoner believed to be hiding in the commune.

The escapee was not found, but a dozen hippies were charged with minor offences, four for drug possession and eight for vagrancy. More seriously, the commune itself was destroyed, despite the hippies' entirely legal occupation of the land. Large and well-built huts were burnt to the ground, along with entire lots of personal possessions, including food and baby clothes. Even the surrounding fruit trees were chopped down.

Initial police reports trumpeting the raid as a great success may have been accepted but for the fact that Steve Gray, who had been working with Stanwell as Triple Zed's promotions coordinator, was holidaying in Cairns at the time. When a friend alerted him to the presence of newly homeless commune members who had straggled into the north's biggest tourist town, Gray put them in touch with the station's newsroom to give their very different account of events.

The Cedar Bay story was tailor-made for Triple Zed. It was highly relevant to its audience: many of the station's listeners still held dear the ideals of the hippie movement. It was also another dramatic demonstration of the Queensland Police's contempt for civil liberties and alternative lifestyles. But the station didn't yet have the national recognition and credibility it needed to publicise its scoop.

The station decided to pass the story on to the ABC. When the late Andrew Olle contacted Gray to ask him to lead a film crew to Cedar Bay, the story began to take on a life of its own. The resulting report, aired nationally on the ABC's *This Day Tonight* program, made Olle's career. The experience was also something of an eye-opener for his crew:

Steve Gray: They thought they were in bloody paradise. At least one of them had his first joint there, and the next day he didn't want to leave! He really did think it was paradise, because there were these extraordinarily beautiful women walking around naked.

The straights at the ABC were not the only ones exposed to a new lifestyle at Cedar Bay. Terry O'Gorman, by then a qualified solicitor, was despatched north by the Queensland Council for Civil Liberties to investigate.

Terry O'Gorman: I met Steve Gray in Cairns, who drove me along a pretty tortuous track to as far as the road went. From there I walked along the beach in my green safari suit carrying my briefcase, to be confronted by two totally naked women who sort of materialised out of the distance. It was a combination of a hippie colony and a nudist colony, and my concession to this milieu was to sit around in my underpants for a couple of days taking witness statements.

The Bjelke-Petersen government suddenly found itself under an unaccustomed level of national scrutiny. A growing chorus of calls for an inquiry into the raid split the state Liberal–National Party coalition. The premier tried his usual crash-through approach – declaring baldly that 'the government would believe the police'[6] – but he hadn't counted on an old adversary, Ray Whitrod, who defied him by opening his own investigation.

On 16 November, summonses were issued against four police officers on more than 20 charges, including arson. That same day, Whitrod held a press conference, announcing his resignation from the force. He would not be the first to query the government's grasp of the ancient Westminster doctrine of the separation of powers:

The government's view seems to be that the police are just another public service department, accountable to the premier

and cabinet through the police minister . . . I believe as a
police commissioner I am answerable not to a person, not to
the executive council, but to the law.

Asked if he thought Queensland was becoming a police
state, Whitrod simply answered, 'I think there are signs of
that development.'[7]
The police were acquitted. This was unsurprising,
given a conservative Cairns jury was being asked to
believe the word of people whom the defence portrayed
as savages. According to O'Gorman, however, the fact the
prosecutions took place at all constituted 'the first serious
challenge to the law-and-order machine which Bjelke-
Petersen had seen work so well in his favour at the time of
the Springboks'.

> **Steve Gray:** I think that incident showed a lot of middle-class
> Queenslanders what the true nature of the Bjelke-Petersen
> government was. Because even though they were hippies,
> even though they were unmarried mothers, even though they
> had minor criminal records, Cedar Bay was their home. And
> obviously, when you get police on charges of arson, it doesn't
> matter whether it's Kenmore or Cedar Bay, that's pretty
> serious in a bourgeois society.

If Triple Zed received little credit for breaking the
story, they certainly copped their share of blame for the
embarrassment it caused the government. For years the
station, its employees and volunteers were subject to
continuous police surveillance and harassment, mainly by
the so-called Special Branch, the tasks of which included
compiling dossiers on known political dissenters.

If Cedar Bay assured the future of Triple Zed's news and
information service, the educational programming that was
a feature of its first months on air was not so lucky. As the

recipient of an educational licence, it was a political imperative for the station to include educational content – not only to keep the masters in Canberra at bay, but also to further the station's philosophy of granting airtime to issues rarely addressed by the mainstream media. This proved a double-edged sword. As the first alternative radio station in a politically repressive climate, everyone wanted a slice of the action.

> **Helen Hambling:** Brisbane had always had a thriving subculture, more so in my experience than Sydney or Melbourne or other places that are bigger and more diffuse. In Brisbane it was smaller, so people tended to know each other more. What I think Triple Zed did was it gave that subculture the capacity to communicate with itself. And there were a number of strands to that: it was a morale booster, it was an information circuit, and it allowed a lot of other things to thrive – the music and the drama and the art, as well as the politics.

The divisions arose over exactly how information was to be presented. While Triple Zed allowed the subculture from which it had been born to 'communicate with itself', most of the staff had little interest in preaching only to the converted. Thus the majority favoured strip programming, meaning that news, information and education would be made to fit around a consistent, if eclectic musical format – music being considered the obvious bridge to a wider audience.

On the other hand, the hard left (which grew out of the station's academic roots) favoured block programming, whereby chunks of airtime were given over to special-interest shows. The collective structure of the station meant that ground had to be given.

> **John Stanwell:** We knew that the small number of very loud voices would not shut up if we didn't give them slabs of time to have the megaphone. So that meant there was a schism

there, in the sense that it was almost like at the end of a music program the subtle message would be 'turn off now'. And at the end of the current affairs thing, the subtle message would be 'turn off now'. It was never as blatant as that, but that kind of feeling was certainly around.

The March 1976 issue of *Radio Times* provides a fair representation of a month's worth of educational programs, running under the name In Depth: a series of readings from the Romantics, a China special featuring glowing interviews with Australians who had recently visited the communist territory (with accompanying music by Ravi Shankar), and a lecture titled 'The Angel in the House: A Critique of the Idealisation of Victorian Women as a Strategy for Maintaining Oppression'.[8]

March 1976 also saw the first appearance of the station logo: a large, cheerful and very bent banana, striking an Elvis-inspired pose with a microphone. The caricature was supplied by Matt Mawson, the station's artist, who acquired something of a reputation as the Invisible Man:

Bill Riner: Matt was like the Phantom! The legend goes that he would show up, deliver a cover for *Radio Times*, no one would even see him, but this thing would be sitting on the desk. I was there for two years before I even knew what Matt Mawson looked like!

The amusing, whimsical and, most importantly, musical image presented by the station logo (which played on the colloquial representation of tropical Queensland as a state of banana benders) did not sit easily with the dour nature of the educational programs. In the May 1976 issue of *Radio Times*, an editorial described the station as 'too humourless', its political values 'often crude and boringly presented'.[9] It sent a blunt message that an on-air extension of university classes was unlikely to attract the mass minority audience the station sought.

Jim Beatson: They didn't know a lot about music. They wanted to have long worthy programs that appealed to a small bunch of committed people surrounded by bucketloads of Bob Dylan, because that was the only musician they knew. And we thought they were completely missing the point of what the station was about – it was supposed to be a celebration of what young people at their most idealistic and creative can be, rather than a bunch of lefties sitting around listening to lectures from people we already agreed with anyway.

By October, In Depth had been axed. The decision was bitterly attacked in the February 1977 issue of the University of Queensland-based feminist journal *Hecate*. Written under the by-line of the Brisbane Women's Media Group, the article savaged what the authors perceived to be Triple Zed's transformation from an open-access broadcaster to an elite boys' club, dedicated only to a 'pseudo-philosophy of rock, rock, rock'. Clearly, a minority at the station felt that politically progressive radio and rock & roll were mutually exclusive forms.

We originally had high hopes for equal participation in and control of the station, but because of the need of certain elements to exercise power, monopolise information and establish hierarchies, the 'tyranny of rock' became hegemonous. We take for granted readers' reservations about rock music: an extended discussion of the problem of the sexism of rock music is not possible in this particular article.[10]

Ironically, one of the station's strongest-performing and most enduring programs was the feminist show, Through The Looking Glass (later Megaherz). Neither was the station above indulging in its own brand of artistic censorship. Helen Hambling remembers the Rolling Stones' *Black And Blue* being among the records unofficially banned from airplay on the grounds of sexism.

Helen Hambling: I think it was a clash not of politics but of using the medium. If it had been a station that had been started by a feminist collective, I think it probably would have been different. But it had a very strong feminist flavour to it, even though some people were criticising it on feminist grounds. Basically anything that was explicitly anti-woman or pro-violence against women, those sorts of things were pretty well blacklisted. In a way it was quite sanctimonious. I was a lot surer about what was good politics and what was bad than I am now.

A more serious censorship threat came from outside the station. Queensland's resident morals campaigner Rona Joyner, founder of the fundamentalist Christian pressure groups Society To Outlaw Pornography (STOP) and Committee Against Regressive Education (CARE), must have been one of Triple Zed's most ardent listeners for the number of obscenity complaints she filed against the station. Joyner had the sympathetic ear of the premier, and news of the station's indiscretions was inevitably forwarded to Canberra, threatening the renewal of the station's licence. As 1976 melted into 1977, and the new music emanating from England and New York began to take on a harder edge, such complaints were bound to increase.

It would be easy to jump to the conclusion that the mutually confrontational agendas of punk and Triple Zed were made for each other. The truth is its rise caused as much division within the station's ranks as it did almost anywhere else. In large part the station had come into existence to play the music that wasn't deemed suitable for AM radio formats. It is one of the ironies of punk that, beyond its obvious rawness, part of the shock of the new lay in its return to AM radio values: short, simple, repetitive songs and, at least in the case of the Ramones, bubblegum melodies to boot.

A glance at Triple Zed's first Hot 100, aired on New Year's

Day 1977 (the start of a long tradition, and the predecessor of Triple J's Hottest 100) is a roll-call of hits and artists still endlessly rotated on commercial FM radio formats today: Led Zeppelin, Deep Purple, Pink Floyd, Santana, Queen.[11] Although its compilation was statistically very dubious – this was long before computers began crunching the numbers – the list is a reliable enough guide to the kind of music then popular at the station.

> **Stuart Matchett:** The stuff that we played early on was incredibly commercial by today's standards. Initially [music programming] was really easy, because you could play Rolling Stones songs and it was regarded as being incredibly avant-garde. At night we used to get into the jazzy fusion stuff, like the Weather Report and Chick Corea and Mahavishnu Orchestra, which looking back now seems really arty and pretentious, but at the time was absolutely de rigueur.

Even more revealing than the Hot 100 was a list of the best 10 albums of 1976 as voted by the station's announcers: Joan Armatrading's self-titled debut, Guy Clark's *Old No. 1*, Ry Cooder's *Chicken Skin Music*, Genesis' *Trick Of The Tail*, Al Jarreau's *Glow*, Graham Parker's *Howlin' Wind*, Boz Scaggs' *Silk Degrees*, Southside Johnny and the Asbury Jukes' *I Don't Want To Go Home* and Steely Dan's *Royal Scam*.[12]

Yet in the previous two months alone, three astonishing singles had been released: the Damned's New Rose, the Sex Pistols' Anarchy In The UK and – most important of all in terms of local context – the Saints' (I'm) Stranded. The station had stated plainly in the first edition of *Radio Times* that Triple Zed would give support, via airplay and promotion of gigs, 'to Australian bands in general and local bands in particular'[13]; the Saints would sorely test that loyalty.

Not that punk was ignored. Indeed, Triple Zed may have been the first radio station in the world to play these songs. A former station-hand, Ross Creighton, had left for England

to work for an independent record label, and from this base
he posted several test pressings of singles and albums back
to the station, often before their release to British radio.
Additionally, new import record stores (the short-lived
Discreet Records, and the enduring Rocking Horse) were
feeding Triple Zed new albums, along with equally vital
editions of *New Musical Express*, *Melody Maker* and *Sounds*.
Jim Beatson dates the length of time it took for punk to
take off in Brisbane as approximate to that of a sea-mail
subscription of the *NME* to reach the country.

> **Jim Beatson:** Again, there were huge divisions within the
> station, almost within six months. And it became big at Triple
> Zed because the most popular presenter by a long way was
> Michael Finucan, and he was a very strong supporter of
> everything that punk represented. So a tremendous argument
> went on between those who argued that the station's audience
> was being alienated by this incoherent, aggressive rubbish,
> and those arguing, with equal force, 'At long last, something
> new and exciting in the world of music.'

The die was soon cast. Quite by accident, Finucan, or more
correctly Finucan's attitude, was to become the embodiment
of Triple Zed's on-air approach.
    As a 17-year-old music fan, Michael Finucan had
first checked into Triple Zed in February 1976, during
the university's orientation festivities. Enrolled as an
economics–law student, he quickly found himself spending
more of his time washing dishes down at the station. At
first he was regarded as something of a hanger-on: he was
just a kid, even by the youthful standards of most of the
staff. But the depth of his musical awareness soon became
apparent.

> **Michael Finucan:** I'd just got out of high school and had been
> a music obsessive for a long time. I probably was buying import
> records at that point, and probably heard about Triple Zed at

one of the import record stores. Anyway, somehow I heard about the station and really liked it. I previously thought I was the only person in Brisbane who was interested in the music they were playing.

Finucan soon found himself helping out Alan Knight, then presenting a request show under the nom de plume Duane Flick. As the obnoxious Flick, Knight had a penchant for abusing subscribers for their less than adventurous taste (those requesting Led Zeppelin's Stairway To Heaven were singled out for particular scorn). When Knight went out for a cigarette one evening and didn't come back, Finucan graduated to announcer. He'd learned his lessons well.

Michael Finucan: I just kept up Alan's tradition of passing judgmental comments on people's choices. I think I was willing to listen to new music a bit more than some people who had more Catholic tastes when it came to what they thought was reasonable rock & roll. I just liked the sound [of punk], it was energetic, and it said, 'Get stuffed.' And the songs were short!

Triple Zed had its first and probably its last genuine radio star.

Abusive, hilarious and spontaneous, Finucan's on-air technique was simply to circle anything in the *Courier-Mail* that looked to have comic potential and go to town. After promoting himself to the breakfast announcer's chair (to the relief of an exhausted John Woods), Finucan literally moved into the studio for six months, sleeping in a narrow brick room out the back known as the Black Hole. This meant that Finucan didn't waste valuable sleeping time commuting to and from the station, as he was woken by the departing graveyard announcer five minutes before commencing his shift.

But it was the music Finucan played that left the most indelible impression on his listeners. Brad Shepherd, of the Fun Things and later the Hoodoo Gurus, is one who

remembers taping one of Finucan's shows. While the
cassette is long lost, such was its influence on the teenage
Shepherd that he recalls to this day the track listing, in its
original sequence: the Ramones' Now I Wanna Sniff Some
Glue, the Stranglers' (Get A) Grip (On Yourself), John Cale's
Leaving It Up To You, the Damned's New Rose, the Stooges'
Real Cool Time, the New York Dolls' Personality Crisis and
the Sex Pistols' Anarchy In The UK.

> **Brad Shepherd:** There'd been a lot of talk about punk rock. By
> that time I'd seen the Sex Pistols on TV, on *Countdown*, and I'd
> heard Radio Birdman talk about the Stooges. But to actually
> hear it myself for the first time, that was something else.

Not all listeners were so appreciative of punk's challenge
to the unwritten conventions of what constituted good
music and, by extension, good radio. Typical was a letter
published in the October 1977 *Radio Times* from a disgruntled
subscriber, begging Finucan not to continue playing harsh-
sounding records at unseemly hours of the morning.
Finucan responded by advising the anonymous listener to
lock themselves in a room with the complete works of James
Taylor; should this be impossible, they should at least 'be
thankful the songs are short'.[14]

The January 1978 issue of *Radio Times* featured a
very different list of albums from the corresponding
edition the previous year. Plainly there was less than
unanimous opinion about the year's best platters among
the announcers, with the list expanded to a wildly
schizophrenic Top 30. Several names appeared a second
time – Joan Armatrading, Graham Parker, Steely Dan
and Peter Gabriel with his first post-Genesis album – and
they are joined by the likes of Bonnie Raitt, Bob Seger
and Linda Ronstadt. But standing alongside them were a
clutch of debuts that pointed the station's way forward:
the Sex Pistols' *Never Mind The Bollocks*, Elvis Costello's
My Aim Is True, Television's *Marquee Moon*, Richard Hell's

Blank Generation, Talking Heads' '77 and, from Sydney, Radio Birdman's *Radios Appear*.[15]

Curiously, the Saints' *(I'm) Stranded* was absent. Stuart Matchett, who would shortly move to Sydney to begin a lengthy career with Triple J, remembers the single's electrifying effect.

> **Stuart Matchett:** I'd grown up listening to all this incredibly rough R&B stuff, and so as soon as the single came out I thought, hang on, this is exactly the same sort of stuff I used to like. And then I realised, if you hadn't already heard all that, then it must sound really wrong and not tuneful and so on.
>
> There was this one listener who used to ring up all the time and ask me questions about what did I think of this record and that record; he was obviously a big jazz-rock fan. And I always remember after I'd played Stranded a few nights in a row, he just rang me up and said, 'What the fuck are you doing? *What are you playing this absolute garbage for*?'

CHAPTER THREE

the most primitive band in the world

The inner western suburbs adjoining the University of Queensland are a leafy mosaic of Brisbane's aspirational middle classes. Set in the foothills of Mt Coot-tha, the houses around Toowong and Indooroopilly are archetypal of the city: high-set, rustic, surrounded by lush vegetation. During summer, the air rings with cicadas as the humidity sinks deep into the gullies.

Over the Indooroopilly Bridge, on the other side of the Brisbane River, it's a different picture. The landscape is flatter, the heat marginally drier. Unconstrained by the ranges that fringe the city's north-west, the suburban sprawl now extends all the way to Ipswich, the gateway to the farming country of the Lockyer Valley and, over the range, the Darling Downs, for years the centre of the National Party's power base.

In the early 1960s the suburbs of Oxley and Inala remained on Brisbane's south-west outskirts. A jumbled mixture of industrial, semi-rural and new residential estates, the area is determinedly pragmatic and blue-collar conservative, a metaphor for the rest of the state. It was in Oxley that Edmund Kuepper's parents settled after emigrating from Bremen, West Germany in 1960. Kuepper was four years old.

Ed Kuepper: I think growing up in Brisbane definitely had an effect on people. Going anywhere else you sort of felt like a poor country cousin. You'd definitely come to other places and be a bit wide-eyed about it. But in a pretty arrogant way. There's a pugnacious element to the city, which I think the Saints had.

Born in Kenya to Irish Catholic parents in 1957, Chris Bailey's family had lived a nomadic existence before also sailing for Australia, stopping in Perth and Adelaide before finally settling in Brisbane. Bailey was eight. His father, who had spent a lifetime in the army, was highly politicised, active on the periphery of the Irish nationalist movement. He also had strong tastes in music, with an extensive collection of rebel songs. By the end of the '60s, Bailey Sr harboured notions of returning to his homeland, intent on signing his children up for the cause.

Bailey's elder sister Margaret was the most obviously influenced by her father. A member of Students In Dissent, she was expelled from Inala High School for wearing a miniskirt. Outraged, her father demonstrated his support for his offspring by chaining Margaret and Chris to the steps of the education department in protest, the latter wearing sandals and his first attempt at long hair. Yet Chris' description of his involvement in Brisbane's political resistance is couched in the terms of an outsider, even an unwelcome interloper.

Chris Bailey: I thought it was a great big middle-class party. I wasn't directly invited but I managed to sneak in the back door. I believed in the possibility of revolution, but after hanging around St Lucia for a couple of weeks I realised that (a) I'd have to get dressed up for it and (b) my table manners weren't quite correct.

I think I was just a teen rebelling. I was fairly politicised, was anti-Vietnam. I used to wear radical feminist badges to school just to piss teachers off. Because Brisbane in those days was, well, a police state, a fascist state.

After beginning his own secondary education at Inala in

1969, Bailey convinced his parents to allow him to cross over to the 'slightly posher' Oxley High School the following year (motivated by a friend's recommendation that the girls there were better looking). In fact, Oxley High was extremely conservative, and equally intolerant of the wearing of moratorium or women's liberation badges, as the insouciant Bailey was wont to do. On his first day he was pulled out of assembly on account of his long hair. Ed Kuepper was taking notes.

> **Ed Kuepper:** There weren't many boys who had long hair and those that did got to know each other, because you got barred from classes and people would pick on you. So you got tough, or at least learned to run. And we had a shared interest in music, not exactly the same sorts of things really, but they seemed close enough at the time.

Kuepper was already a voracious music fan. Somewhat alienated from his peers, resulting in the creation of an arch, omniscient persona – 'I was fairly condescending towards what was going on around me. I definitely felt above it' – Kuepper's discovery of the Stooges' second album *Fun House*, released in 1970, was a pivotal moment:

> **Ed Kuepper:** *Fun House* had a quality that transcended everything. An unbelievable simplicity, for starters, which was actually shocking to people at the time. People would be like, 'What the fuck is this?' They were like cavemen, and yet obviously they weren't stupid. When you move into your teens, if you're in an environment where you're not feeling a part of what's going on in society, to have a record like that come along is a real life-saver. At the very least it can help point you somewhere.

Tall and lanky, with prematurely thinning blond hair, Ivor Hay was another Oxley teenager who was learning to play piano when aspiring guitarist Kuepper met him at local hangout Oxley Station. Hay was practising his pick-up lines, a skill that would prove invaluable for his future bandmates.

> **Ed Kuepper:** That was one of the great things about having Ivor around. He could set everybody up! I don't think Bailey and I could get a date if we carried enormous amounts of money in those days. But Ivor was the man. There's a place and a purpose for everyone in a band. Apart from that, he was the only one who could drive.

Hay was studying at Corinda High, a far more liberal school to which both Kuepper and Bailey would eventually decamp for their final years. Again, the motivation for joining Hay at Corinda probably had little to do with politics: one urban myth suggested the school then had the highest rate of teenage pregnancies in the state. Either way, Corinda High was to become something of a breeding ground for the first wave of Brisbane's musical talent.

One student enthralled by this emerging scene, and who later became its most earnest chronicler, was a young Clinton Walker. He quickly fell under the spell of these 'antisocial young longhairs', of whom Hay, Kuepper and Bailey were the most driven. There was already, Walker later wrote, an aura about them, 'an absolute arrogance, a contempt not only for the adult world of authority generally but everything else as well, especially the music you were supposed to like'.[1]

> **Clinton Walker:** They were terrifying! Because their hair was so long, and they were so haughty, basically. Ed always kept himself at a height and a distance; he was most at home with his record collection. And Chris was this cavalier vagabond who even in grade 11 had cultivated this image of a wine bottle in one hand and a cigarette in the other.

* *

In 1973 Bailey, Kuepper and Hay began playing together as a three-piece, under the name of Kid Galahad and the Eternals (Kid Galahad from the Elvis movie *Kid Creole*; the Eternals from the science fiction film *Zardoz*). Bailey – a natural frontman with a nascent willingness to push everything, and everyone, to the limit – would sing as Hay pounded the keys and Kuepper thrashed away over the top. Walker witnessed an early rehearsal in Hay's mother's garage. As he later described the event, perhaps a little romantically:

> I was trembling with excitement. I knew I was privy to the birth of a whole new future for rock & roll . . . In possession of this secret knowledge, I felt an absolute certainty that eventually the hippy world would be overturned, that all the squares and naysayers would be shown up for what they were and real rock & roll would prevail.[2]

Whether the birth of 'a whole new future' or not, it is true that these rehearsals took place before the release of the New York Dolls' debut in July. The band's aesthetic and sound was already taking shape, along with prototypes of many of the songs that would later appear on their first album. The first two songs the band wrote were its most elaborate: Messin' With The Kid was a traditional, Stones-styled ballad, while the far more daring Nights In Venice was built around a jagged machine-gun riff that dissolved into a maelstrom of white noise.

The band's line-up was still unsettled. Abandoning the piano, Hay initially moved to bass as the Eternals tried out a succession of drummers. One of them, Bruce Anthon, would soon make his own mark on Brisbane's music scene as a member of the Survivors; another, Jeffrey Wegener, later built a reputation as one of the country's best drummers in Kuepper's post-Saints outfit, the Laughing Clowns. But Wegener had yet to develop his signature style, and his casual approach ensured his tenure in the Saints was brief.

> **Ed Kuepper:** I kicked Jeff out of the band. He was just too unreliable, he wasn't turning up to rehearsals, wasn't treating it seriously. Of course, he denies all this, but it's true! He just wasn't turning up, and when he did he was pissed.

With the band thinking it would be easier to acquire a bassist than a drummer, Ivor Hay decided to settle back behind the kit.

The band's first official gig was at the Chelmer Hall. With next to no chance of getting a gig in conventional venues, the band was forced to play in the few Brisbane locations potentially open to new sounds and ideas. Suburban halls were to become the newly christened Saints' salvation, and they began to book their own shows under the name of Eternal Promotions. The venues were cheap to hire, and there were fewer questions to be answered – at least until the morning after the show, as the Saints pursued the musical equivalent of a scorched-earth policy.

A show at the University of Queensland, organised courtesy of Margaret Bailey's leftist connections, cemented the Saints' reputation as local enfants terribles. By this time, the group had attracted a tiny but devoted following, consisting almost entirely of high school friends and friends of friends. Some, like Walker, gravitated mainly towards the music; others interpreted the wildness of the band's sound as a cue for another kind of auto-destruction. Triple Zed was keen to demonstrate its support for local music, but found itself thoroughly unprepared for the musical and personal hurricane it encountered.

> **John Stanwell:** The Saints, particularly Chris Bailey, just had this real thing about them. They were *angry*. Now, that anger may well have been totally genuine, but for people who

had to deal with them, it was difficult. They set out to make themselves unpopular.

Ed Kuepper: Our relationship with Triple Zed was pretty bumpy. I think the Saints were maybe just a little too extreme for them. They were touting themselves as supporters of the local industry, and looking back on it now I can see things from a slightly different perspective, but at the time they struck me as being fairly gutless and unsupportive, really. But I'd qualify all that – the Saints were a pretty anarchic band.

John Stanwell: Basically what happened in those days was people would go and smash up toilets; that was the kind of thing they did. So the venues would just chuck the bands out, and the bands had nowhere to go. A fair bit of damage was done to the room, which we were held responsible for, and that led to a lot of ill feeling.

Chris Bailey: They were panicking about their funding, and we were a little bit too outré for their tastes. Because they were a little bit Jackson Browne, West Coast, touchy-feely if memory serves me correctly, and we weren't considered to be musically kosher. Also, we weren't on campus, we weren't university students, so [therefore] we were just scumbag troublemakers from the wrong side of the tracks interested in their women. Which of course we were!

At the junction of Milton Road and Petrie Terrace, on the north-west edge of the city centre, is a small house that is now home to a photographic studio. Situated at the top of Paddington, originally a poor area that would later become one of the first inner-city suburbs to fall to the creep of gentrification, the building looks directly across to a foreboding brick building that was once the city's police headquarters. Four hundred metres further down Milton

Road is the Castlemaine Perkins brewery, its crimson neon XXXX logo visible for miles around.

In early 1976 Chris Bailey moved into the house that was then being rented by Margaret. When she moved out shortly afterwards, Ivor Hay moved in, and the band continued rehearsals in the long front room – this time with the addition of a permanent bass player, Kym Bradshaw. It was a strictly pragmatic choice.

> **Chris Bailey:** [Kym] had a job; he had money. I think we might have used his credit to buy a van. I think he got marginalised fairly early on. It's a terrible thing to say, but I think he was just being used, actually.

But the addition of Bradshaw to the line-up supplied the necessary gravity to the Saints' high-octane sound. Ivor Hay had developed a unique style on the drums that was almost bottomless: with little use of the kick drum for backbeat, Hay instead provided an instinctive, manic whirl of snare and cymbals that at times – most notably on Nights In Venice – pushed the band's sound to the brink of derailment. In short, Hay played to the guitar rather than the bass.

The band's dedication was beginning to pay off.

> **Bill Riner:** I used to live in Paddington, and I'd hear them on the way home on my bicycle. I'd stop there and I'd hear them, thrashing and bashing and making the most awful noise. But boy, they practised hard. And often. They got good in a short space of time.

Few others were so appreciative of the group's development. When a plate-glass window at the building's front required boarding up after being smashed by a disgruntled neighbour, it was Kuepper who suggested daubing the words 'Club 76' over the top and using the house as a venue, albeit one with neither a bar nor an admission fee.

The Saints' now legendary performances at Club
76 – described by Clinton Walker as 'a humbling, thundering
thing to experience'[3] – were essentially band rehearsals
or parties at which the band would play: up to three sets a
night, including roaring, hyper-extended covers of Ike and
Tina Turner's River Deep, Mountain High and Del Shannon's
Runaway. But the 'venue' was short-lived. The noise inevitably
drew the attention of the constabulary on the other side of
Petrie Terrace. So did the crowd that spilled into the busy
street between sets. And many of the band's fans would make
their own fun that often had very little to do with the music.

> **Ed Kuepper:** It started off with maybe a dozen people coming
> along and ended up with literally a full house in a fairly short
> period of time. So the police and the health department closed
> us down, because for starters we didn't have a licence, and
> secondly there weren't adequate fire exits and toilets, that sort
> of thing.
>
> There wasn't much to do in Brisbane, so we got a pretty
> wide cross-section of people. I didn't witness it, but I heard
> that on the last night a girl was raped there. We were starting
> to get some fairly violent people; people that we really didn't
> want to have anything to do with.

Just as the band's sound was coming into focus, there
appeared an album by a New York group whose short,
bullet-point songs and street-gang image was uncomfortably
close to the Saints'. Released in May 1976, the Ramones had
effectively beaten the Saints to the punch. Kuepper was
crushed.

> **Ed Kuepper:** I was immensely depressed by that. Up until
> that point, really we had no contemporary musical parallels.
> We started around the same time as the New York Dolls, but
> they'd broken up, and [at the time] there wasn't anything else
> around anywhere to my knowledge that was vaguely like what
> we were doing. I just thought, fuck, this is not going to do

us any good, because obviously every man and his donkey is going to see these provincial kids from Brisbane as being the copyists here.

Ed Kuepper had been lucky since leaving school at the end of 1974. He'd landed a job in the warehouse of the now defunct Astor Records, where he furthered his musical education, helping himself to an extensive back catalogue of '60s pop and sundry deleted records that would otherwise have been destroyed. He was appointed the sales representative for north Queensland, a role he didn't treat with a great deal of enthusiasm.

He also had the task of looking after custom pressings of records. Kuepper found he would commonly receive tapes from people, often truckers in outback Queensland who played a little country and western in their spare time and wanted their songs pressed up as singles for use in local juke joints. Kuepper would send the tapes to Melbourne and later be astounded to receive a box full of records back, which he would then return to the songs' creators.

Ed Kuepper: I'd actually left Astor before it dawned on me that it was an incredibly easy thing to do to have a tape and turn it into a record. So while the Saints are credited for putting out the first independent record, there were a lot of hobbyists that were doing it beforehand. It's always happened; it just hadn't really been done by a rock & roll band at that point in time. Of course, a very short period of time after that, everybody was doing it. But for a long time beforehand we were playing and there would be this acknowledgment, 'Yes, here we are making this sound', and then you'd look at your record collection and see these objects, and everything in between would be a bit of a mystery.

Encouraged, in June the Saints booked themselves two

hours in Bruce Window's 16-track studios at West End, on
the south side of the Brisbane River, with the intention
of making a single. Mark Moffatt was billed as producer.
The studio, later known as Sunshine and now based in
Fortitude Valley, was (and still is) primarily used for
recording jingles. Kuepper estimates the cost of the session
at around $200.

Now with over a dozen songs to choose from, the band
conducted a straw poll of friends to determine a likely hit
single. With its anthemic, rallying chorus, (I'm) Stranded
emerged the clear winner. Certainly, if alienation and
escape are key rock & roll themes, (I'm) Stranded remains
as emblematic as any song of its era.

Kuepper's sheet-metal guitar sets the breakneck tempo,
pushed all the way by Hay. There is no solo, just Bailey
howling into the gale. The recording quality is raw
(the distinctive chink heard at the song's conclusion is
the sound of Hay knocking over a bottle[4]) but captures
perfectly the sound of a band on the cusp of greatness.

With no label or distributor to call on, 500 copies of
the single were pressed on the Saints' own Fatal Records
imprint. There was no picture sleeve, no frills. Even the
name Fatal was a misnomer: Kuepper had originally
suggested Fay-Tel, a pun on the cheap K-Tel label. It didn't
matter. 'By the time I got the record, I just played it about
a hundred times,' Kuepper says. 'I was pretty happy with
it.'

A few copies were dropped off at Rocking Horse and
Discreet Records in the city. Most of the remainder were
shipped around the country and overseas, to record
companies and journalists, with Kuepper listing his
parents' home in Oxley as a mailing address. The band
even shot a primitive but charged video for the single in a
disused house on Petrie Terrace, spraying the words '(I'm)
Stranded' over the top of the fireplace. The video begins
with the obvious if unintended metaphor of Hay kicking
the door open.

It was now September 1976. The same month, in London, the 100 Club held a festival featuring a colourful assortment of new bands, all playing variations on a new kind of amphetamine-fuelled rock, as vaudevillian as it was vitriolic. These new groups – the Sex Pistols, the Clash, the Damned, the Banshees and more – were channelling their own anger into a new kind of musical energy.

SOUNDS SINGLE OF THIS AND EVERY WEEK

THE SAINTS: (I'm) Stranded (Fatal). There's a tendency to blabber mindlessly about this single, it's so bloody incredible. This Queensland combo had to record and release on their own label; for some reason Australian record companies think the band lack commercial potential. What a bunch of idiots.

You like Quo or the Ramones? This pounds them into the dirt. Hear it once and you'll never forget it. The singing's flat and disinterested, the guitars are on full stun. There's no such thing as a middle eight. It's fabulous.

The flip, No Time, isn't quite as cataclysmic, but the guitars are great, a manic grind that winds up faster and faster until it blows your head off. Made to play REAL LOUD. Until some record company gets wise to the best single this year you'll have to send 90p for the first one and 60p for each additional copy to: Eternal Productions, 20 Lawson St, Oxley 4075, Queensland, Australia.

Do it today.[5]

Even the ABC radio newsreader sounded surprised by what he was reading. 'An unknown band from Brisbane, by the name of the Saints, has earned rave reviews in England for a record it made itself,' he intoned.[6] For most Brisbane listeners, it was the first they had heard of the band. While Jonh Ingham's review for British weekly *Sounds* virtually assured the Saints' status from the outset – as decisive a prediction of rock & roll future as Jon Landau's famous 1974 assessment of Bruce Springsteen – its significance went largely unrecognised at the time.

> **Chris Bailey:** I was actually listening to the radio at the time and I thought, 'That's odd. I'm in that group. I don't recall becoming instantly famous in the UK.' And then Ed called up and said, 'Have you heard the news?' and I said, 'Yes, it sounds a bit weird. What's going on?' And then a telegram came, probably the Power Exchange offering us a deal. And then lots of telegrams started to arrive. And then ultimately after the telegrams arrived we were sent a copy of the magazine. By that stage we had the impression that something was up, because even EMI here had been in touch.

The short-lived Power Exchange label's enthusiasm won them the licence to reissue the single locally in England. By the time of its eventual release in December, punk had reached a crescendo of public hysteria. The Sex Pistols had already been sacked from EMI in the wake of their expletive-flecked confrontation with Bill Grundy on the *Today* show. Slammed for caving into a tabloid-led moral panic, the label was desperate to claw back lost credibility. Seduced by Ingham's endorsement, EMI instructed its baffled representatives in Sydney to sign the Saints.

Thus Sydney artist & repertoire manager Chris Barnes along with EMI house producer Rod Coe were packed off to Brisbane to meet the band. With an album being demanded by their bosses in London, they had little choice. More time – this time an entire weekend – was booked at Window Studios. Rod Coe, who had made his mark working with Slim Dusty, found he didn't have a great deal to do. His lasting contribution was to let the band go: the Saints' inexperience in the studio didn't translate to an ignorance of what they were trying to achieve. 'Musically,' Kuepper insists, 'we knew exactly what we were doing.'

Rod Coe: It was incredibly raw, and that was confronting, because my natural instinct was to smooth it over. But they were really strong, they had their own chemistry going, they had their sound and their energy. It wasn't like you had to pick the songs apart and rearrange them and present them in studio form – it was very much a garage-type situation. I just had to get it while it was hot.

Ed Kuepper: Rod came along and sat there with a bemused look on his face for a couple of days. I don't think he had much of a clue what we were doing, but he was a really nice guy, and he let us do what we wanted to do. The other thing I really liked about Rod – still do – was that he became kind of an ally at EMI. He was a friendly face there, whereas a lot of people weren't.

Rod Coe: It pisses me off sometimes when people say that the producer just sat there and did nothing, because sometimes that's the very best thing to do! But I did feel at the time I was contributing nothing, other than making sure the job got done.

Regardless of the extent of his musical contribution, the rocket-fuelled intensity of the eight new tracks Coe recorded for *(I'm) Stranded* outstripped even the two single cuts, which were redeployed to open each side of the album. More disciplined than *Damned Damned Damned*, as nihilistic as *Never Mind The Bollocks*, *Stranded*'s raw fury was nevertheless closer in spirit to the English bands than anything to come out of New York.

Ed Kuepper: Well, the Saints were a working-class band. The New York bands, as much as I liked them, were all well-off kids working in a very safe environment. I mean, they could play CBGBs and play to 50 people and it would all be very cool. Whereas we might play the Sherwood RSL and risk getting our heads bashed in. Anything goes in New York, whereas here, not very much goes.

The pole position of the two single sides notwithstanding, *Stranded* revolves around the band's first two compositions. A slow, chugging hymn to adolescent frustration, Messin' With The Kid is raised to towering proportions by Kuepper's long outro solo. But Nights In Venice is the tour de force, propelled by a blinding performance from the untutored Hay. Hay's jousting with Kuepper provided the key to the album's rapier cut-and-thrust sound, a musical relationship that Kuepper would extend further with Jeffrey Wegener in the jazz-inspired Laughing Clowns.

Ed Kuepper: Nights In Venice was a distilled version of what a lot of the live sets at various times consisted of. The instrumental section with Bailey ad-libbing over it was something we did in a few songs, but it only got put onto record with that one. There were a couple of others that had a similar kind of feel. Messin' With The Kid was there to counter the total expressionism of Nights In Venice.

In early 1977 EMI assigned the Saints their first manager, a budding music entrepreneur called Chris Gilbey. The band was already being pulled in different directions. With zero commercial interest in what either the Saints or their Sydney counterparts, Radio Birdman, were doing in Australia, a move was inevitable. England was the obvious place for both bands to go.

Ed Kuepper: It was a difficult relationship with EMI in Australia, and we ended up signing directly to [EMI subsidiary] Harvest in the UK. They were keen to have us over there, and they paid for it. EMI in Australia didn't really have a clue what to do with the band.

Chris Bailey: I think there were several buses being chartered and driven at the same time. Chris [Gilbey] was a real careerist, a bit of a wide-boy. When things were going well he was on side. Ed's a megalomaniac, I'm sure he thought he was in control of everything, but that's not strictly true. It was quite fragmented, and it started to fragment very quickly.

Following a brief tour to Melbourne, the band played its final gig in Australia with Radio Birdman at the Paddington Town Hall on 3 April 1977. The performances of both bands on that night – the Saints in their sloppy street clothes, Birdman with their uniforms and symbols – have since gone down in history. So has the mutual distrust that bordered on enmity between the two bands: in Vivien Johnson's biography of Birdman, guitarist Deniz Tek remembers Kuepper's 'brooding hostility', and dismisses Bailey as a 'drunken Irishman'.[7] While the feud has long since passed, it was real enough at the time.

Chris Bailey: It's pretty overblown, and quite amusing. But there was animosity, and I'm sure they'd say the same thing. I thought it was more from their side, even though I've heard the quote 'They came down like hillbillies, and were really obnoxious and we just welcomed them with open arms!' Which I think is kind of true.

Filmed by the ABC, the show is the best existing document of the original Saints in full flight. There's Kuepper, sleeves rolled up, nodding his head with each downstroke on his cherry-red Gibson, dispensing with lead guitar flourish in favour of jagged rhythm, maximum distortion and lightning bursts of feedback. At the back, Hay barely holds down the beat, his face painfully contorted. Bradshaw remains in the background, unobtrusive, perhaps already superfluous to requirements.

At the front is Bailey, his hair a dripping tangle of sweat.

Occasionally he shimmies self-consciously, but mostly he remains still, gripping the microphone tightly. His vocals, though, are explosive, each syllable a verbal grenade. Between songs he thanks 'the local chapter of the Hitler youth' for the stage props, a reference to Radio Birdman's quasi-militaristic logo.

As Nights In Venice descends into the abyss, Bailey drops from the stage. He sings the remainder of the song slumped below its lip. As the camera moves in for a close-up, he forgets himself, stares, and swipes. There is a momentary loss of vision. Regaining his feet, he charges; screams; reels back and, in a gesture of the most supreme indifference, actually *thumbs his nose* at the audience, before plunging headlong into the song's last verse:

> East side, west side it all looks the same now
> Don't need nobody and you don't care nohow
> Don't need no love and you don't need no hate
> You were screaming so loud but it was much too late

The song finally topples in on itself. The spent singer staggers off into the crowd, offering one final sign-off before tossing his microphone aside:

'WHAT A FUCKING WASTE OF TIME!'

The Saints arrived in England in the last days of May 1977. Punk was already a fashionable contrivance, a prisoner of its three chords. In London, the image – somewhere between the Ramones' leather jackets and the Pistols' cut-and-paste juxtapositions – had become a uniform. EMI was making noises about designing a 'Saints Suit': lime-green shirts, ripped pants and spiky hair.[8] The band blanched at the suggestion. Bailey's long, tousled mop remained in place.

Outside London, the new music, and its accompanying garb, had yet to take hold.

Ed Kuepper: It hadn't hit the provinces yet. We did a couple of shows in London and then did a tour around the country, and once you got out of London . . . If the mark of a punk is a particular look, then they didn't exist outside the capital cities. Maybe there might have been a token punk in the medium-sized towns, but you didn't see many of them. In fact, our first tour around, people looked pretty much the way people did in Australia.

This dichotomy cut against the Saints both ways. Punk was moving so fast that inside the capital the band found itself scorned by the same British weeklies that had fêted it six months earlier. Elsewhere, they remained unknown. EMI's patronage, too, was the source of press accusations that the Saints were mere hangers-on. The band's unwillingness to be corralled into anything that resembled an organised movement would ultimately cruel its prospects.

Ed Kuepper: [After the Sex Pistols] there seemed to be a view that if you were going to be on EMI then you were some kind of class traitor or something. The fact that the Clash were on CBS didn't seem to offend anybody nearly as much.

Chris Bailey: We weren't really part of that whole stream. I didn't really relate to punk rock. I liked the soft aspects of it – the little gothic kids in their funny make-up; I thought that was quite sweet. As far as it being a philosophy, I mean, that's all bollocks, it was just a marketing exercise.

The Saints' first London shows were prestigious. Interest in the group post-*Stranded* was such that Seymour Stein had, via EMI, signed them for the American market to his own Sire Records, home of the Ramones and Talking Heads. Accordingly the band was booked to support their new label-mates at the Roundhouse on 5 and 6 June. What should have been a dream debut turned into a debacle: unused to the big stage, nervous and jetlagged, the band was pitifully off-form, a situation not helped by Kuepper's amps blowing up on both nights. And, sure enough, the press denounced the Saints as Ramones plagiarists. Kuepper's earlier fears were swiftly materialising.

After a brief regional tour, the band retreated to the studio. This Perfect Day was among the band's toughest moments, its serrated riff echoing the Stones' Paint It, Black; Bailey's lyrics a series of denials as potent as any penned by John Lydon: 'I don't need no one to tell me what I don't already know!' It was a relentless track, impossible to assimilate into the more pop-friendly marketing strategy of the new wave. It says much for Britain's dark humour in the summer of 1977 that, incredibly, the single took off following the band's appearance on the UK television institution *Top Of The Pops*.

This Perfect Day sold a staggering 75,000 copies in two weeks, pushing the band to number 34 on the British charts. It would climb no higher: anticipating a smaller return, EMI had run out of stock. How such a blunder was allowed to happen is a mystery, for the label had taken the trouble to issue both 7-inch and 12-inch formats of the single, with the latter containing a bonus track.[9] The sleeve's disclaimer warning that the third song, Do The Robot, had been added 'due to an administrative error' was an obvious promotional ruse, but it worked. By the time stores were supplied with additional copies, however, it was too late: the song had already slipped off the radar.

By this time Bradshaw was gone, sacked by Kuepper after the first tour. Bradshaw had remained on the periphery of the initial triumvirate. Suffering from what Kuepper euphemistically describes as 'personal problems' and unable to fulfil his bass duties to requirements, he had outstayed his welcome. His replacement, Alasdair Ward, was close at hand.

Ed Kuepper: Alasdair was the brother of a roadie that we had working for us. He was obviously aware of the fact that the situation with Kym wasn't all that good and took the first

opportunity he could to put his brother forward. Alasdair came
along, did an audition and he knew all the stuff, he was a much
tighter bass player than Kym. So he got the job.

Attempting to regain their momentum, in July the band
gathered in AIR studios in London to record a second EP,
One Two Three Four. Featuring two covers and superfluous
second takes of Demolition Girl and One Way Street, it was
plainly a stopgap. The highlight, a thrilling version of River
Deep, Mountain High, had been in the band's set from the
early days. But playing standards at a time when history
had been cast aside only furthered the impression that the
band was out of step.

Ed Kuepper: There weren't enough new songs around
that I can remember. And it just seemed like a really good
opportunity to record songs that had worked fantastically
live. River Deep, Mountain High was a real standout. If we
were trying to align ourselves with the fashion-conscious
punk element, then sure, it was a major blunder. But even
with that knowledge we would have gone ahead, because
one of the things that I certainly rejected was the denial of
the past.

There were plenty of new songs by the time the band
embarked upon a brief tour to support the EP's release in
October. One month earlier, the band had laid down 11
tracks in Wessex Studios that would form the backbone of
their second album, provisionally titled *International Robots*.
With tracks like Lost And Found, Misunderstood and Run
Down, along with streamlined new recordings of This
Perfect Day and Do The Robot, musically the album didn't
promise to be any great extension of *Stranded*.[10]

On 28 October *Never Mind The Bollocks* was released. The
Sex Pistols' only complete album, it remains the definitive

artefact of the punk era. But with lesser bands content to regard *Bollocks* as a blueprint rather than a full stop, and with the Saints having already made one album the equal of the Pistols in sound and fury anyway, Kuepper recognised the need to start again.

> **Ed Kuepper:** I don't think you can keep making a record like *Stranded*. Because it would be like [the Stooges'] LA Blues, you can hear it once but you don't want to constantly hear it. It has to go somewhere else to retain any sort of validity.

The Saints returned to Wessex at the conclusion of the tour. The extra money and time available to the band, courtesy of EMI's patronage, would be used to full advantage. Inspired by Otis Redding's horn-fuelled rearrangement of the Rolling Stones' Satisfaction, Kuepper began experimenting with a punching brass arrangement for a new song, welded to an explosive riff. The result, Know Your Product, would take the Saints in an entirely new direction and provide the necessary focal point for what would become *Eternally Yours*.

With Kuepper still only 22 and Bailey barely 21, the novelty of being imported rock stars had scarcely worn off.

> **Ed Kuepper:** I wasn't happy with what we had before we added Know Your Product, and the idea of having a bit more time in the studio was great. Having an EMI car or cab picking us up to go to the studio to do the recording, all that stuff was incredibly exciting and really got me into the whole idea of being a recording band, as opposed to just a band who played live.

Eternally Yours captures the Saints in transition. Know Your Product bridges the unbridled force of *Stranded* with the driving R&B of *Prehistoric Sounds*, while the acoustic Memories Are Made Of This, Untitled and A Minor Aversion look ahead to the more considered solo careers of both

Kuepper and Bailey. If the overall results are less focused than *Stranded*, what holds the album together are Bailey's lyrics, a pinpoint satire on punk's commercial incorporation.

But EMI was unprepared for such a departure. Ill feeling between band and label (fomented by the latter's mishandling of This Perfect Day) was already simmering. Audiences were similarly affronted, reacting with bemusement when the group toured with a brass section in January. When Know Your Product went nowhere on its release as a single the next month, the writing was on the wall. The Saints, too young to appreciate that the merits of what they were setting out to accomplish might just be lost on others, were stunned by the injustice of it all.

> **Chris Bailey:** We went to Paris, and nobody turned up. We went to Amsterdam, and nobody turned up. So Ed and I got a bit sulky and didn't want to tour any more. I think we kind of made the wrong decision, because we probably should have actually slogged it out a little bit longer. But I think we thought we'd already arrived, and that was a mistake.

Convinced the band was going nowhere, Bailey's girlfriend tried to persuade the singer to retire from music to become a publican in Cornwall. Bailey duly left after the tour, a fact concealed from EMI. But Kuepper, his creative muse ignited by Know Your Product, had already commenced writing material even further away from the band's roots. Barely a month after *Eternally Yours* finally crept out in April, the band was back in the studio. It was their last chance.

> **Ed Kuepper:** I just said to Chris, 'Look, you haven't made this departure public, come back and do the vocals, write some lyrics.' So *Prehistoric Sounds* was a more extended recording session, because he didn't have much in the way of lyrics initially.

Chris Bailey: It was pretty obvious EMI was going to drop us. I'd decided I was going to scarper because it was just in the too-hard basket. Ed takes credit for this, but Gilbey actually talked me into not going, because I was the voice of the band and if I left I'd be letting everybody down, and I thought yeah, OK, he's got a point. So I came back to the flock, and the flock disintegrated after the record, which we knew was going to happen.

Released posthumously in November 1978, *Prehistoric Sounds* was the Saints' final album in their original incarnation. It may as well have been the work of an entirely different band to that which made *Stranded* only 18 months previously. The Stax-style horn arrangements prefigured by Know Your Product is given full vent, with the authentic R&B soulfulness of All Times Through Paradise, Swing For The Crime and The Chameleon reinforced by covers of Otis Redding's Security and Aretha Franklin's Save Me.

Most crucially, the slower tempos and extra space in the sound freed Bailey, who responded magnificently, in spite of Kuepper's insistence that he was less than enthusiastic about the new material. But while in Australia *Prehistoric Sounds* is widely regarded as the Saints' masterpiece – in Clinton Walker's words, 'an extraordinary collision of brass, guitars and attitude'[11] – in the UK it was viewed as the work of a band that had lost touch with what made it great in the first place. The album was never released by Sire in America.

Ed Kuepper: I was really focused on *Prehistoric Sounds*; I really started to feel that I was getting into stride on that record. The more subdued sound is totally intentional; it wasn't an oversight. Everyone was using distorted guitars in those days, and that was something that I wanted to move away from.

Ironically, given the poor reception of the covers on *One Two Three Four*, EMI was convinced the album's best chance lay with the recording of the Otis Redding chestnut, Security.

It was indicative of the label's loss of faith in the band's direction, and was compounded by A&R changes that are the scourge of any new band.

> **Chris Bailey:** EMI were *not* pleased. I really thought Swing For The Crime should have been the single, but that wasn't the case. We got our marching orders – you know, your wages will stop in a month from now. And then it all just fell to pieces.

> **Ed Kuepper:** I kind of didn't care after we'd done that album. If we were going to end, it was a really good record to end on. I was actually contemplating chucking it in for a short period of time.

Kuepper and Bailey had grown apart. The horns on *Prehistoric Sounds* – especially the saxophone on Kuepper's solo composition Brisbane (Security City) – had reflected his fascination with jazz, particularly the work of Archie Shepp and John Coltrane. Lyrically, the song's subject matter drifted homeward.

> Thirteen hot nights in a row
> The cops drive past but they move slow
> A million people staying low
> With mangoes ripe who needs to grow

Bailey was unmoved. A far more traditional writer, he had begun to assert himself with his own solo contribution to *Prehistoric Sounds*, Take This Heart Of Mine (a song Kuepper would have preferred omitted). Further, Bailey had no intention of returning to Brisbane. And he had already completed demos for what would become his personal triumph, the *Paralytic Tonight, Dublin Tomorrow* EP.

> **Chris Bailey:** Ed just didn't want to be in London anymore, and I did. And even though Ed never mentions this, I already had the basis of a new group.

> He came down for one rehearsal, sat there with a guitar
> in his hand for about 20 minutes, then said, 'I don't like this,'
> and left.

Kuepper returned to Brisbane, where he would form the Laughing Clowns with Jeffrey Wegener in 1979. Bailey retained the Saints name, making a number of fine records with a floating line-up of very different bands.

The relationship between the two songwriters never recovered.

CHAPTER FOUR

the striped sunlight sound

If the Saints' working-class origins in Brisbane's south-west were a factor in the band's self-described 'obnoxious demeanour', then the opposite was the case for Brisbane's other pre-eminent band of the late 1970s. Forged at the University of Queensland by two former private school teenagers, the Go-Betweens were inspired more by the Saints' willingness to go against the grain than their sound. Although by no means the first group to emerge from Brisbane in the wake of the Saints' departure, the Go-Betweens also harboured ambitions beyond what their country was able to provide. By the early '80s they too would decamp for London.

> **Robert Forster:** I think we all felt a little bit brushed by the Saints' wings. They certainly made Brisbane seem a bit more like a place where you could do something tangible. Before that, the previous band from here that had put out an album was Railroad Gin, and they were from a whole other era – they were like *musos*, you know? The fact that these four delinquents from Oxley and Inala had got together and flipped out a city was a huge thing.

Robert Forster grew up in The Gap, a sprawling new suburb situated at the foot of the forested slopes of Mt Nebo. The son of a fitter and turner and a physical education teacher, Forster was educated at Brisbane Boys Grammar in inner-city Spring Hill. Not surprisingly his upbringing was steeped in sport rather than music, and he played in the school's first XI cricket team, even attending state trials.

In 1975 Forster became one of the first members of his family to attend university. He had excelled academically and was initially accepted into the University of Queensland's law school before settling on arts, much to his family's chagrin.

> **Robert Forster:** I was 17, which I think is miles too young. I probably knew somewhere in my gut that I never wanted to work in a normal job, but that was hard to articulate at the time, or even understand. So I just went and did an arts degree basically to buy time.

Grant McLennan was born in Rockhampton, a cattle town in central Queensland. His father died when he was four, and the family subsequently relocated to Cairns in the state's far north. At the age of 12 McLennan was sent to Brisbane as a boarder at the Anglican Church Grammar School. Growing up in the country, in a climate hotter and even more humid than Brisbane, meant that McLennan viewed the city with greater charity than many of the locals.

> **Grant McLennan:** As a kid I remember being very impressed by Brisbane. It meant the Gabba, because I was interested in sport at school. It meant bookshops; it meant anything that Cairns wasn't, [because] Cairns just seemed so hot and boring to me at that stage. And very racist. There were definitely parts of north Queensland where there were black pubs and white pubs. There were even pubs that were black on one side and white on the other.

Despite their mutual love of cricket, both Forster and McLennan had gravitated to literature and the arts from their teenage years. Forster had picked up the guitar in his final school years and begun writing poetry. What transpired in the next few years could have been a classic study of wasted potential, as the former high achiever struggled to reconcile his burgeoning interests with both his parents and his own expectations. He never graduated.

McLennan was more sure-footed. Although he too came from a family comparatively untouched by art, his love of reading and, especially, film had been encouraged. Enrolling in an arts degree the same year as Forster, McLennan pursued journalism and drama as majors. It was during drama classes that the future creative partners in the Go-Betweens met in their second year.

> **Grant McLennan:** Drama courses were split into two classes, and at the end of semester each class put on a play. My class did *Hamlet*, and I played Polonius. And Robert's class did *The Rocky Horror Show*, and he played the monster. Typecasting, I thought!

Tall and preternaturally handsome, Forster had the air of a 1940s Hollywood star. The active construction of a public persona was very much part of the developing Forster (and indeed the McLennan) aesthetic. David Bowie was at the peak of his fame; Lou Reed had undergone his post-Velvet Underground transformation. The songwriter who most captured Forster and McLennan's imagination, however, was an even more compelling combination of the decadent and the poetic: the young Bob Dylan.

And the city that brought Bowie, Reed and Dylan together was New York, where the music scene was exploding. Figures such as Patti Smith, Tom Verlaine and Richard Hell all held artistic pretensions that would take their work, and their reputations, beyond the narrow confines of rock & roll.

> **Grant McLennan:** I noticed that Robert was carrying around records that I was interested in, and vice versa. He was reading

NME and I was reading *NME*. We were both into *New York Rocker*, an awesome magazine at the time. The New York scene was a mixture of rock & rollers who wanted to be artists, and artists who wanted to be rock & rollers.

1975 was in some respects a watershed year for Brisbane's first wave of musical talent. Six months prior to Triple Zed's establishment in December, a tiny shop had opened in Rowes Arcade, off Adelaide Street in the city centre. Rocking Horse Records (closely followed by Discreet, in the bohemian oasis of Elizabeth Arcade) was Brisbane's first import record store. Its timing was perfect: by the middle of the '70s, pop music had reached a crossroads, about to shed the endless layers it had accumulated since the Beatles' ultimate pop-as-art statement *Sgt Pepper* in 1967.

Rocking Horse swiftly became something of a meeting place (and an employer) of young musicians, and its range of magazines were certainly more important, at least in terms of local development, than the deluxe imported copies of Eagles and Jackson Browne albums cramming its racks. Its founder, Warwick Vere, still manages the store today.

Warwick Vere: At the time there was an enormous undersupply by the Australian record companies of what should have been available. Kids were reading things like *Rolling Stone*, which was a very good magazine back in those days – it had Hunter S Thompson, William Burroughs, people like that writing for it. There was lots of interesting stuff, and music reviews of stuff that just wasn't available here locally.

Both Forster and McLennan were avid followers of *NME*'s Nick Kent, whose espousal of 'the dark stuff' was arguably as important to punk's philosophical development as Lester Bangs. But no matter how difficult a place Brisbane may have been for many young people in the '70s, the Go-Betweens were in no way a product of that darkness. Forster's early musical memories were dominated not by the Beatles or the Stones – much less the Stooges and the MC5 – but by Donovan and early '70s bubblegum. McLennan, for his part, was introduced to music chiefly through television and *The Monkees*.

The obvious bridge between these extremes was Jonathan Richman, whose band the Modern Lovers married a refreshingly positive lyrical sensibility with driving Velvets-inspired rock & roll. Songs like Modern World and Roadrunner were to have a profound influence on Forster's early songwriting. By 1975, before he met McLennan, Forster had formed his first band, the Mosquitoes, followed by the Godots, a name that inspired the wry caption 'the band everyone's waiting for'. The literary overtones of the Godots were reinforced by Forster's first notable original composition, Karen, a love song to a librarian:

> She helps me find Hemingway
> Helps me find Genet
> Helps me find Brecht
> Helps me find Chandler
> Helps me find James Joyce, she always makes the right choice

As Go-Betweens biographer David Nichols has pointed out, Forster's denial of his desire for any 'Queen Street sex thing' with the fictitious Karen makes two radical statements: first, the song is specifically located in Brisbane; and second, his interest is intellectual, not carnal (carnal knowledge still being very much a mystery at that point to the 18-year-old Forster[1]). The self-deprecation of another Forster original, Lee Remick, was even more striking: Forster's juxtaposition of the film starlet's aura with the lyric 'I come from Brisbane, and I'm quite plain' is probably the first explicit manifestation of the kind of place-specific irony that, many years later, was captured in the term Brisvegas.

Forster's muse was too eccentric, and quite possibly too sexually ambiguous, for the series of would-be 'musos' he initially auditioned to join his band. As well as his own nascent original material, covers of songs by the early Beatles and stripped-down versions of disco classics like KC and the Sunshine Band's Shake Your Booty – even Hot Chocolate's Sexy Thing – reflected a camp sensibility totally alien to any self-respecting Deep Purple fan.[2] If Forster were to develop, he would need to find someone more sympathetic to his vision.

> **Robert Forster:** I just realised towards the end that I'd never find the musicians. We'd have guitarists come down, guys that would play in cover bands, and it never worked. So what I had to do was teach my best friend. That's what Tom Verlaine did with Richard Hell, he taught him to play bass, and so I did the same thing.

Grant McLennan was a reluctant musician. Unlike Forster, he was committed to his studies and was sailing through university with distinction. His first love was film, and while working at the Schonell Theatre on campus, he also wrote reviews for the student newspaper, *Semper*. His ultimate plan was to attend film and television school, but on application was told to come back when he turned 21. After finishing his arts degree in the minimum three years, aged 19, he finally acquiesced to Forster's repeated requests to start a band. He had no previous musical experience.

The Go-Betweens – the name echoing LP Hartley's classic novel – were one of many new bands on the Brisbane scene at the beginning of 1978. The Survivors, whose set consisted largely of full-throttle versions of '60s pop classics by the early Who, Kinks and Small Faces, were already gigging. So too were the Leftovers, the most obvious group to pick up the punk baton (and its attendant attire) discarded by the Saints. Although poles apart stylistically, what the Go-Betweens shared with the Saints was a disdain for music as fashion statement.

> **Robert Forster:** I think right from the start we could see that being in leather and chains was exactly not what punk was about. Punk was more the New York thing, where you could have hair down to here, like Joey Ramone. It's variety; it's individual expression; it's diversity.

The group that provided the most immediate assistance to the Go-Betweens was the Numbers, soon to become the Riptides. Fronted by Mark 'Cal' Callaghan and featuring future Go-Between Robert Vickers on bass, the Numbers' snappy surf-pop songs and winning sense of irony made them natural allies to Forster and McLennan, and it was at a Numbers show in early April 1978 that the Go-Betweens made their first public appearance, at Baroona Hall, just around the corner from the long-gone Club 76. Forster simply asked permission for the band to get up and perform two songs during a break following the Numbers' support act (the delightfully named Ronnie Ribbitt and the Toadettes). Forster felt like a debutante.

> **Robert Forster:** We played the two songs, and as soon as we got off stage, Mark Callaghan, Robert Vickers – we met them all, in five minutes . . . They immediately asked us to play a second show. On a personal level, I went from having very few friends to suddenly knowing 100 people. It was incredible, it was like a coming-out, like some sort of old-fashioned Victorian belle or something . . . Life suddenly had a purpose. It just flowered. And it flowered right from the start – right from us playing Lee Remick.

Baroona Hall had originally been secured as a venue

by one John Reid in order to raise money for the *Cane Toad Times*, a local anarchist paper produced by various Triple Zed alumni, including *Radio Times* illustrators Matt Mawson and Damien Ledwich. The fact that the hall was owned by the Paddington branch of the Labor Party was an important consideration: by late 1977, punk gigs were being routinely targeted by police. Although barely a stone's throw from the barracks on Petrie Terrace, Reid hoped that the hall's status would afford the venue, and its patrons, a degree of political protection from further harassment.

> **John Reid:** They'd been trying to have these punk dances in places like Hamilton Hall and Darra Hall, and police would descend upon them all the time. At Baroona we never had a phalanx of police invading the hall. They kept their patrols to the outside. Every other hall dance, the police would come in – I'm talking at least 30 – to shut it down.

Forster and McLennan were still minus a drummer. They had borrowed local author and part-time Toadette Gerard Lee for their first, unplanned show at Baroona Hall. The Survivors' Bruce Anthon also played several early gigs with the band, and his consummate skills probably helped boost the credibility of Forster and McLennan, at that point still extremely limited musicians. But Anthon was committed to his own group.

What Forster and McLennan really wanted was a female drummer. As both freely admit, this had more to do with appearances than talent.

> **Robert Forster:** Grant and I very much liked [Talking Heads' bassist] Tina Weymouth, and we also liked a show called *The Mod Squad*, on TV, which had two guys and a girl. We just liked the chemistry. I think if Grant had have taken to playing drums, we would have had to get a girl on bass. It was like casting.

By this time Forster and McLennan were living together in an old Queenslander in Golding Street, Toowong, not far from the university. Shortly after the Go-Betweens' debut, Grant McLennan wandered into a struggling record store located in a small arcade off the suburb's main shopping precinct of Sherwood Road.

> **Damian Nelson:** My father bought a record shop. And for some reason he looked at me and said, 'Damian, you can manage this record shop' . . . One day Grant McLennan came in and was searching through the records and started advising me about the records I should have, and the next day he came in and asked for a job. And I said OK. No job interviews or résumés! I've often said that if they held an Olympics for the world's worst businessman, I would be the Mark Spitz of that Olympics.

Damian Nelson would become the Go-Betweens' friend, driver and, within his limited means, financial benefactor. He baulks at the term manager – 'I couldn't manage a piss-up in a brewery' – but that is in effect what he became when McLennan showed up at the store one evening with a bottle of wine and told him that the Go-Betweens were going to cut a single. The band had been in existence less than six months.

Registering the name the Able Label (again, its moniker a vehicle for the rather daggy caption, 'If it's ready, it's Able'), the band was booked into Window Studios in May 1978, where *(I'm) Stranded* had been cut 18 months earlier. Like the Saints' first effort, the creation of the first Able Label single was an almost totally DIY operation.

> **Damian Nelson:** We got 700 of these singles back, then we got the labels for the A-side and the B-side. And we just sat around the table, sticking them on.

Eventually released in September, Lee Remick/Karen exposed a band still barely competent on their instruments: Forster chops through the chord changes, McLennan plunks away earnestly on bass behind him, and ring-in drummer Dennis Cantwell, of the Numbers, struggles to keep time with either of them. On the other hand, it captured perfectly the Go-Betweens' brazen mixture of naivety and self-belief. The sleeve – which depicts Forster and McLennan alongside portraits of Dylan, Che Guevara and, naturally, Lee Remick herself – dedicates the record 'to John Fogerty, Phil Ochs, Michael Cole, Natalie Wood, and that striped sunlight sound'.

As the Numbers' bass player Robert Vickers packed a suitcase full of copies to tote around to record shops in Sydney and Melbourne (along with his own band's debut effort, Sunset Strip, recorded in July), the Go-Betweens set about sending most of the remaining platters around the world, not only to journalists and record companies, but also to many of their idols, including Remick, the Byrds' Roger McGuinn and producer Kim Fowley.

The label that responded most enthusiastically (predictably, no local record companies were interested) was the British arm of America's Beserkley Records, whose most famous previous signing was no less than Jonathan Richman.

The group had acquired their first real drummer. Cyprus-born Temucin (Tim) Mustafa was recruited shortly after the recording of Lee Remick, and he appears on the picture sleeve, although Dennis Cantwell is credited 'for the beat'. (Earlier, one Lissa Ross had appeared as the band's drummer in their first press article, but Forster claims she only ever practised with the group.[3]) Mustafa hadn't played in a band before, but his skills were at least comparable to his new band-mates.

The Go-Betweens were looking to expand their sound even further. They had met Peter Milton Walsh, songwriter and guitarist for another new band, the Apartments, in Damian Nelson's shop. A dapper, charismatic figure, Walsh was similarly besotted with Dylan and the New York scene. Moreover, he had just returned from England, where he had witnessed the British punk explosion first-hand: 'It was phenomenally exciting to come back to Brisbane and think there was no reason why I couldn't do it.' He was also slightly older and, in every sense, more worldly than the Go-Betweens.

> **Robert Forster:** He was very much a character. We were characters in the making, but he was more fully formed. He'd been overseas, he'd even been to *Morocco*, which to a couple of boys who'd never been out of Brisbane . . . He was flamboyant, like someone out of a novel, and we liked him. He was enormously funny, very quick-witted, very sharp-tongued.

Walsh's impression of the young Go-Betweens validates Forster's appraisal entirely.

> **Peter Milton Walsh:** They were wholesome, upbeat, sunny people. But everything was mediated for them, nothing was ever experienced, and that was reflected in the sort of songs that they wrote. They were masters of the vicarious!

Beserkley had offered the band a contract that proposed the reissue of both Lee Remick and Karen as two single A-sides, followed by an eight-album deal. Seduced, the band sent not only their signatures but also the master tapes of the single off to England. They were never seen again. Nelson, as green as his band, unfairly blames himself for the debacle.

> **Damian Nelson:** I remember they sent over this huge contract. The guy [from Beserkley], the first time I heard his voice, I had this feeling of dread. But I honestly just felt so happy for Grant and Robert. We took it in to see a lawyer, and he went through

it with us. 'Yeah, it's a standard contract.' And they signed
it . . . God, I was an idiot. The naivety, the absolute naivety.

Forster had visions of being booked into larger venues in
London, and it was with this in mind that he approached
Walsh to help fill out the band as a second guitarist. The
shimmering sounds Walsh contributed to the two songs the
band recorded for Beserkley in November 1978 – especially
The Sound Of Rain – represented an enormous advance.
But when Beserkley went bust only weeks later, the basis
for his recruitment evaporated. Walsh was also starting to
write excellent songs of his own and needed his own avenue
to present them.

> **Robert Forster:** Musically, it was too big a jump for us. And
> Walsh realised as soon as he wasn't going to London with us
> that his playing guitar in the Go-Betweens just wasn't going to
> work, so it just sort of fizzled out. And he went off and formed
> the Apartments, which was entirely the right thing to do.

Walsh remained friends with Forster and McLennan, and
Don't Let Him Come Back (the B-side to the Go-Betweens'
next single for Able, People Say, recorded with Mustafa on
drums in May 1979) is both a fond and funny farewell, its
reedy harmonica playing a good-humoured nod to their
shared love of Bob Dylan.

Tim Mustafa had also decided his time was up. Despite
recording a series of demos recorded at Golding Street
with Gerald Teekman (the so-called 'Teeki Tapes', a crucial
document of the band's early sound[4]), Forster and McLennan
were still making noises about finding a female drummer: in
fact, they had already found one. Mustafa, who at that stage
wasn't even sure that he wanted to be in a band, graciously
vacated his stool.

*   *

Belinda Morrison had seen a great deal more of life than either Robert Forster or Grant McLennan by the time she joined the Go-Betweens in 1980. Born in 1951 in Sydney, she was a full six years older than Forster, and very nearly as tall, standing just over six feet. She was also highly politicised, with a background in social work. In 1973 she had taken a job in the Aboriginal and Islander Legal Service, where the house lawyer was future Labor premier Wayne Goss, and where she had a relationship with radical activist Denis Walker, the son of Aboriginal poet Kath Walker (Oodgeroo Noonuccal).

> **Lindy Morrison:** He took me all over Queensland, he showed me all the communities, everything. I can't tell you the number of times we were stopped . . . We couldn't get a drink in a bar, because Denis was black. We couldn't get motels to stay in, but the biggest thing for me was that I just lost so many of my white friends. I was completely tainted by having had an affair with an Aboriginal man in Brisbane.

Morrison was sharing a house in the inner-west suburb of Auchenflower with Stuart Matchett (then in the process of helping set up Triple Zed) and a trio of budding actors, Geoffrey Rush, Bille Browne and Trevor Stuart. The house featured a dedicated music room, and Morrison started banging the drums, simply because they were 'the easiest to pick up, as far as I was concerned. I didn't understand guitars or amplifiers. And also they were physical, and I wanted to do something that was physically active.'

After a period spent travelling through Europe, Morrison joined her first band in 1978, an acoustic women's group called Shrew. However, it was as a member of Xero (then Zero) that she would first make her mark. Xero also began life as an all-female band, although they were soon joined by guitarist John Willsteed who, along with singer Irena Luckus, would become the creative nucleus of the group (and who, many years later, would himself become a Go-Between).

Xero were defiantly experimental, taking their cues from the fractured sounds of British bands such as the Slits, the Raincoats and the early Cure. Already a veteran of political demonstrations in Queensland, Morrison responded enthusiastically to punk, and most of the singles she took to her heart emanated not from New York but from London: the Slits' Typical Girls; X-Ray Spex's Oh Bondage Up Yours!; and, of course, the Sex Pistols' Anarchy In The UK and God Save The Queen. 'I'd found a way to be political artistically,' Morrison says, 'which was what I was looking for in those days.'

Xero had found a rehearsal space behind the *Sun's* newspaper offices on Brunswick Street in Fortitude Valley, which many other bands, including the Go-Betweens, would soon share. And Morrison had found, in the Go-Betweens, a group that both shared and complemented her interests.

Lindy Morrison: This sounds really snobbish, but I just couldn't find any intellectual satisfaction in the music scene . . . Grant and Robert introduced me to a whole new cultural world, because they knew all the American film-makers, and all the American writers, and all the American groups like Television, and Bob Dylan. And in many ways I was introducing them to my culture too, but with the arrogance of youth, they weren't so interested in what I was trying to show them!

Morrison's passage into the Go-Betweens was far from smooth. Even as she and Forster became inseparable, rehearsing together daily (and Forster, briefly, wrote songs and played for Xero), she unsuccessfully attempted to persuade other drummers around town to join the band. It was, in fact, Morrison's very personal interest in Forster that made her as reluctant to become a Go-Between as McLennan initially had been. Forster himself took some time to twig to Morrison's intentions.

Lindy Morrison: It took me ages to realise. We went to see the

Apartments at the University of Queensland, and I was asking him about girlfriends, and he was being really obscure with me, and vague, and evasive, and suddenly it just clicked. And I said, 'You're not – you're a virgin!' And after I found that out, of course, it was all really easy!

Despite the Beserkley debacle, not to mention the consummation of the Forster–Morrison relationship, Forster and McLennan decided to try their luck in England, travelling there in late 1979. Carrying no equipment other than two acoustic guitars, the plan was to shop their songs from record company to record company simply by visiting their offices and playing them.

Such a guileless strategy would have been an abject failure if not for the tiny Glasgow-based Postcard label, operated by Alan Horne. Horne was the manager of Orange Juice, whose singer Edwyn Collins would become a long-time associate of the Go-Betweens. On 28 April 1980 the Go-Betweens cut their only single for the label, I Need Two Heads, with Orange Juice's Steven Daly sitting in on drums for the session.

The single marked an important shift in direction for the Go-Betweens. Forster, who at that stage was still writing the bulk of the Go-Betweens' material, was himself coming under the spell of some of the post-punk groups he had been introduced to by Morrison. Bands like the Gang of Four, the Pop Group and Melbourne's Boys Next Door, soon to become the Birthday Party, were taking punk in new directions. Catchy but less straightforward than either Lee Remick or People Say, I Need Two Heads formed the bridge to the more angular material that the Go-Betweens would begin writing for their first album, 1981's Send Me A Lullaby.

Although separation had ended their liaison, Forster and Morrison continued to correspond intensely. This did not stop Forster and McLennan putting up yet another advertisement for a female drummer in a local record store

during a brief stay in Paris. Even after returning alone to
Australia in June 1980 – McLennan continued his pilgrimage
to New York, where Robert Vickers was staying following his
departure from the Numbers – Forster didn't immediately
invite Morrison to join the band. Instead, he recruited
another Xero associate in Clare McKenna, whose apparent
loathing for Bob Dylan probably killed off any prospect of
permanent membership.[5] It was Morrison who finally made
the first move.

> **Lindy Morrison:** When he came back, I had to go around to
> his place – he didn't contact me – and we went out one night
> pretty soon after that. And he got incredibly upset. I didn't
> think he wanted me, which he did. And at the same time the
> band wanted a drummer – a female drummer – and I was just
> there.

When McLennan finally came home to find Morrison had
been anointed as the new drummer for the Go-Betweens,
he was distinctly unimpressed. Apart from the fact that
his opinion hadn't been sought, Morrison was, after all,
coming between him and his best friend. (Unsurprisingly,
McLennan suggests it was Morrison who resented his
closeness to Forster; either way, of course, Forster was caught
in the middle.) The incident that Morrison believes betrayed
McLennan's hurt has stuck in her memory.

> **Lindy Morrison:** Grant lent me one of his books, and I have
> always read in the bath. He came over one night – we used
> to just rehearse every single night – and he screamed at me,
> 'What's that, what's that?' And I said, 'It's your book.' It was
> all wet, and there was no way it was going to dry properly.
> And I just laughed – I mean, I love books, but to me the
> more mucked up they get the better. But Grant is absolutely
> meticulous about his book collection, obsessional. He never
> did lend me another book again. But basically he was just
> incredibly jealous of the fact that I took Robert away from him.

Peter Milton Walsh: Well, Grant would always like you to envy his bookshelf rather than his experiences. That was how he saw himself – you measured him by the films he'd seen, or what he'd received rather than what he'd experienced.

Grant McLennan: I remember the book! It was a Penguin paperback; I think it was *The Crying Of Lot 49*, by Thomas Pynchon. And she did drop it in the bath. I probably overreacted just to get a response. But there's no acrimony because of that. There are other things I could probably single out, but it certainly wasn't the book in the bath incident!

With Morrison on board, the Go-Betweens would finally become a real, and very different, band.

CHAPTER FIVE

task force versus the brisbane punks

There's two of us here. Does that constitute a crowd?
— The Go-Betweens, Don't Let Him Come Back

In September 1977, Joh Bjelke-Petersen was searching for some appropriately flammable material on which to fight the looming state election in November. Noting the rise of the anti-uranium movement in other states – and protective of an industry in which he and many of his peers held shares – the premier decided that law and order would again form the key plank of his re-election strategy. Invoking the spectre of the 1971 Springbok demonstrations, he declared protest marches to be a thing of the past.

> Nobody, including the Communist Party or anyone else, is going to turn the streets of Brisbane into a forum . . . Don't bother applying for a permit. You won't get one. That's government policy now.[1]

In fact there had never been a genuine right to peaceful assembly in the first place. The police had long held the discretion to grant or refuse permits for street processions, a power tempered only by the right of appeal to a magistrate. Bjelke-Petersen's tactic was to remove this right of appeal, making police commissioner Terry Lewis, then less than a year into the job, the sole arbiter on such matters.

A slope-shouldered, rubbery-looking figure, Lewis had long been the subject of well-sourced rumours that he was part of a 'rat pack' of corrupt police. He was also a staunch government loyalist, having been curiously promoted to the top job ahead of a field of more highly credentialed candidates. He was, above all, a yes-man: Bjelke-Petersen's stand had effectively predetermined his own ability to make decisions on the matter of street marches anyway.

The timing and public nature of Bjelke-Petersen's announcement – not to mention his identification of Brisbane as the principle source of troublemakers – invites speculation that the street march proclamation was really an electoral stunt, designed to appeal to the National Party's rural constituency. The party held only a single parliamentary seat in the capital (which it subsequently lost on the election of 12 November), but it mattered not: the electoral system ensured the party won easily, on the strength of 27.4 per cent of the primary vote.

The Right to March campaign became the longest civil liberties action in Queensland's history. Over the next two years dozens of protests led to thousands of arrests and the laying of over 4500 charges by police. At each demonstration, hundreds of police were deployed to quell anti-government sentiment. Police brutality was rife, extending to undercover Special Branch squad members provoking violence by 'running through the crowd and stirring them up, pushing people over and going hysterical'.[2]

Empowering the police as political shock troopers enabled the government to step up its attacks on minorities and dissenters.[3] And the police proved willing enforcers, prepared to stamp out the slightest disturbance. So-called punk dances, frequented by groups of garishly dressed young people, were the easiest of small targets.

* *

Jim Dickson had arrived in Townsville from England as a
teenager in 1968, eventually moving to Brisbane in 1972.
A few years later the lean bass player was recruited by
Railroad Gin, whose mellow, Jethro Tull-influenced sound
was well established. The group tried their luck in Sydney
but were already disintegrating, their ambitions thwarted
by the departure of original singer Carol Lloyd. Dickson
was more interested in the Blue Öyster Cult anyway, and
while in Sydney he immersed himself in the beginnings of
a new music scene obsessed with Detroit-style rock & roll.

In early 1977 Dickson returned to Brisbane, where
he found a more stable line of employment behind the
counter of Rocking Horse. One day drummer Bruce
Anthon walked in and immediately established a rapport
with Dickson over a copy of an album by British group the
Nice. As a rhythm section with a shared passion for the
'60s mods in general and the Who in particular, the pair
shared a perfect musical symmetry. Dickson played bass
like a sledgehammer, while Anthon – he who was almost a
Saint – was an enormous if unfulfilled talent.

> **Jim Dickson:** Bruce is a complete drummer, he doesn't really
> think about anything else. He's one of those few people I've met
> who's completely devoted – not only does he want to play but
> he wants to learn, and then he wants to share his knowledge,
> so he teaches as well. And not only does he want to share his
> knowledge, he wants to share his talent, by playing.

> **Bruce Anthon:** I'm essentially a player. I still am a player,
> I'll always be a player, and I always played with the view of
> wanting to improve.

Completed by the recruitment of former Tintern
Abbey guitarist and fellow Pete Townshend fanatic Greg
Williamson, the Survivors were essentially a covers
band with one important difference: they played mainly
for themselves, their zeal for what they considered to be

the primary virtues of rock & roll largely overwhelming audience considerations. A typical set list would consist of a few keepers (Eddie Cochran's Something Else, Otis Blackwell's Daddy Rollin' Stone) interspersed with selections plundered mainly from the Who, Kinks and Small Faces songbooks.

The band received an early break when they were asked to play at a new restaurant in a downstairs room at the lower end of George Street in the city. Proprietor Kevin Hayes (who as an architecture student had directed construction of Triple Zed's studios two years earlier) set up the Curry Shop to add some spice to a city of limited culinary options. But the enterprise was struggling, and Hayes approached Dickson with a new idea for attracting patrons.

> **Jim Dickson:** They said, 'There's no one coming to our shop, we've got this little space in the corner, do you guys want to come and play?' We said sure, and the first time we played there the place was packed, and we made more money than we'd ever made before. And Kevin came up to us later and said, 'You guys have a good night, did you?' and we said yeah, we did. And he said, 'We didn't have a good night at all,' and I asked why, and he said, 'Because people couldn't get to the food!' We split the door money after that, and it developed into a venue.

The group's timing was perfect. New bands were appearing on the scene, sporting names like the Leftovers, the Sex Haters, the Trash (later the Same 13), the Disposable Fits, the X-Men and the Hard-Ons.[4] What the Survivors' high-energy performances helped provide was the necessary musical context through which the new bands could be viewed: both the intellectual and the unschooled wings of punk found common ground in the Survivors' feral brand of classic rock & roll.

The most important and certainly the most notorious of

the new bands to emerge in 1977 was the Leftovers, who
hailed from the deadbeat north-eastern suburb of Sandgate,
nestled against the mudflats of Moreton Bay. Miles from
the city, boredom was the highest motivating factor to do
anything. And boredom, denied any more appropriate
outlet, is a recipe for trouble.

The Leftovers, Clinton Walker wrote in his *Pulp* fanzine,
'are the first new group I've met who actually stick safety
pins in their ears'.[5] They were, essentially, Australia's first
uniformed punks in the mould of the Sex Pistols. In a later
edition of the fanzine, Walker appraised their musical
abilities in a review of a gig at Sandgate Town Hall:

> The Leftovers don't 'play', or even put on a 'show', rather, they
> consider the whole affair a 'performance'. Heavy (deep) stuff (?).
> This is the scene: a large hall, containing at most 19 people
> (I know cos I counted them). There are some Roxy-style
> Leftovers fans throwing chairs and breaking bottles (ho hum).
> The Leftovers, dressed to punkly excess as usual, are on
> stage warming up (i.e. feeding back). The 'performance' has
> begun.
> Vocalist Warren lies on the stage floor, and screams
> inaudibly. Glen leans against his amp and nonchalantly picks
> out his bass lines. Jim prowls around the stage, intent on his
> guitar playing. Eddie, their new drummer and old friend, sits
> behind his kit, and simply doesn't play! He just leans back and
> laughs, or smokes and drinks, or even wanders around.
> They play songs, but you wouldn't know it – nothing is
> recognisable or discernible, it's just a big fuzz of noise that
> has little to do with music.[6]

In fact, Warren Lamond, Glen Smith, Jim Shoebridge and
Ed Wreckage were all avid music fans, with a deep and
equal appreciation of both Jerry Lee Lewis–Little Richard-
style '50s rock and early '60s teenage pop. Later, as their

skills improved, they would perform a medley of the Velvet Underground's Run Run Run and the (very different) song of the same title by psychedelic band the Third Rail. Early on, though, there is no doubt the band suffered from terrible technical shortcomings.

John Reid: I know the whole beauty of punk is non-musicality, but the Leftovers used to stop in the middle of songs! Glen was a hopeless bass player, absolutely hopeless. He only had four strings and he still couldn't work 'em out! And they would have these huge fights. Warren would stop a song in the middle, fly across the stage at Shoebridge and say, 'You swished your hair during your lead break, we don't allow swished hair here' – thump! They were always at one another's throats like that. They were personalities before they were musicians.

The Leftovers or, as they sometimes referred to themselves, the Fucken Leftovers, were certainly unique to Brisbane at the time. Lamond cut a somewhat monkey-like figure, with a large head on a small body. Smith towered over him, well over six feet tall, with a long pink fringe hanging over his face. Ed Wreckage – the youngest at 19 – looked like a teenage Frankenstein. Shoebridge, for his part, was relatively normal, which soon eventuated in his dismissal from the band. He simply didn't fit.

Jim Dickson: The great thing about the Leftovers was that whereas everybody else paid lip-service to punk, the Leftovers lived it. Of all of the bands in Brisbane that could actually say that they related to it the most, they'd be it. And they were scary in that way, because they were genuinely unhinged . . . I mean, they had problems where they'd come from, they had problems with the people they hung around with, they had problems with alcohol, they had problems with drugs – these guys were problem magnets! But somehow they could siphon this energy into something that they liked,

which was music, and very often they had problems with
that too.

Yet as self-destructive as the Leftovers could be, they
were also victims. On 17 August 1977, the night Elvis Presley
died, Ed Wreckage experienced the fear and loathing his
band engendered in brutally first-hand fashion when he
was severely beaten with a fence paling.

Ed Wreckage: Me and Glen, Warren, Jim and Robert
Perkins, Tex's older brother, were at this hotel in Shorncliffe,
near Sandgate. Somebody took a dislike to us and they
came and beat the fuck out of us. I had massive internal
injuries – ruptured spleen, perforated stomach, ruptured
intestines. I had to have parts of my organs and ribcage
removed. Very nasty. That's the sort of shit we had to put
up with. It wasn't just the cops; it was the locals in our
neighbourhoods, too, who were just as vicious.

The violence was not all one-sided. An early October gig
at Darra Hall, featuring the Survivors and the Same 13 (the
latter including Ed Kuepper's younger brother, Wolfgang),
degenerated into a showdown between Saints and
Leftovers fans. Brawling – both on and off stage – either
blighted or enhanced performances, depending on
one's point of view. And persistent vandalism of venues
undercut everyone's efforts. Rocking Horse's Warwick
Vere remembers one Curry Shop gig where a piece of
porcelain washbasin went sailing past his head, hurled
from an upstairs bathroom.

Warwick Vere: There were a lot of problems with those early
punk gigs. Glen from the Leftovers had a particularly obnoxious
brother, Gary, who used to make it his business to smash
toilets up. So of course any venue you secured where bands
could play, like little halls, you were never invited back again,
because there would be so much damage. And that led to

police presences at gigs, dog squads, raids, all sorts of terrible things.

Ed Wreckage: We never accepted responsibility for any vandalism. It wasn't our doing. But the cost of destroying venues wasn't a consideration of most dedicated punks in those years. The band never retained a bond for any venue we hired, so we also bore those financial losses.

Drugs, too, were becoming a serious problem. Throughout 1977 Brisbane had been in the grip of a severe marijuana drought. When heroin became the alternative of choice, musicians began dropping like flies. The Leftovers, who derived a significant amount of their charisma from their status as rock & roll animals, were quickly swept into the drug's vortex. So too were many other bands, promoters and record store personnel. Discreet Records' Phil Smith, a victim of sustained harassment over the importing of stock for which local record companies held the rights, found himself fighting on too many fronts to survive. The much-loved store folded in 1979.

Phil Smith: Things seemed to explode at different times. Weird things would happen, and I think it became harder to concentrate on running a store. If you're running a store you've got to keep your eye on the ball. I think that being young . . . Well, it's hard for me to reflect on those things without seeming like I'm making excuses, you know. It was up to me to change things.

The Task Force had its origins in an early random breath-testing unit, colloquially known as Murphy's Marauders. Originally stationed in downtown Fortitude Valley a kilo-metre from the CBD, the Marauders were there to maintain a visible presence in a precinct where, in March 1973, 15 people were burned alive in the firebombing of the

Whiskey Au-Go-Go nightclub. But putting police on every corner of the city's red-light district only helped further the spread of corruption into illegal vice and gaming over the next decade.

It was in the Valley that the Leftovers first began rehearsals in late 1976, next to a brothel known as Pinky's. The area was almost a no-go zone, dominated by the crime bosses and Licensing Branch officers that a decade later would become the star witnesses of the Fitzgerald Inquiry. But it was one place where the Leftovers could (almost) blend in.

Ed Wreckage: You were walking into gangster territory there, and we were just kids. We were wearing our own version of rock & roll clothes, and they must have thought we were totally nuts, with balls this fucking big – 'Can we rent this place for a week to rehearse?'

By 1978 Murphy's Marauders had mutated into the Task Force, a specially uniformed squad. A smaller undercover coterie of male and female police – pigs and sows, as they were often referred to – had their own casual, gendered code of clothing: while the pigs would wear Hawaiian shirts in summer and lumberjackets in winter, sows alternated between tracksuits and light frocks (with modesty culottes beneath). Cruising the streets in paddy wagons, the Task Force had a roving brief to assist in the breaking up of demonstrations and any other designated trouble spots more or less as they saw fit.[7]

In a political climate where dissent was actively and often violently quelled, it should be no surprise that punk dances became a target, and would have become so even had those attending them behaved like angels. The tabloid frenzy surrounding punk in the UK had reached the Australian media, and the police were quick to catch on. As John Reid writes, tongue well in cheek:

The Task Force had a new social evil identified to them: young, fashionably skinny, green-haired ratbags. Age and sex indeterminate but usually 15 to 20 years old, these were not long-haired university radicals, but street kids mixed with students mixed with clerks mixed with hairdressers.[8]

In early January, two months after the government's re-election, four people were arrested at a dance at Hamilton Hall featuring the Survivors and the Leftovers. About 30 people were present. At roughly 9pm – two hours before proceedings were due to end – an equivalent number of police, backed by dogs and the vice squad, descended on the venue, allegedly acting on a noise complaint.[9]

Jim Dickson: There's a great anecdote about that gig. There was this guy who saw all the cops out the front of the hall, so he raced out the back door and started jumping the fences of Hamilton, and as he was jumping the fences he was pulling clothing off people's Hill's Hoists and dressing himself in this clothing. And once he'd actually got himself an attire that looked normal, he went back to the hall. Just walked past the police and they didn't bat an eyelid!

But for a teenage Brad Shepherd – by then fronting his own band, the Aliens – the experience was no laughing matter.

Brad Shepherd: I got put in a headlock and chucked in the back of a paddy wagon, supposedly for public profanity, which was just bullshit. This bloke on the street said, 'You've left your headlights on, mate.' I said, 'Oh thanks,' and that was it – before I knew it I was chucked into the van. The bloke was an undercover cop, and they were just cracking down, intimidating these young kids.

My dad had to come and bail me out of jail. It was pretty dreadful. All those horror stories that you used to hear about Aborigines being beaten by the cops, I saw all of that while I was just sitting in the cell for an hour. I saw them pick this black guy up and spear him into the corner of the jail cell, knocked him unconscious. He was in the cell across from me. They dragged him out by his hair and left this trail of gore along the floor of the watch-house.

It was pretty terrifying. I thought I was next.

The song to capture this era most vividly – indeed, written immediately after the Hamilton Hall bust – was Razar's Task Force (Undercover Cops), which opened with a siren-like peal of guitar:

> We're having fun, people are swearing
> You and your haircuts, you're arrested
> You put our friends away overnight
> But hey, Mr Task Force, that's all right!

The song's author and singer, Marty Burke, was all of 16. Razar – Burke, guitarist Steven Mee, drummer Greg 'Keg' Wackley and younger brother Bob on bass – were a high school band from the southern suburb of Mt Gravatt. Completely taken by the noise of British punk, especially the Damned, the band was a virtual punk jukebox, filling out their set by covering new singles almost as soon as they were released. But it was the topical irreverence of Razar's original material (other songs included I Hate Abba, Stamp Out Disco and Shutdown Countdown) that stood out.

Marty Burke: We wanted to write about things that people were going to connect with in Brisbane – you know, 'I come from Brisbane and I'm quite plain', lines like that. We knew that we wanted to write stuff about what was going on here, because it was truly unusual and pretty exciting, especially what was going on with the political situation.

Razar, however, wanted nothing to do with Go-Betweens-style whimsy, despite performing several times with the band at Baroona Hall (John Reid, who became Razar's manager, once dubbed the Go-Betweens 'armchair rock', prompting Forster and McLennan to play a short set standing on their own furniture). From their first gig on 25 February 1978, supporting the Survivors at the Atcherley Hotel, Razar's motto – 'young, fast and non-boring' – was backed up by better than average playing skills.

> **John Reid:** I have to give it to them, they were the only punk band I ever saw who could play an hour and a half from the first time they got on a stage. And tight! None of this 'My string's broken so I'm stopping'.

In fact, so tight were Razar that the band earned several high-profile support slots to the likes of Jo Jo Zep, the Angels and even Cold Chisel, where their rabble-rousing style kept hecklers at bay. At one memorable gig supporting the Angels, Burke won over the rabid crowd by feeding them a life-size masonite effigy of *Saturday Night Fever*-era John Travolta during Stamp Out Disco. They tore it to pieces, hurling chunks back at the band.

> **Marty Burke:** Years later this guy came up to me and said, 'Mate, you remember that night with the Angels?' I said, you mean the one with John Travolta? And he goes, 'Yeah! *I've got the kneecap!*' I thought that was really great.

Other gigs are remembered less fondly. In April 1978 Razar were booked to play a medical students' ball in one of the function rooms of Lang Park, Queensland's home of rugby league. The result was a catastrophe, as original Leftovers guitarist Johnny Burnaway and Brisbane's resident cartoon punk, known as V2, ran amok. The gig lasted 18 minutes.

> **Warwick Vere:** They smashed up the bathroom and smeared

themselves with blood. They smashed all the photos of the
football heroes that lined the stairs, and smeared them with
blood. Understandably the wallopers were called, and they
cleared everybody out. As of course they would, having seen
the damage.

This incident, which remarkably was scarcely reported,
could have done irreparable damage to the fledgling scene,
yet little over a month later it received a vital boost. Triple
Zed had been raising revenue through its Joint Efforts
(boasting the unsubtle slogan 'you'd be a dope to miss it')
since early 1976 at the University of Queensland, featuring
the likes of Carol Lloyd and deathly jazz-rock groups such
as Quasar and Moonlight. But with the station's commercial
viability on the rise along with street-level rock & roll, the
events soon migrated to the pubs.

On 24 May 1978 Skyhooks and the Survivors played the
first Joint Effort held at the Queen's Hotel on the corner
of Charlotte and Creek Street in the city. With nearly 800
people crammed into the room, the Queen's was exactly
the mid-sized venue Brisbane needed. The aftermath of
the gig was described by Rob Cameron in *Semper*:

> Half deaf and three quarters off our faces, we step out into
> the cool autumn night. Parked in the driveway between
> the hotel entrance and the car park is a police paddy
> wagon . . . Two plain-clothed police and a few uniformed
> police start arresting people, at least three, maybe four. What
> the charges were is still a matter of conjecture as the police
> at the watch-house were not inclined to give you the time of
> day, let alone giving reasons for dragging young kids off in
> the middle of the night.[10]

Despite the inevitable police presence, the opening of
the Queen's and the Exchange (a mere block away, on the
corner of Charlotte and Edward Street) to new bands was
a turning point for live music in Brisbane. Not only did

the venues provide fresh stages for local acts, Triple Zed was able to begin attracting overseas bands to play in the city. A few fans were misguided in their attempts to show their appreciation of their punk heroes. When the Stranglers came to town, V2 made the serious mistake of spitting on bassist and karate exponent Jean-Jacques Burnel.

> **Bill Riner:** Burnel just stepped off the stage and whacked V2 over the head with his bass. I actually have it on tape, they're playing, there's all this noise and then they stop – thump! – and then they start playing again!

The first of the new groups to commit to vinyl was the Survivors, whose debut single Baby Come Back/Mr Record Man was released in January 1978 on their own Real Records imprint. It was a disappointment – the two original songs hampered by weak lyrics and production – but the band was nevertheless approached by Melbourne-based label Suicide, a new offshoot of Mushroom.

Sadly, a five-year deal, and a reissue of the two songs on the label's *Lethal Weapons* compilation in July, only helped kill off the band's prospects. The two songs were toned down even further by a tame remix, and the album was widely panned as an attempt to cash in on the punk boom with second-rate bands, marketed under the friendlier 'new wave' tag.[11] After the label collapsed ignominiously, the Survivors split following a Sydney tour in September 1978. Bruce Anthon has no regrets.

> **Bruce Anthon:** We had a really good little tour in Sydney, actually, we came out ahead – the Survivors is the only band I've ever made money out of! It wasn't like the end of our world. We parted extremely good friends.

Razar fared better, at least on record, despite a curious

anomaly surrounding the release of their first single, Task Force/Stamp Out Disco, in September. A brilliant spurt of teenage enthusiasm, the single was recorded in between the Go-Betweens' Lee Remick (May) and the Numbers' Sunset Strip (July), both of which were released by the Able Label.

Marty Burke: Bob and Steven used to hang around Toowong Music. Now, we used to put shit on the Go-Betweens when we used to see them play – 'You're fucking boring, why are you here, you're pissing us off!' – there was definitely a lack of respect! But Bob, I think, said to Damian Nelson something like, 'We're going to release a single, we want to do it ourselves, but what's the go with your label?' and Damian just said, 'Oh, we don't really want you,' and we just said, 'Whatever, it doesn't matter.'

When Razar's single came back with the inscription AB002 – marking it as the second Able single, with Lee Remick as 001 and Sunset Strip as 003 – the band were accused of falsely appropriating the label's name. With all three singles recorded within two months of each other at Window Studios, the more likely explanation is a simple manufacturing error at the M7 plant in Sydney, where all three records were pressed at around the same time.

Marty Burke: Sure enough people started to take on the notion that we'd done this on purpose. What must have happened was, the guy who cut the platters would have got all the tapes together, and saw they'd all come down from rural, hick, big country town Brisbane. 'Oh, three Brisbane bands! They must be all together!' There was always this notion that bands from up north were hicks.

But the band to make the most successful transition to vinyl, against all expectations, was the Leftovers. Cigarettes And Alcohol – the band's solitary recorded contribution to musical history – was nothing short of miraculous.

> **Warwick Vere:** Having attended their gigs, when I heard they were putting out a single, I thought, oh my God, this is gonna be the acid test. And I was shocked. I was very pleasantly surprised by how good it was.

> **Ed Wreckage:** We wanted it to sound insane. I think we did it. I guess that's where we were coming from at the time. It's the life we led.

Perhaps the group knew it was their only shot. After recording two songs for what became the B-side in August 1977 (No Complaints and I Only Panic When There's Nothing To Do), the band was unable to finance the recording of Cigarettes And Alcohol until April 1978.[12] Picture sleeves were designed but never printed and even the imprint Punji Stick records – named after a Viet Cong booby trap – disappeared after objections from EMI, who custom-pressed the single.

In June 1979, 500 copies of Cigarettes And Alcohol were finally released with a generic sleeve and label. A select few were emblazoned with the stamped message, 'The Fucken Leftovers Hate You'. All four members then took it upon themselves to destroy 50 copies each as they saw fit, both for fun and to enhance their collectable status. Ed Wreckage personally disposed of his share by hurling the platters off the Indooroopilly Bridge, into one of the muddier reaches of the Brisbane River.

By this time Shoebridge had been sacked, his list of offences allegedly including bringing his mum to a rehearsal. Ed Wreckage moved to guitar, while Razar's Greg Wackley filled in on drums. It was this line-up that played the infamous Great Brain Robbery at the Colossus Hall in West End on 15 June 1979, along with Razar and up-and-coming Melbourne band, the Models.

The gig was ruthlessly targeted by police. As the Leftovers

launched into their set with No Complaints, a lumberjacket-wearing undercover officer approached the stage. When Warren Lamond let fly with the first of several expletives, the officer simply picked the smaller man up and attempted to carry him out. The result was bedlam. With paddy wagons reversed up outside the door in readiness, 25 people were arrested in the ensuing melee.

Marty Burke: Greg [Wackley] jumped his kit, and in combination with three lesbian feminists who shall remain nameless – I can't name them, but they were legendary for their heart and what they did that night – they jumped this guy and kicked the fuck out of him. And we're all standing back going, whoa, hang on, what's gonna happen now? And within probably two minutes, the cops at the door realised something was wrong, and bang, it was on.

The Models came up to [promoter] Dave Darling, and Sean Kelly and Ash Wednesday were saying, 'Fucking hell, this really *is* punk city. What have you got next, have you got another punk band?' And David said yeah – because we were due on next – and they said, 'Well, we want to play now, because we're out of here, man, this is bad news.' They were freaked out!

Razar had just released a second EP featuring Shutdown Countdown, but the band disintegrated soon after, a victim of their own strictly imposed parameters.

Marty Burke: Steven wrote a lot of the music, but he was the one who was changing and we just didn't like what he was getting into. The songs that he was writing didn't spit any venom of any sort; they didn't say anything.

The punk scene was splintering as it grew, like the brittle bones of an undernourished child. After the breakup of the Survivors, Jim Dickson moved to Sydney, playing with the

Passengers, and later with the Barracudas in England. On his return to Sydney in early 1982, he bumped into Warren Lamond at the bus shelters on Broadway. Lamond and Glen Smith had also made the trek south.

Jim Dickson: Warren said to me, 'Hey Jim, have a look at this' – and showed me the roof of his mouth. I said, 'What's that mate?' And he said, 'That's where I tried to blow my head off last time.'

Ed Wreckage: Warren wasn't so humoured by his own predicament. He suffered immensely during that period.

Miraculously, Lamond had survived the attempt on his own life, with the .22 calibre bullet lodging behind his cheekbone. The delicate placement of the projectile meant it stayed where it was until 12 October 1989 when, after years spent rebuilding his life, Lamond died in his sleep of a brain haemorrhage following a minor car accident.

The year earlier, original guitarist Johnny Burnaway had hanged himself in Sydney, where he had been having some success with his band the Plug Uglies under his real name, John Gorman.

Gorman's brother Michael Hiron (the Leftovers' first drummer, who later played with the Riptides) never got over the shock. He died suddenly in 2001, unaware even of the existence of the stomach ulcer that claimed his life.

Glen and Gary Smith, whose individual stories are as grotesque as they are tragic, are dead too, after pursuing the cosseted punk ideal all the way to its logical conclusion in their quest for musical and personal self-annihilation.

Jim Shoebridge and Ed Wreckage are now all that remains of the Leftovers. After years in and out of jail, where he served time for a variety of offences, Ed Wreckage has returned to Sandgate, and seems to have found a kind of peace.[13]

Ed Wreckage: I didn't shake my skin in jail. I still consider myself a punk, in every sense of the word. That's my life. It's always been the same.

CHAPTER SIX

swept away

Although several Brisbane bands released independent singles throughout 1978, the Able Label was the first local label to cater for a number of like-minded acts. Its six singles and four bands – the Go-Betweens, the Riptides, the Apartments and the short-lived Four Gods – came to represent an entire aesthetic: romantic, yearning, undeniably self-conscious. The music of these groups shared a fragile, sparse quality that some dubbed the Brisbane sound. Being barely able to play was a mere technicality that need not interfere with one's breadth of vision.

> **Robert Vickers:** I remember talking to Mark Callaghan once about why we thought the Go-Betweens were so great. If you were the Numbers or the Saints, you could be doing something that was very good, but it was difficult for you to step outside that. Whereas it seemed like the Go-Betweens could do absolutely anything. They weren't trapped in any genre.

Like Chris Bailey, Mark Callaghan's father had been in the army and had taken the family from England to Africa and back before retiring and emigrating to Australia in 1972. Callaghan was 14. After initially settling at Bundaberg on Queensland's central coast, he relocated to Brisbane in 1976 to study architecture at the University of Queensland. There he met Scott Matheson who, along with Robert Vickers, was yet another graduate of Corinda High.

The architecture faculty was to be Brisbane's next hotbed of musical activity: Callaghan remembers that of the 40 students starting their degrees that year, more than a quarter played the guitar. Like almost everybody else at the time, Callaghan was initially inspired by the Saints: 'We used to go over to Triple Zed and hassle them to play Stranded when Michael Finucan was on air.' Formed in the winter of 1977 – first as the Grudge and then the Neon Steal – the Numbers were a band before they could play. The practical skills learned on campus, however, allowed a degree of DIY enterprise unusual even in punk circles.

> **Mark Callaghan:** In our first year at uni we had this explosion of wanting to do everything, because it was available there for us in the faculty. We took our own photographs, we developed them, we did our own sculpture and woodwork and painting and drawing and putting on shows. And then . . . We didn't exactly get serious about it, but we wanted to do more playing, and we started writing our own songs.

With fellow architecture students Dennis Cantwell borrowing a friend's drum kit and Allan Rielly joining as lead guitarist, the band solidified as a five-piece, with Callaghan on vocals, Matheson on rhythm guitar and Vickers on bass. As the Grudge, the group had started life as a full-tilt punk band. As the Numbers, they developed a much lighter mod aesthetic, complete with suits and a fatefully generic name, mirroring the British transition from punk to new wave.

Tall and rangy, with an open rather than guttural singing style, the genial Callaghan quickly realised he couldn't relate with any honesty to punk's negative energy. With its '60s television references, ripe melody and sunny, youthful demeanour, Callaghan's first notable song, Sunset Strip, confirmed the Numbers' shift from angst to romance, and from realism to irony.

Mark Callaghan: My family lived in Africa from 1964 to 1968, and we still heard a lot of music over there, Beatles and Stones and so forth. And then we came back to England from '68 to '72 . . . It was the golden age of English pop and rock. It was everywhere, we were watching *Top Of The Pops*, and it just sunk right in.

When his band played host to the first impromptu Go-Betweens performance at Baroona Hall, Callaghan was enthused by Robert Forster's quaint songs about forgotten film starlets and chaste librarians. The rapport between the Numbers and the Go-Betweens – which extended to games of backyard cricket, and even a partial merging of the two bands for two shows as the Lemons[1] – made them the next group to officially record for the Able Label (disregarding Razar's Task Force).

With Sunset Strip the obvious standout, the band entered Window Studios on 4 July 1978. Callaghan looks back on his early classic with a mixture of embarrassment and wonder.

Mark Callaghan: I don't even think it's a really good song! It's naivety, that's what it is. I couldn't write a song like that now because I had no idea what I was doing then. Of course, the more you work in music and the more you write songs, the more you realise what an obvious chord progression it is, and what cheesy lyrics, but it worked. It was the second song I ever wrote.

Robert Vickers: There's a certain naivety that you have when you're first writing songs. It allows you to use very simple chord progressions . . . Later on in people's careers, they want to be more complicated, and it doesn't necessarily produce the

best songs. I think a lot of people's first songs are by far their
best . . . [Sunset Strip] was definitely our best song.

Backed by Matheson's spunky Magic Castle and another
Callaghan original, Rules Of Love, Sunset Strip was released
almost simultaneously with Lee Remick, in a pressing of
500. With a picture sleeve of the band in matching suits,
the look was gimmicky, but the group's raw garage-pop
enthusiasm is contagious: the single remains one of the
most highly priced Australian collectables of its era.

By this point the band had become aware of the
existence of another Sydney band calling themselves
the Numbers, who were less than amenable to making
concessions to a bunch of upstarts from Queensland. In
any event, the Brisbane group's change of name to the
Riptides (a reference to the dismal late '60s beaches-and-
bikinis television soap *Riptide*, produced in Australia, but
with minimal Australian input[2]) was an inspired one,
perfectly suited to their joyous but still developing hybrid
of surf, ska and power pop.

It also marked Callaghan's burgeoning ambition. Upon
his return from Sydney, Vickers was ousted from the band
on account of his rudimentary bass playing, and plans
were made to remix and reissue Sunset Strip under the
new name. Probably Vickers suffered for being more easily
replaced, since the primary purpose of the remix was to
tame his equally erratic rhythmic counterpart, drummer
Dennis Cantwell.

Mark Callaghan: The main difference with the remix was we
turned off Dennis' hi-hat microphone, because at that stage
he didn't realise you were supposed to clamp the hat down
when you did a drum roll, so you had the cymbals spilling out
over everything!

Robert Vickers: It was funny, because the last show that I
played with them I finally began to realise what I should have

been doing, you know, how to play scales around chords. But by that time it was too late.

Vickers was untroubled. A genuine dandy, with his Beatles mop-top, preference for suits (off stage as well as on) and fondness for Burt Bacharach and Dionne Warwick, he unsurprisingly found Brisbane stifling, and not just for the heat. Having already been to London in 1977, he set off for New York. There he formed a new band, the Colors, before himself becoming a Go-Between in 1982.

Robert Vickers: I had already begun to feel that Brisbane was a place I had to get out of. You started to see things on television, or read in books, that other cities had that Brisbane simply didn't have. There were no restaurants in Brisbane, for example. It seemed a really barren place in a lot of ways.

Another dandy about town, Peter Milton Walsh, was equally desperate to escape.

Peter Milton Walsh: Anybody with a pulse would have felt they were trapped in a scene from *In The Heat Of The Night*. It was like a northern version of a southern American state; it was the cops against people who were alive.

Born in 1956 in Sydney, Walsh was slightly older than most of his contemporaries on the Brisbane scene when he formed the Apartments (with fellow guitarist Michael O'Connell, Peter Martin on drums and former school friend and 'old drug connection' Peter Whitby on bass) in October 1978. Both Walsh and O'Connell had prodigious record collections – the latter worked for some time behind the counter at Rocking Horse – and although galvanised by punk, both were interested in rather more exotic fare than what was coming out of England circa 1977.

Peter Milton Walsh: I had a turntable that could stack, and I never found it odd that I could have on Big Star's *Third*, and on top of that I'd have Burt Bacharach's greatest hits, and on top of that I might have, you know, *Nuggets*.

Walsh's brief induction and swift departure from the Go-Betweens, shortly after the Apartments' birth, was to prove fortuitous for both parties. Walsh shared much in common with Forster and McLennan, but he was too much of an individualist to be comfortable playing a supporting role for long. He needed an outlet for his own material, which was, if anything, even more eccentric than Forster's. Influenced by the slow, wounded ballads on Dylan's *Blood On The Tracks* and the third Velvet Underground album, the prickly delicacy of Walsh's music was completely out of place and time. Some concessions were required to present the songs on stage.

Peter Milton Walsh: We sped them up! I was terrified of doing my own stuff, because it was so slow, and because it was intimate. And essentially, the thing that I liked about that time was everything felt like it was all amphetamine-driven and it was a great rock experience . . . [Whereas] a song like Nobody Like You, I could play it on the piano now and it's a big, slow ballad. It wasn't lounge music in the sense of the commodity that lounge is now, but very much like playing in your living room.

Walsh describes the single turbulent year that was the original Apartments' existence as 'just an event. It flared, and then it was gone, and then it was just smoke and ruins.' Such a poetic sense of haphazard creation and combustion was, for Walsh, simply a function of living in a town where there wasn't a great deal to do. This was punk's greatest gift to Brisbane: far more crucial than any specific political refusal was the impetus that it provided to a bored youth to create its own history.

By this time, however, the music alone wasn't going to be

enough. As heroin swept through Brisbane, it slowly picked the group off one by one.

> **Peter Milton Walsh:** That definitely worked against keeping the band together, because it becomes a much bigger demand than anything else. It was never a big problem with me, but it wasn't productive either. If you turn up to rehearsal and somebody's stoned, that's fabulous if you're stoned, but if you're not stoned, it's just gruesome. You are rigid with boredom, looking at pinned eyes.

The solitary EP recorded by the Apartments in May 1979, *The Return Of The Hypnotist*, was released shortly after the group's break-up in October. Its lead track, Help – its longing mood carried by some beautiful lead guitar – saw Walsh return the compliment originally paid him by the Go-Betweens on Don't Let Him Come Back:

> I've seen the choirboys dancing cheek to cheek
> I could sell it all, talk about the world, but talk's so cheap!

Walsh insists he was joking with these lines, which are certainly in keeping with the ironic farewell at the heart of Don't Let Him Come Back. The remainder of the song, however, confirmed that Walsh wanted out – not just of the Apartments, much less the Go-Betweens, but Brisbane itself.

The Riptides had slimmed to a four-piece following the departure of Robert Vickers, with Mark Callaghan taking over bass duties. Gone also were the suits as the band dispensed with further affectations in favour of a more suburban, everyday appeal. The blue-collar approach won the Riptides few admirers among the scene's more ideological adherents, but otherwise only broadened their already wide appeal.

Mark Callaghan: We had a very genuine egalitarian attitude. We really wanted our music to be successful, even if it was a suburban pub in Brisbane . . . We didn't really like the exclusive attitudes of these bands that wanted to be successful in the inner cities of Brisbane and Sydney but thought it was demeaning to play in a pub in the western suburbs.

After the reissue of Sunset Strip in July 1979 (again on Able, this time in a whopping pressing of 2000 copies), Allan Rielly left to concentrate on his architecture studies. His replacement, Andrew Leitch, was exactly the foil Callaghan needed. An exceptionally talented guitarist and keyboard player, Leitch's addition to the line-up helped flesh out Callaghan's songs, as well as giving them the necessary room to breathe.

The band's next single, Tomorrow's Tears – released on the Flat label on Valentine's Day, 1980 – may be the Riptides' finest moment. Infectious and exuberant, it should have creamed the charts. But the Riptides remained a guitar band, and guitars still spelt punk to the local music industry. Commercial radio wouldn't touch the song.

Investing in the band's prospects in Australia would, in the long term, prove the Riptides' downfall. The band's move to Sydney was, in hindsight, the beginning of the end.

Mark Callaghan: This is a true story, and I'm still amazed by it to this day. We'd built our own PA and rehearsal rooms, we did all that ourselves. Incredible! And then we went down to do some gigs in Sydney that had been arranged by our agent up in Brisbane, and we got there and there were no gigs. We'd driven all the way down, with our gear and our PA and it all fell over. I think we did one gig at a place called the Rock Garden and there were maybe six people there.

We went back to our hotel, a place down in Bondi where we were staying. And I remember sitting around this milk bar on the corner of Campbell Parade the next day and saying, 'Look, this is stupid, we're never going to get to play in Sydney unless we move to Sydney.' And so we all decided then and there to move to Sydney. It's the sort of thing you do when you're 20 years old and don't know any better.

So that's what we did. We got a newspaper, and found a house, right there. We went and rented the house and said, 'Right, you – get all the stuff out of the van. You – drive back to Brisbane, go to all of our houses and pick up all our gear.' I'm sure to this day I lost heaps of stuff in that move. I didn't go back to Brisbane for a long time after that.

And we absolutely starved. I'm serious; we absolutely starved for about six to eight weeks. We couldn't get any gigs in Sydney at first; we got the occasional gig but it was very, very tough. And whenever we did the gigs we'd go straight up to the Cross and buy hamburgers, because we had no money. We did it all literally on bread and black sauce, which was all that was in the house for a while.

After a few months the Riptides' courage looked like paying off. The band was scoring consistently good reviews and had matured into a surprisingly tight musical unit without sacrificing the fragile chemistry that gave the shows their edge. Most of all, the natural humour and warmth of Callaghan's songs radiated from the stage. The band soon became one of the most popular draws in town.

Mark Callaghan: We'd go out and support the Sports or Skyhooks or some other rock band, and the audience would be very sceptical. And you know, they might not have been raging fans by the end of the night, but we saw other bands trying to do the same thing and they would have things thrown at them! We never had things thrown at us. People were amused, and they enjoyed themselves, you could see them laughing and having a good time.

After signing with Festival offshoot Regular Records, the Riptides began recording demos for a six-track mini-album,

Swept Away. But the band was already pulling apart at the seams. Living under the one roof on a diet of bread and black sauce was hardly conducive to group harmony; drinking and playing by night, no matter how good the gigs, only poisoned the cocktail further.

First to leave was Matheson, beginning a chain reaction of departures that would destroy the band. He was replaced with one-time Leftovers drummer Michael Hiron on bass, allowing Callaghan to switch to guitar. But when such eminently melodic and danceable material as Holiday Time couldn't crack Australian radio playlists upon *Swept Away*'s eventual release in late 1981, the cracks finally opened, then swallowed the group. Cantwell and Leitch followed Matheson.

While Callaghan soldiered on with Hiron, recording the darkly gorgeous Hearts And Flowers single in 1982, the Riptides' spirit had been broken. The group had been tarred commercially by their initial association with punk, but their fan base on the live circuit was so strong, the question of what might have been still lingers.

> **Mark Callaghan:** The line-up changes derailed us, without a doubt. It was so stupid in retrospect. See, that's where you want a good manager – someone to say don't worry about the hassles you're having now, they're not important. Just don't share a house, move out, have a bit of space – come together to play and think about the things that you like about each other. I think in retrospect that was what stopped our momentum.

Mark Callaghan was too clever a songwriter to be stifled permanently by the breakup of the Riptides. With his new group, GANGgajang, he achieved deserved commercial success, writing a string of hits throughout the '80s, experiencing a roughly equivalent measure of spoils and compromises along the way: the classic Sounds Of Then was even used as the soundtrack for both Coke and Channel Nine commercials.

After a brief stint with the Colors in New York with Robert Vickers, and with the Laughing Clowns in London, Peter Milton Walsh assembled a new version of the Apartments. The album he cut in London for Rough Trade in 1985, *The Evening Visits . . . And Stays For Years*, has become a cult classic, cementing Walsh's reputation in Europe. Never even released locally in Australia, the album's highlight was the soft-sung elegy Mr Somewhere, later covered by British ensemble This Mortal Coil. Like Ed Kuepper's Brisbane (Security City), the song was a bitter lament for his former home.

> A boat from the river takes you out
> Cross the other side of town, to get out, to get out,
> You'll take the tide, any tide, any tide
> Like there isn't gonna be any tide

The brief rise and messy dissolution of the Riptides and the Apartments were important signposts in Brisbane's musical history. Both *The Return Of The Hypnotist* and Tomorrow's Tears marked not just the end of the '70s but also the beginning of a new era. Over the next decade, as the city's horizon darkened, countless groups left town, only to dash themselves against the rocks of foreign shores. Those that remained retreated into different forms of musical insularity, tracing ever-diminishing circles of parochial punk noise and exclusive avant-garde experimentation to an increasingly disillusioned, frightened audience.

ups and downs
(1980–1989)

CHAPTER SEVEN

last of the leather age

Ron Peno was on his way to the social security office when he was stopped by police. After relocating from Sydney at the end of 1979 friends had warned him about the reputation of Brisbane's finest, but he had brushed them off. 'I was told that you had to be very careful,' he remembers, 'and I would say, "What? What are you talking about?" And they would say, "No, really, look out, police are patrolling." "What do you mean police are patrolling? I'm getting a cab now, I'm going home." "Well, don't get taken to the watch-house!"'

After explaining his mission – even showing his tormentors the unemployment form in his hand – the conversation took a predictably downward turn. 'So,' said the first cop after a pause, 'you take drugs.' It was not really a question, not even an accusation, but a presumption: Peno had long hair. In fact, Peno was sober at the time, albeit hungover; it was, after all, barely 9.30 in the morning. It made no difference. They took a full description. Eyes: bloodshot. Hair: dirty.

Ron Peno: They had me there for like half an hour by the side of the road. It was just amazing; I could not believe it. And then it all sort of fell into place – like, yeah, you do have to be careful going out in Brisbane! You actually have to watch yourself

when you go out . . . [Before that] I was like, 'Hey, I'm from
Sydney! Rock and roll!'

Looking like a rock & roll star, Peno realised, could get
you into serious trouble in Queensland.

By the turn of the decade, Sydney was undergoing an
independent music boom hitherto unseen in Australia.
Radio Birdman's musical scope was not as broad as the
Saints – lead guitarist Deniz Tek was a Michigan native,
and his songs were unapologetically derived from the
Detroit noise of the Stooges and the MC5 – but the band
had succeeded where their northern cousins hadn't: they
had won over a large and devoted fan base in their home
city. After leaving for England in early 1978 (where, like the
Saints, they soon fell apart), Birdman left behind a legion
of fans, associates and hangers-on. From their ashes rose
the Other Side, the Hellcats, the Hitmen, the Passengers,
the Visitors, New Race and the New Christs. Hundreds of
others were directly inspired by their influence.

The fact that Sydney was the CBD of the Australian
music industry was immaterial to the boom. Punk, by
definition, was not a mainstream movement. Those
that didn't form their own bands, or didn't last in them,
instead formed record labels, partly to provide an outlet
for groups the major labels had no interest in, partly as a
way of immortalising their friends on plastic, and partly,
if they were lucky, to make some pocket money. Names
like Phantom, Citadel and Hot began to flourish. The late
George Wayne, then the breakfast DJ on Triple J, gave
the records heavy rotation. Venues opened their doors to
original bands in every inner-city suburb and most of the
suburban ones. The crowds came.

The combination of venues, audiences, recording
opportunities and the lack of police harassment in Sydney
would prove a magnet to aspiring Brisbane musicians,

especially those drawn into the maelstrom of the hard-rock Detroit sound. A few would go on to play in some of the most revered Australian bands of the 1980s. The Screaming Tribesmen, Died Pretty and even the Hoodoo Gurus (whose leader, Dave Faulkner, hailed from Perth) all shared significant roots in the post-Saints Brisbane scene, evolving from three crucial groups: the Fun Things, the 31st and the End.

The most obviously enthralled by the Detroit connection were the Fun Things, whose leader, Brad Shepherd, was a card-carrying member of Radio Birdman's fan club.[1]

Brad Shepherd: I read *RAM* magazine and I saw this article on Radio Birdman, at around about the same time as *Countdown* showed the Sex Pistols doing Anarchy In The UK . . . Birdman were listing songs that they covered by bands that influenced them, and there was this ton of stuff that I'd never heard of before – the Stooges, the MC5, the Blue Öyster Cult, and they had these amazing song titles like Kick Out The Jams and Search And Destroy. It was like this great, entire universe had opened up.

Cheerfully well adjusted, Brad Shepherd was not a punk in the Leftovers mould. Like Robert Forster, he grew up in The Gap, attending school at Brisbane Boys Grammar in Spring Hill. Moreover, his parents were exceptionally supportive of his musical ambitions, although he does remember unsuccessfully trying to persuade his mother to take him to see the Master's Apprentices in 1971 when he was 10. He acquired his first guitar shortly thereafter, quickly becoming proficient on the instrument.

Like many a suburban teenager growing up in the mid '70s, Shepherd cut his teeth on early heavy metal: Black Sabbath, Deep Purple and Alice Cooper. At high school he formed his first band, Overkill, with younger brother Murray and new friend John Hartley, who picked up the bass. The Shepherds' mother – perhaps feeling guilty about denying her music-obsessed eldest son the chance to see the Master's – dutifully drove her sons to Hartley's home in the southern suburb of Tarragindi for rehearsals.

When punk broke, Brad Shepherd persuaded an initially reluctant Hartley to start incorporating Sex Pistols songs into their set. By 1978 the band had changed its name to the Aliens. Shepherd had seen several performances by the Grudge and the Neon Steal, and it was Mark Callaghan who introduced Shepherd to the history on his doorstep.

> **Brad Shepherd:** He tipped me off to where that place was on the front cover of the Saints album, and I went and had my photograph taken there in front of the fireplace. Which was a big thrill, because in the iconography of rock it was very cool to have something that was so seminal – the front cover of the first Saints album – and we just idolised that record. And there it was, just down the road, just across from my old bloody school!

The Fun Things were completed when the original trio were joined by Graeme Beavis on additional guitar. Beavis was, as Shepherd recalls, 'a belligerent son of a bitch, which is perfect for a punk rock band'. Beavis was also a big fan of glam rock, and the extra firepower he provided, combined with the caveman stomp of drummer Murray, immediately distinguished the band from others around town. Playing a mixture of Stooges, Dolls and Radio Birdman covers alongside original material, the Fun Things' sound was wilder and louder than anything else on the scene. Mick Medew, who would soon be joined by Brad Shepherd in his own band, the 31st, remembers him as 'quite a sight to behold':

> **Mick Medew:** Watching Brad in the Fun Things was like watching the devil. He used to stamp his foot so hard you'd think he was going to drive a hole in the stage with his boots!

He had the sound, the presence and the voice. He's probably got one of the loudest voices in Australian rock, Brad. He certainly had the fire in him.

Brad Shepherd: I was actually very serious about music, and in many respects I had to de-evolve. When punk came along I was so impressed by the raw energy of it, the stuff I'd been learning in Spanish guitar classes sort of fell by the wayside! I had to relearn again once I realised that essentially it was folly to play as badly as you could.

The Fun Things were not built to last. By Shepherd's estimation the band played a maximum of a dozen performances around town in their entire existence, including as the Aliens. The only recording by the group – an infamous self-titled four-track EP – was recorded in February 1980 at a jingle studio at Buderim on the Sunshine Coast for the princely sum of $200, provided by the Shepherds' parents. With the band having already decided to break up, it was no more than a postscript.

Issued in the standard pressing of 500 copies, the EP has since been bootlegged many times. Shepherd, understandably frustrated by the ridiculously high prices the artefact continues to attract on the collectors' market, eventually reissued a newly mastered version on Spanish label Pennimann in 2000, dedicating the record 'To the memory of Glen and Gary Smith, Warren Lamond and Johnny Burnaway – REAL fuckin' punks.'[2]

'I was just trying desperately to be Iggy Pop circa *Metallic KO,*' he laughs, 'with mixed results!' With its roaring, heavily compressed sound, the final track Savage – on which Shepherd declares his band the 'last of the leather age' – features a guitar solo as pure as anything James Williamson committed to the Stooges' *Raw Power*. 'Cheap, idiotic, amateurish and hilarious,' Shepherd writes in the liner notes to the reissue, 'after all these years I can finally admit, for a bunch of green teenagers from the arse end of the world, it ain't bad at all.'[3]

Ron Peno had been the singer of Sydney covers band the Hellcats, in which he had performed under the alias of Ronnie Pop. Like his hero, Peno was not much over five foot one, but his stage presence belied his stature, and his reputation had spread. In late 1979 he took a call from Bruce Anthon, inviting him to come to Brisbane to try out for his new band, the Credits. By then Peno was bumming around Gosford, on the Central Coast of New South Wales, and had nothing to lose.

In the end, Anthon was indifferent to Peno's dramatic vocals, but the Credits' bass player, Tony Robertson, saw potential and introduced the singer to his high school chum, Mick Medew. The slender, jockey-voiced Medew was no bigger than Peno but was possessed of similarly outlandish charisma. He was also a fine guitarist. Another school friend, Chris Welsh, was recruited on drums. The band was christened by Peno, shortening the name of an obscure '60s group, the 31st of February.

Playing mainly at the 279 Club (at the Exchange Hotel) and the Silver Dollar in Fortitude Valley, the 31st found themselves the subject of some carping: like the Fun Things, the group could really play and didn't mind showing it off. Further, the band's brash taste in covers tended towards American hard rock – the Dictators, Blue Öyster Cult and Sonic's Rendezvous Band – alongside psychedelic '60s nuggets like the Vogues' Five O'Clock World. Neither style was of much interest to a music scene desperately trying to recreate London 1977.

More impressive were the 31st's originals, which managed an unlikely marriage between these two very different musical streams. Two early songs in particular stood out from the pack. They also introduced the world to the unique lyrical sensibility of Ron Peno.

Ron Peno: Mick and I sat down in a lounge room one day and we wrote Igloo, and then A Stand Alone . . . I'd read *Metamorphosis* by Franz Kafka, and that's where I got the idea for Igloo, just about alienation and isolation.[4]

It was at about this time that Brad Shepherd – fresh from the breakup of the Fun Things and a trip to England, where he was dismayed to find punk's energy to have long since evaporated – was brought to the 31st by Peno. Peno had also fallen hard for another new local band, the End, led by gangling, square-jawed guitarist Brett Myers. Myers was similarly enthralled by Peno's shamanistic stage antics.

Brett Myers: He was actually wilder back then, when he was young and cocky. When he was on stage it was like, fuck, what the hell is this? I'd never seen anything like him before. I guess we were all very Stooges-fixated at that time, and Ron fitted right into that mould, with these wild spastic stage movements . . . You couldn't help but watch him.

Myers was another product of The Gap, growing up only blocks away from Brad Shepherd, whom he would not meet until years later. By the time he formed the End in 1979, he was nursing a serious Velvet Underground crush. Patti Smith and Television were equally important reference points. Introducing the sounds of urban New York to the brick veneer and backyard pools of The Gap, however, would be a next to impossible task. The heavy metal/proto-punk practised by the Fun Things was easier to understand for most teenagers, and it was certainly easier to play. For a long time Myers' musical ambitions were ahead of his band's abilities.

Brett Myers: I didn't know anyone who liked any of this stuff, except for the people at Discreet, and I really wanted to play it. I'd learned how to play guitar and I basically just found some guys at high school – a guy called Murray Davis who played keyboards, another guy called Andrew Massey who lived about three blocks away, and Colin Barwick, the drummer, lived about 20 metres away. That was the End.

Mick Medew: They were just a catastrophe waiting to happen live, that band, though they ended up being incredibly tight and very musical by the end of it. But boy, when they started, it was organised chaos, although I guess that was part of their appeal too.

Certainly it appealed to Peno, whose allegiance to the 31st didn't prevent him from offering his services to Myers immediately after seeing the band play at a new Fortitude Valley dive called Kisses. Myers, though charmed, was taken aback.

Brett Myers: I guess what made me really like Ron . . . He was a lot more rock than I was, and when [the 31st] played it was all Dictators, Stooges, obscure '60s punk bands, and he was really fantastic at it. But when we talked, he said something like, 'Oh, [John Cale's] *Paris 1919* is one of my favourite ever albums,' and it was just *not* what I expected to come out of his mouth . . . That made me really warm to him and realise he was a bit more multi-dimensional than just this screaming rock-god guy. The only thing I wasn't keen on was that the End was my band, and I didn't like the idea of him being the singer in that!

Ron Peno: I tried desperately! 'Brett, please, let me join as lead singer!' And Brett being Brett would say no, no, this is my band. 'But Brett, it'll be *great* if you let me be the lead singer!' He softened a little bit and let me do Goo Goo Muck with them, by the Cramps. It was the fucking highlight of the show!

The bond formed between Myers and Peno would ultimately result in the mutation of both the 31st and the End into new, more powerful combinations.

* *

In early 1981 Brad Shepherd and Ron Peno travelled to Sydney in the hope of booking some shows for the 31st. Shepherd in particular took to the city's Rock & Roll All Night credo with unrestrained gusto.

Brad Shepherd: I was very fortunate to meet some great people in the first week that I was in Sydney. Ron had arranged to meet Jim Dickson – he had become part of the post-Birdman scene in Sydney and was playing in the Passengers with Angie Pepper. And Jim brought Clyde Bramley along, who I ended up playing with in the Hoodoo Gurus. He was originally from Toowoomba.

It became apparent to me that I couldn't go back to Brisbane. Sydney was just a ball of energy – places would stay open, there were all-night bars, there was a lot going on creatively with music, and it was all very much the sort of thing that appealed to me personally. It was all American-based rock & roll, you know. So I attempted to get the other guys from the 31st to move down and make something of the band. They weren't into the idea, so I gracefully submitted my resignation.

Shepherd was immediately snapped up by the Hitmen, later to be joined by 31st bassist Tony Robertson. When Brett Myers also decided to take the End to Sydney little more than six months later, shortly after the release of their only single (the brooding My Confession/White World, released in a tiny pressing of 300), Peno could stand it no longer. He was already torn between his favourite bands, but Sydney versus Brisbane was a no-contest. He was a Sydney native anyway.

Mick Medew's reluctance to leave his home town had left him marooned without a band, but what could have been a terminal setback proved his making. Recruited by former Fun Things Murray Shepherd and John Hartley, the Screaming Tribesmen gave him the vehicle – and the confidence – to take centre stage. He was a good enough guitarist to cover Brad Shepherd's loss, a more than capable singer, and the power-trio format was better suited to the spacious dynamics of his songs.

The band's shared history also ensured the Tribesmen a ready-made fan base. Unfortunately the new group's first offering, a self-titled four-track EP recorded in March 1982 at Speak Studios in Milton, showed only glimpses of their potential.[5]

Mick Medew: We had troubles recording our first EP. We went to a couple of different studios and couldn't get a good sound. We really just made it for the fans in Brisbane, because we had a bit of a following, and it was building. So it's all a bit embarrassing. You could pick it up in London now for a couple of hundred pounds though.

The reality was the Tribesmen hit the ceiling in Brisbane almost as soon as they were born. Medew bowed to the inevitable. In Sydney they would immediately find themselves among friends and fans. Brisbane, by contrast, was about to touch bottom: venues were closing, another state election was looming, and the grip of the government's law-and-order campaign was tighter than ever.

Mick Medew: A lot of people were leaving town. It was pretty sad. The police-state mentality was upsetting a lot of people. I don't know, I always liked Brisbane, but it just seemed like Sydney was the happening place.

Brett Myers: We had to get out of Brisbane. It was just so oppressive, with the political situation and the cops – you couldn't go out; there were no venues; everything closed at 10 o'clock. Sydney was like going to New York by comparison.

The recording of Igloo in December 1982 was a turning

point for the Screaming Tribesmen. With a cavernous, echoing production courtesy of former Radio Birdman guitarist Chris Masuak, the single established the band's Detroit-via-San Francisco template: a mixture of tough garage rock and spangled psychedelic pop, 'floating on a guitar sound like a space-age heavy metal Byrds'.[6] The combination oozed commercial potential. Released on the Citadel label, Igloo was among the biggest selling independent releases of 1983.

But the chemistry of the first, classic Tribesmen line-up was to be short-lived. By the release of the thundering follow-up single A Stand Alone in May 1984, Hartley and Murray Shepherd had returned to Brisbane and obscurity, leaving Medew to carry on with a succession of personnel, including Masuak and former Razar bassist Bob Wackley. With Masuak on board, the Tribesmen enjoyed some success, especially in America, where by the late '80s the band's fashion sense (leather jackets, leopard print, shag-pile hair and iron crosses) seemed to fit right in:

Mick Medew: When we went to Los Angeles everyone looked like Axl Rose. Not just people in bands. I mean people on the streets everywhere.

The End had not fared so well. Like the Screaming Tribesmen, the original line-up had disintegrated not long after arriving in Sydney, and a second version of the group was struggling to make headway. Brett Myers was becoming stale.

Brett Myers: I had a whole new band – I had a new drummer, new bass player and a second guitarist and they were all from Sydney. And then I met Frank Brunetti, he was a journalist from *RAM* at the time, and he did a couple of interviews with me. He really liked the band, and we became friends.

He and I and Ron were all having a drink one day, and I was talking about some problems I was having with the band and

Frank said, 'Well, get rid of them.' I went, really? Then what'll
I do? And Frank said 'Well, you can get into a new band with
Ron and I, I'll be your keyboard player and Ron will be the
singer.' And it actually sounded pretty attractive, to be honest!

Thus were born Died Pretty who, Brunetti and Peno aside,
were soon made up entirely of Brisbane personnel, with
the original trio joined by Mark Lock on bass and former
31st drummer Chris Welsh. And Peno was right: the band
was great with him singing, his flamboyant presence and
cryptic lyrical imagery proving the ideal foil to Myers' heady
musical ambitions. With a cluster of the End's leftovers and
a fresh brace of new songs, Died Pretty became the spiritual
hub of the burgeoning Sydney scene, centred on the Trade
Union club in Surry Hills.[7]

Just as Sydney was the place to go, Brisbane had become
the place to leave.

CHAPTER EIGHT

everybody moves

Brisbane you have to leave. You come out of your mother, you
go to school, and then you think, oh shit, what am I doing here?
— Tex Perkins[1]

Since the Second World War, Brisbane's skyline had been
overlooked by an eccentric structure at the top of the inner
industrial suburb of Bowen Hills. The Cloudland Ballroom
had a distinguished history. Originally intended as a
Luna Park development, the site was initially serviced by
a so-called alpine railway running from Breakfast Creek
Road all the way up to the high-set location. In 1942, by
which time Brisbane was a garrison town, Cloudland was
set aside as a defence facility for the American military.

After the war's end and the venue's reopening in 1947,
Cloudland became a social Mecca. Generations of young
people courted and caroused there; it was once mischievously
suggested that a third of the city's population had been
conceived in the car park.[2] After Buddy Holly brought rock
& roll to town on February 1958, the venue regularly hosted
bands and was also used for end-of-year university exams.

The building itself was striking, to say the least. Its arched,
laminated entrance was a full 18 metres high and by night was
rather tackily lit in various fluorescent shades that, combined

with its prestigious location, made Cloudland visible for miles. Inside, thick columns supported the high ceiling. Most famous of all was the magnificently sprung dance floor.

Such self-conscious glamour in an otherwise barren town captured the irony that lay at the heart of Brisbane. Had the sails of the Sydney Opera House flown atop Bowen Hills, they would scarcely have appeared any more anomalous than Cloudland. Journalist Linden Woodward, who had joined the Triple Zed newsroom in 1980, remembers:

Linden Woodward: I'd grown up seeing pictures of my mum and her sisters in these gorgeous ball gowns, and I remember saying, 'Mum, where is this, you look so beautiful', and her saying it was at a dance at Cloudland. You could sit there with this big arch above you and look down over Brisbane. I remember once doing that – I think it could have been when UB40 were playing – and sitting there, having a joint on the stairs, and looking down on this police dog spectacular at the Exhibition grounds. So it was a fantastic place, this whimsical symbol of lightness and fun up on the hill, above what could be a fairly harsh and arid city for a lot of people.

After the Queensland Licensing Commission put paid to the Queen's Hotel as a live venue in March 1979, Triple Zed had successfully relocated its Joint Efforts to Cloudland. This was a coup for the station. Brisbane's other medium-sized venue, Festival Hall in the city, was prohibitively expensive to hire. Following the Stranglers' appearance at the Queen's, Cloudland allowed Triple Zed to attract bigger international and national acts, with local bands providing support. In the latter months of 1979, thousands of madly pogoing fans tested out the sprung floor for themselves to the sounds of Graham Parker and XTC.

The live music scene was still subject to constant harassment. A show featuring the Sharks at the Caxton (formerly Baroona) Hall on 30 November 1979 was particularly hard hit when patrons began spilling onto the street after the show. The unforgiving heat, lateness of the hour, alcohol and seething frustration had all taken their toll. Anne Jones, who was playing bass on the bottom of the bill with the Toesuckers, witnessed the violent aftermath.

Anne Jones: About seven police cars came, and as you'd imagine in that situation, people in the crowd were yelling 'Fucking pigs!' And then the police started laying into the crowd and it was on for young and old. I was actually with these two young guys, and one of them came running past with a cop chasing on foot, followed by a police car.

So we raced after them, and they'd caught up with my friend and were beating him up. And his friend went, 'Oh, this is terrible,' and walked over to them – 'Excuse me, officer, you can't do that!' and of course you can imagine what happened. He got walloped as well, they both get arrested, and I'm sitting on the footpath in my taffeta petticoat watching the whole thing.

At trial, the magistrate dismissed Jones' evidence as unreliable. Many years later, after years of court battles, her friend finally had his conviction quashed. He subsequently, and successfully, took civil action against the police.

The Go-Betweens were in a state of transition. Since acquiring Lindy Morrison, the band had completely deconstructed its original sound. Their music had become angular, based on shifting rhythms and tones rather than naive melodies. Robert Forster had no interest in rewriting Lee Remick, but for some time found himself unsure of which musical path to pursue: through 1980 and into 1981, by his own admission, 'I didn't write a really good song for two years.' The band was practising obsessively and becoming stale.

Robert Forster: It was *dreadful* . . . It was the harsh wind of a new decade, and Brisbane was just not ready for it at all. And there we were, practising five days a week, playing this deconstructed, fractured music. For a year and a half Grant, Lindy and I played in a practice room in Brisbane and we were playing rubbish, absolute rubbish. But we got very good at playing with each other. We became a band.

The internal dynamics of the group were evolving too. Pushed to one side by the relationship between Forster and Morrison, Grant McLennan had begun writing his own songs. When Forster did the vocals on McLennan's first major contribution, Your Turn, My Turn, the latter's ambition began to surface. McLennan's voice was plaintive but pleasing and, although Forster was the greater presence, he was determined to establish himself. Predictably, Forster and Morrison's perspectives on this development differ.

Lindy Morrison: Grant quickly made it clear that he wanted to move onto guitar to be able to sing his songs, and Robert didn't like that at all. He didn't want to share [the spotlight] with Grant, no way. I remember saying to Robert, if you don't share it, you're going to lose him.

Robert Forster: If I really [wanted] to be powerful I would have got rid of Grant after three weeks. I knew, just through Grant's personality, that he was an intensely creative person. The fact that he started to write songs came to me as no surprise.

There was a big world waiting for the Go-Betweens' music beyond Brisbane. In November 1980 the band played their first Sydney show at the Paris Theatre, pitting their frail sound against the monstrous noise of the Birthday Party and the Laughing Clowns. When the Go-Betweens emerged with their reputations enhanced, their confidence was boosted immeasurably. Keith Glass, whose Melbourne-based label

Missing Link boasted both the Birthday Party and the Clowns, had reissued the Go-Betweens' Postcard single I Need Two Heads for the Australian market; now he offered to record another single for the band. In April 1981 Your Turn, My Turn was recorded in Sydney with Tony Cohen, then establishing a name for himself as the Birthday Party's producer.

In July the band travelled to Melbourne to record their debut album, for which Glass' wife unkindly volunteered the working title *Two Wimps And A Witch*. Following Your Turn, My Turn's release as a single in October, the reinvigorated group decided to make the move permanent. Almost immediately, Forster overcame his writer's block with a clutch of new songs.

The drain of creative energy out of Brisbane was becoming all too familiar.

Warwick Vere: I don't know how many Sundays I spent waving people goodbye at the airport, leaving for parts unknown. There's probably a Brisbane ghetto of people my age in just about every major city in the world. We lost an enormous number of talented people during that time, and only a few of them would have filtered back.

Lindy Morrison: Why did we leave Brisbane? That was the one thing that all three of us agreed about, that's what really made the group. We knew we had to get out of town. We were equally ambitious, and we were prepared to sacrifice everything for the band.

Next to the albums that followed, *Send Me A Lullaby*, as the Go-Betweens' debut was eventually titled, is often dismissed as amateurish and tentative. It is in fact ripe for rediscovery, making far more sense when viewed in the context of the band's immediate post-punk peers. Still, the band was only beginning to find its feet. 'It's us,' says McLennan, who contributed five of the 12 songs but sang on just three, 'not fully realising it's us.'[3]

> **Grant McLennan:** Both Robert and I have incredible reservations about *Send Me A Lullaby*. It's an inauspicious debut. But it certainly sounds like no one else! Robert's since said, and I know, that he was a bit lost then. He really felt like he wanted to make a statement at that time, and it wasn't until *Before Hollywood* that he found his voice.

With neither the band nor Keith Glass much taken with the results, *Send Me A Lullaby* was released by Missing Link in November 1981 as an eight-track mini-album. But when Missing Link's UK distributors Rough Trade released the album three months later in its intended 12-track format, import copies began to outsell the local version. It was becoming obvious that the Go-Betweens' future lay offshore. Enticed by Rough Trade, the band followed the Birthday Party to London, moving into a squat in Ladbroke Grove. They were soon joined by a fellow Brisbane émigré, Clinton Walker, who later wrote:

> Grant McLennan and I lived on a diet of speed, beer, Kentucky Fried Chicken and Richard Pryor tapes. This lasted only until the reality of the heroin situation hit home. There was truckloads of it around, it was good and it was cheap.[4]

In fairness, the Go-Betweens were mere dabblers compared to the Birthday Party (and Walker), but neither were they immune. In the middle of an English winter, scraping together an existence from one gig to the next, drugs could be more sustaining than a hot meal.

> **Lindy Morrison:** I was a pot smoker. [The Birthday Party's] Nick Cave used to rubbish me to death about it, he used to say why didn't I take a risk and use other drugs? And heroin was the drug of choice, because it made you feel so warm.

You'd be freezing and hungry, living in these disgusting
places, and you'd take heroin and everything was fabulous.
You can see why people did it.

Yet the band was making steady progress. Another
McLennan-penned single, Hammer The Hammer, did
well when released by Rough Trade in July. The B-side
was Forster's By Chance, a song he regarded as a personal
breakthrough. The Go-Betweens' identity was being
reconfigured around the partnership between two very
different songwriters. The British press were fascinated
by these opinionated yet effete Australians, denizens of
a country they thought populated mainly by sheep and
kangaroos. And the outsized personalities of Forster and
Morrison gave the band genuine charisma.

Rough Trade found an unusual venue for the recording
of the band's second album, the International Christian
Communications Studio in the seaside retirement village
of Eastbourne. It was hardly rock & roll, but the decaying
atmosphere suited the album the band cut with English
producer John Brand. Refining the edgy arrangements
of *Send Me A Lullaby*, *Before Hollywood*'s impressionistic
lyrics and sparkling blend of acoustic and electric textures
recalled earlier folk influences – Simon and Garfunkel,
the Byrds and, especially, Bob Dylan's *Bringing It All Back
Home*. Even *Before Hollywood*'s sleeve design nods towards
the Dylan album, with the Go-Betweens framed by a
collection of antiques.

Appropriately, the songs were suffused with
homesickness, nostalgia and beauty, like the yellowing
pages of an old photo album. The touchstone was the
band's first classic, McLennan's Cattle And Cane. In both
this song and the exquisite Dusty In Here, he moves
through a series of vignettes drawn from his childhood in
far north Queensland:

I recall a schoolboy coming home

Through fields of cane, to a house of tin and timber
And in the sky, a rain of falling cinders

Robert Vickers, who joined the band on bass immediately after *Before Hollywood*, allowing McLennan to shift to guitar, was astounded by the group's development.

Robert Vickers: I'd heard *Send Me A Lullaby* and thought it was quite different, obviously, to the early material. It was interesting, but it sounded like they were trying to work something out. So I was very happy when I heard *Before Hollywood*, because it was obvious that they had worked it out. It contained a lot of the melody that was in the early songs, but it was more intelligently put together. The structures of the songs were complex but also memorable, which is an almost impossible thing to do in music.

The rapid growth of the two songwriters aside, at the heart of *Before Hollywood*'s sound is Morrison, who picks her way through the songs' changes with the nervy concentration of a tightrope walker: Cattle And Cane may have become lost but for her remarkable rhythmic undertow. Her influence on the group's sound was never greater.

Lindy Morrison: I remember talking to Bruce Anthon, who played drums with them before me, and I asked him what he did when they played him songs that were in 7/4 time. And he told me to play straight through them in 4/4 time, and they will eventually come back around to where you are. And I consciously said to myself, I'm not going to do that. And that's why the first two albums have so many songs with bizarre timings. But they're so lovely.

Things were not getting any better in Brisbane. For a year the city had been readying itself for the Commonwealth Games in September, and the atmosphere was more paranoid than ever. The government had quietly wound back its prohibition of street marches due to the associated enforcement costs; now, conscious of upcoming Aboriginal protests, it enacted special legislation increasing police powers to freshly absurd levels. So vaguely drafted was the bill that for the three weeks surrounding the games it became illegal to be in possession of a 'prohibited thing' in 'notified areas'.[5] But what and where such things were to be prohibited remained at the discretion of the police minister Russ Hinze.

It is telling that this difficult period saw Triple Zed at the apex of its influence on Queensland political life. Supported by Joint Efforts and subscriber-boosting radiothons, the station employed 13 full-time paid staff. It had also attracted an extraordinary amount of talent, particularly to its newsroom. Between 1980 and 1983 (by which time most of the original station-hands had moved on and musicians were frantically bailing out of the city) several aspiring journalists and broadcasters – Andy Nehl, Tony Collins, Linda Wallace, Nicola Joseph, Louise Butt and Amanda Collinge – actually made the move *from* Sydney to further their careers in the Sunshine State.

Andy Nehl: I think I was the first of what became known as the Sydney invasion. The next couple of people that came up were Tony Collins and Nicola Joseph, and I guess part of what prompted quite a few other people to come up was the reputation Triple Zed then had from those of us that had gone back.

Amanda Collinge: Brisbane was a great place to learn to be a practising journalist, because there was so much going on politically . . . We used to have a rigorous early morning editorial meeting, apportioning stories, discussing those stories, and off we'd go with our recording material. It was very diligent; it was a proper newsroom.

Although Triple Zed's core audience was small, its

newsroom was putting the government under some pressure, concentrating on allegations of political and police corruption, giving a timid mainstream media numerous leads along the way. Often, the day would begin with an early morning call to the premier, down on the farm at Kingaroy. Remarkably, Bjelke-Petersen played the game, and his uniquely garbled way of fielding questions – combined with the out-of-context lunacy of hearing him hold forth each morning in between a brace of punk tracks – meant that the precious minutes he would grant the station invariably became the breakfast laugh track.

Linden Woodward: It was quite surreal. It seemed to me he'd been raised to be very polite to women. Other than that, he dealt with everyone pretty much the same way, and it was almost like with each conversation you were starting afresh with him, so he would start out answering your questions, and then it would degenerate into, 'Oh I know where you work, young lady; I know what kind of organisation you're in,' and eventually he'd hang up. Tony Collins loved it when he hung up on me, because then he could play [Blondie's] Hanging On The Telephone. Because I have blonde hair, he thought that was a particularly amusing joke!

Not everyone appreciated the humour. Most of the station's staff, particularly journalists, were finding themselves under increasing levels of surveillance. Some suffered the frightening experience of having their homes raided at dawn by the Special Branch. Others were subjected to more subtle means of intimidation.

Amanda Collinge: I was at this Russ Hinze press conference one day, which was an eye-opener in itself, and I was approached by someone who started asking me questions that indicated he knew a hell of a lot about me. He asked me first how I was finding my lodgings at 8 Broadway Street in Red Hill.

Then he asked me if my Datsun 180B was giving me a problem.
And the third question was how was I managing to survive on
whatever it was we were paid at Triple Zed at the time.

On 7 November 1982 the city awoke to find the queer old
archway on the hill was gone. There was no warning of the
pre-dawn attack on the much-loved ballroom: no permit
was ever issued for its destruction, and the building had
been listed by the National Trust. The Deen Brothers, a
no-questions-asked demolition outfit who had infamously
destroyed the Bellevue Hotel in George Street three years
earlier, took a little less than an hour to level the site. For
some, it was the final straw. John Stanwell and partner
Helen Hambling, both of whom had fought so hard for
Triple Zed's establishment in 1975, no longer had the energy
to continue.

John Stanwell: Cloudland was a sheer act of political
vandalism. It was knocked down to build high-rise apartments,
for which they didn't have approval, and they never got
approval because it was under a flight path. So that was the
proof positive it was an act of vandalism; it was real dick-on-
the-table stuff. It was Joh showing that he didn't even have to
care about what anyone in Brisbane thought, and that was just
too much. So we left.

Linden Woodward: It was depressing, because the bastards
outwitted us. They snuck up on us in the middle of the night
and we didn't catch them. For me as a journalist, in Brisbane,
the big thing was the importance of just witnessing things that
were happening and saying, I'm watching you.

By now Triple Zed's operations were becoming
unsustainable. With other music promoters beginning to
establish themselves – among them former station staff
striking out to make a living on their own – competition

rose for the decreasing number of gigs around town. As the number of venues shrank and crowd-pulling international tours declined, the brightest local talent also left. While a few good bands remained, they were mostly divided between hardcore punk (Mystery of Sixes, Public Execution, the Vampire Lovers), the avant-garde (the Pits, Pork, Pictish Blood) and the simply lame. None of them was especially listenable.

Since its launch in 1980 Triple M had established itself as the city's first commercial FM station, attracting two of Triple Zed's best presenters, Bill Riner and Mark Bracken. Many of Triple Zed's more conservative listeners shifted their radio dials accordingly to the right. Further, several talented journalists and broadcasters who established their careers at Triple Zed defected to Triple J: Andy Nehl, Tony Collins, Tony Biggs, Linden Woodward and Amanda Collinge all made the jump.

Amanda Collinge: I became aware of why some people resented Sydney people coming up, because it was so much easier to leave. I do remember feeling that little bit guilty, because Triple Zed had started to go through rough times, and when you're a part of something like that you do feel committed. To just up and go, I felt like I was abandoning ship a bit.

In early 1983 Collinge had assisted fellow journalist Jon Baird in breaking Triple Zed's biggest story since Cedar Bay, exposing subhuman conditions in the notorious Boggo Road jail. Months later – with almost all the inmates on an extended hunger strike – Corrective Services Minister Geoff Muntz unwisely declared in a press conference that the prisoners 'could starve for all I care'.[6] The jail was almost immediately torched beyond recognition in response. The government was forced into extensive penal reforms; for its part, Triple Zed won the Public (now Community) Broadcasting Association's annual Golden Reel Award, and considerable new respect.

> **Jon Baird:** Before Boggo Road, we were always the ratbag left-wing media. Afterwards, we started to get journalists ringing Triple Zed up, saying I'm onto a jail story or a criminal justice story, to see if we had anything to help, because we'd become established as a credible media source in areas like the criminal justice system and police corruption.

It was to be Triple Zed's last major political strike against the government. Bled dry of funds, it began an inexorable shift from paid to volunteer labour. Unable to adequately replace its outgoing talent, the station – in particular the newsroom – would never be the same force again.

> **Amanda Collinge:** There was a very proud history of good journalism in that newsroom, from people like Marian Wilkinson right through to Lindy Woodward. Sloppy journalism was not tolerated there, and nor was sloppy presenting. And all that went out the window when the wages were lost, unfortunately. That edge of professionalism disappeared, so it was no longer attractive to people who wanted to be media professionals.

> **Jon Baird:** When you're relying on volunteers to do jobs, you can't really blame them if things fuck up. It does make things a hell of a lot harder, and at Triple Zed we were really battling [after that]. Just paying the bills was enough.

In August 1983 a Festival Hall show by Californian punks the Dead Kennedys was again blighted by police harassment. Possibly apocryphal was the story of the person arrested outside the venue for carrying a concealed weapon: a pineapple. Embarrassingly factual was the arrest of the band's African-American drummer Darren Peligro after the show, allegedly for drinking on the street along with other (white) band members and fans.

The police thought him a drunken Aborigine. The band's singer, Jello Biafra, later wrote that he 'felt safer walking around on the streets of East Berlin than Brisbane'.[7]

The same month, veteran political activist Tony Kneipp entered the studios of Triple Zed with the intention of making a recording. He had no band, just a song he wanted to knock out before the upcoming state election in October. Payment was made via some construction work around the station, and recording was completed in dribs and drabs over a fortnight, with Kneipp laying down vocals, rhythm and slide guitar, and a honking saxophone. Former Swell Guy Steven Pritchard filled in on drums, while Ian Graham contributed a scorching lead guitar solo over some very wobbly bass. With each line a chorus of friends chanted the song's title – Pig City – over and over.

The ad-hoc band, which never played again, called itself the Parameters. Although the resulting single was not released for nearly a year (it took Kneipp a while to come up with the B-side), his song received extensive airplay during the election campaign. Kneipp's protest didn't stop the National Party winning the election in its own right for the first time in its history: the Queensland Liberal Party, a dismal minority of metropolitan conservatives, had torn up the coalition agreement with the Nationals two months earlier. The Nationals didn't need them anyway. The opposition was routed, with the Nationals snaring 41 seats from 39 per cent of the vote, while Labor managed 32 seats from 44.4 per cent. Bjelke-Petersen appeared impregnable.

Pig City was a paranoid masterpiece, a genuine Queensland blues.

If you go downtown, just beware
There's a demonstration in the square
The boys in blue are everywhere

See the blacks in the park

Hear the doors slam, hear the dogs bark
They're keeping the city safe after dark

The minister for corruption's working late
He wants a piece of the action in race eight
No SP here, he's ringing interstate

The blacks at Aurukun have to go
To keep big business on the go
While Joh gets shares in Comalco![8]

Who was the bagman, who was the hit man?
Who were the front men, who were the big men?
In the National scam

Hello, hello, is that you dear?
What's that clicking noise I hear?
Walls have eyes and phones have ears

Go to a dance to have some fun
Here come the boys with their dogs and guns
They don't like punks – run, Johnny, run!

Who's that knocking at the door?
At 6am it must be the law!
'Right, you know what we're looking for'

State of emergency for the 'Boks
And then to show the workers who's boss
If you think you've got rights, they're already lost

So you don't want to know, you've heard it before
But if you cop this lot you'll sure get more
Where to now from '84?

CHAPTER NINE

brisbane blacks

The most famous Triple Zed gig to be played at Cloudland was also one of the last. Touted as 'the only band that matters', the Clash were quick to tap into the local political dialect on their arrival in Australia, and for their set on 20 February 1982 they invited local Aboriginal activist Bob Weatherall to address the crowd. The Commonwealth Games were fast approaching, and the land rights movement was gaining momentum.

Despite the passing of the spectacularly draconian Commonwealth Games Act in March, the opportunity to bring the cause of Indigenous Australia to international attention during the games was compelling. The police force was arguably never more openly politicised than during this time. At one point Russ Hinze (who held the portfolios of police, local government, main roads and racing, earning him the nickname Minister for Everything) even suggested that fans attending the so-called 'Friendly Games' might be encouraged to set upon demonstrators themselves, under the approving gaze of his commissioner, Terry Lewis:

> I'll get my police officers to get into the ring first and let it be known to the fans that 2000 or 3000 gangsters are walking down the street . . . I'll say to my police officers and Terry [Lewis], 'Let's stand aside and watch what happens' . . . Two

or three thousand young bucks out of the stand . . . Let them
come down and meet the demonstrators in the centre. We'll
stand by and watch fair play.[1]

With the possible exception of Western Australia,
Queensland lagged significantly behind the rest of the
country in its relations with its original inhabitants.
While the federal government had years earlier dropped
its assimilation policy in favour of self-determination
for Aboriginal and Torres Strait Islander people, the
Queensland government regarded any such moves as
a promotion of separatism akin to apartheid. Bjelke-
Petersen – who blamed the sorry state of Aboriginal health
on the twin evils of alcohol and 'sin' – was implacable in
his resistance.

Considering the majority of the state cabinet shared a
background in the primary industries, and that many
held significant mining interests, the government's
hostility towards land rights was unsurprising, although
the rhetoric used to attack it was at times naked in its
racism. Ken Tomkins, then the minister for Aboriginal and
Islander advancement, infamously stated he did not believe
Aboriginal people were 'ready' for freehold title, concluding
hopefully, 'What I'm saying now mightn't apply in 50 years'
time. In 50 years evolution, they could be quite a different
proposition to what they are today.'[2]

The irony was that for decades the system of Aboriginal
reserves in Queensland effectively *did* comprise a nation
within a nation, closely comparable to apartheid-era South
Africa in that they were entirely administered by the
white bureaucracy. Just as the cheap labour provided by
blacks propped up the white economy in South Africa,
so too Aboriginal people on the outstations and reserves
in Queensland were expected to work for token wages, a
situation that continued long after the Whitlam Government's
passing of the Racial Discrimination Act in 1975.

Such persecution, along with strictly controlled freedom of movement and appalling standards of health and housing, resulted in an inevitable drift of Aboriginal people to the cities, where a combination of poor education standards, few employment skills, the effects of displacement and outright racism made survival even more difficult. Unsurprisingly, Aboriginal people were massively over-represented in state custody; by 1980 the number of Aboriginal and Torres Strait Islander males in Queensland prisons was seven times their proportion to the state's population. Moreover, the chances of being arrested for trivial offences was exponentially greater: the *Courier-Mail* once reported that Aboriginal people were 200 times more likely to be arrested for drunkenness in Brisbane than whites.[3] Tiga Bayles, who came to the city in 1969 from the township of Theodore in the central Queensland goldfields, was one who received his share of summary justice, Queensland-style.

Tiga Bayles: One of their favourite spots was under the Grey Street [William Jolly] Bridge on the south side. It'd be midnight and you'd be trying to make your way home from being out, you'd get picked up and taken down there in a paddy wagon or police car and given a bit of a serve. It didn't matter whether you were drunk or not; the fact that you were black was good enough to qualify you for a ride to the watch-house. My mother was locked up more than once, and she doesn't drink!

Lindy Morrison, working at the Aboriginal and Islander legal service in the early '70s, saw more of black life in Brisbane during this time than most whites.

Lindy Morrison: We used to do what we called Pig Patrol at 10 o'clock every night, where we'd go out and try to stop people getting picked up by police, because the police were so vicious to Aboriginal people at that time.

Tiga Bayles left Brisbane in 1976, beginning a long career in radio on Sydney's 2SER, one of the original dozen community stations which had received its licence from the federal government at the same time as Triple Zed. In early 1982 he began presenting the Aboriginal music program Black Perspectives, while also managing Aboriginal group Us Mob. At the same time he began working with 2SER journalist Louise Butt on an independent documentary, *The Whole World's Watching*, aimed at rallying Aboriginal people and white supporters to attend protests against the Commonwealth Games beginning on 30 September.

Butt had conducted several interviews for the documentary at a pre-games land rights conference in Brisbane, then relocated from Sydney shortly afterwards to take up a position at Triple Zed. Her interest in indigenous politics quickly proved influential at the station.

Louise Butt: There was a lot of political unrest within the Aboriginal community and a feeling that they needed to have a focus for expressing their aspirations and discontent. The last big thing had been the tent embassy in Canberra, which had been some time earlier [1972], and then there had been a lot of political work in terms of setting up self-determination organisations. But there was a feeling around at the time, particularly among younger people, that there needed to be some sort of major public event that was a focal point for the Aboriginal community.

By 23 September hundreds of Aboriginal people from around the country had begun arriving in Brisbane. Three days later, following a march from the Roma Street Forum, a tent city of more than 300 people took root in the traditional Aboriginal meeting place of Musgrave Park in South Brisbane. The 'city' began as a cheap solution to the lack of organised accommodation, but over the next three weeks it doubled as the nerve centre of discussion and decision-making.

The tent city also facilitated an unprecedented degree of contact and collaboration between blacks and whites in Brisbane. A Rock Against Racism gig was staged by Triple Zed on 25 September at Souths rugby league club in West End, and a radiothon was held to raise money to provide food for those camping in the park. But most of the funds were diverted into bailing nearly 320 demonstrators out of jail following two more marches on 4 and 7 October, by which time the games were underway.

'Even though the Deep North is the home of indigenous jazz, blues and soul,' Clinton Walker writes in his account of Aboriginal country music, *Buried Country*, 'in the rest of the sunshine state the country is drier, and the music is country.' Given the survival of Aboriginal culture is based on its connection to the land and the passing down of oral history, it makes sense that Aboriginal people identified most strongly with country music's storytelling traditions. (Of course, as Walker also points out, the fact that most Aboriginal people grew up far from the city meant that country music was ubiquitous anyway.[4])

The most potent wellspring of Aboriginal country music in Queensland was Cherbourg, ironically situated just outside Murgon, half an hour north of Bjelke-Petersen's home base, Kingaroy. Cherbourg had already produced several local heroes, including opera singer Harold Blair, Les Collins and Angus Rabbit. As a raw teenager in the late '60s, Dennis 'Mop' Conlon began his first band, the Magpies, with his uncle Doodie Bond. The Magpies quickly became a popular draw in the black communities of the South Burnett.

At the age of 14, Conlon moved to Brisbane in search of new opportunities. A new version of the Magpies was soon assembled around the core of Conlon, Bond and Hedley Johnson, playing regular gigs at Aboriginal-run venue the

Open Doors on Herschel Street and at the Ship Inn in South Brisbane. By the late '70s they were even playing occasional punk bills with Razar; as Walker notes, 'the Task Force didn't know who to bust first'.[5]

With band members constantly drifting back and forth between Brisbane and the towns and communities of the South Burnett, the Magpies was neither a permanent ensemble nor name, and frequently gigs were billed as Dennis Conlon (or Dennis, or Mop) 'and his band'. One night, after a blazing row with his nephew, Doodie Bond walked out on a gig at the Ship Inn. Spying a poster, he crossed out 'band' and substituted 'Dropouts' in a fit of pique.[6] Bond soon returned and the name stuck, even though not all the members were keen on the tag.

> **Dennis Conlon:** There were a few of the fellows who took it a bit hard there; they didn't want to be called the Dropouts. I said, 'Get a grip on yourself, look at the black community now – we're not welcome in the mainstream, we *are* the Dropouts!'

By early 1982 Conlon was spending most of his time back in Murgon. One night watching television, he saw a current affairs piece about Aboriginal people living and drinking in Musgrave Park.

> **Dennis Conlon:** It looked good on TV, you know, but the story was just gonna die the next day. I thought, oh well, I'll write something and give people something to remember it. So I wrote Brisbane Blacks. I had that many pages, it was like a really big story.

The resulting song – Conlon's first original composition, set to a slow, lilting melodic refrain – was as plain-spoken and emotionally direct as anything in the Hank Williams canon:

> You look down through your noses to see
> The black man grovelling down at your feet
> With weary eyes looking up at you
> Waiting for the message to get through

Brisbane Blacks – originally released by Sundown Records under the name of Dennis Conlon and the Magpies, later as Mop and the Dropouts – didn't quite make it out in time for the Commonwealth Games, although the band did play the aforementioned Rock Against Racism gig. The song's impact, however, was immediate and far-reaching. The Dropouts were soon in heavy demand nationally.

Dennis Conlon: We did a lot of fundraisers for black organisations like Born Free in Brisbane, a lot of organisations that were struggling – kindergartens, football clubs, and really we did it because . . . Well, we needed to support them somehow, but really we needed the practice! And what better way to practise than straight on stage? Out of all the years we've been together, I can only remember one practice that we've ever had at home.

In 1983 Sydney's Radio Skid Row received its community broadcasting licence, and immediately offered the Aboriginal community six hours of airtime per week. Tiga Bayles took on the job of programming. The demand for Aboriginal radio in the city was such that six hours quickly became 30, eventually resulting in a satellite station, Radio Redfern.

Similar calls were being heard in Brisbane. Awareness of Aboriginal issues was at a high after the games protests, and one of Triple Zed's original aims had been to provide a voice to those inadequately represented by the mainstream media. The movement of former 2SER broadcasters to Triple Zed (including Louise Butt and Amanda Collinge) was also crucial. In mid 1983 Butt approached local community leader Ross Watson about presenting a new show on Triple Zed.

Charismatic and outspoken, Watson had formed a black protest committee prior to the games, and put together two issues of an independent newspaper, *Black Nation*. He was also aware of the potential power of black radio: the fact that it was an oral medium, and allowed Aboriginal people the opportunity to speak for themselves, was irresistible.

> **Ross Watson:** Radio's a pretty quick medium for communicating to people; it's effective, it's oral, it's much quicker than the printed word, and it was much more appropriate to us culturally.

Watson began organising a team of people, commencing workshops at the station and identifying Aboriginal music: No Fixed Address and Us Mob's split soundtrack album *Wrong Side Of The Road*, and the various artists cassette *Rebel Voices*, produced by the Central Australian Aboriginal Media Association (CAAMA).

The Murri Hour finally made its debut on Triple Zed (with Brisbane Blacks serving as the obvious theme song) in mid 1984, going to air as a pre-recorded one-hour tape. Announcer Liz Willis, who helped train the new broadcasters, remembers the initial response from the station's white audience – and from sections within Triple Zed itself – was befuddled, to say the least.

> **Liz Willis:** The complaint was 'they talk about football and they play country music'. I mean, that's standard now, everyone talks about football, but back then no one talked about sport at Triple Zed. And *no one* played country music, except at a radiothon to make people subscribe so they would take it off!

> **Amanda Collinge:** It was a real challenge to people, because [although] people said they wanted to be part of this progressive

community radio station, when it really happened – when real
people from the community got on air – people didn't like it,
because they didn't sound slick. [And] Aboriginal people have
a different way of speaking; they often speak at a different
pace; a few had quite thick accents, and we met a fair amount
of resistance [because] some people thought it was a real
turn-off.

The Aboriginal community, however, was enraptured.

Ross Watson: We'd tape the show on Friday and play it on
the Saturday morning. Later we'd go somewhere, to a party
on a Saturday night, and we'd hear our program just being
replayed. People would tape it off the radio and just keep
playing it over and over.

Although the rise of Aboriginal broadcasting in the early
'80s coincided with an upsurge of interest in contemporary
Aboriginal music, precious little had yet been committed
to tape. *Wrong Side Of The Road*, released in late 1981, was
one of the few contemporary Aboriginal recordings, if not
the first, since Jimmy Little's heyday. The Warumpi Band's
debut single, Jailanguru Parkarnu, didn't appear until
October 1983; Coloured Stone followed with Black Boy in
May 1984.

The short-term solution to circumvent the lack of music
was to invite Aboriginal songwriters into the Triple Zed
studios to perform. The most prominent was Kev Carmody.
Born in 1946 on the Darling Downs west of Brisbane to an
Irish father and Aboriginal mother, Carmody was taken
from his parents at the age of 10 and placed in a Christian
school on account of his mixed heritage. Emerging from
school functionally illiterate, he spent 17 years working
as a farm labourer before managing to blag his way into
the Darling Downs Institute of Technology in Toowoomba
(now the University of Southern Queensland) thanks to his
prodigious gifts as a guitarist.

Kev Carmody: I studied music at night; I did the Australian Music Board exams. I got to a stage where my teacher said you're miles ahead of the institute out there as far as entry goes, so I went out and I auditioned for it – in my overalls! – and they had to accept me because I was so advanced in theory, but they didn't have a classical guitar teacher of the standard they required. So they said 'Look, do this BA in history, philosophy and geography, and take a third of your course in music,' so that's how I got in.

I was lucky; I had great lecturers. For the first tutorial, I said, 'Can I bring my guitar in?' I was damn sure within six months I could get this writing thing right, so that was the trade-off – I could put oral history in by using the guitar, it was bloody great, and after about six months I had the skills and just went from there. I didn't know how to get a book out of a library. I'd never even seen a library!

Carmody's ability to improvise solutions in this manner went back to his labouring days.

Kev Carmody: Through the '50s we used to have packhorses, and they couldn't carry a guitar, but there was still music around the campfire every night, you know, mouth organ. But when we got a truck, we could actually carry a guitar, and my uncle knew a few chords. That's why country music was so important to blackfellas, because you only needed two or three chords and you could put your own words to it. And of course the old uncle, he was very interested in the old African-American stuff like Huddie Ledbetter [Leadbelly]. And the merchant marine mob, after the war the African-American sailors would come over and they used to bring over old jukebox records from America, with the big hole in the middle. You'd get a lump of pipe and put it on the old gramophone that you used to wind up. We used the lump of pipe to fill up the big hole on the jukebox vinyl.

Unlike Dennis Conlon, Carmody had been composing

his own material from early on: steeped equally in rural blues and the urban protest music of Woody Guthrie and early Bob Dylan, his ear for language was as fine-tuned as his guitar playing. Thou Shalt Not Steal – one of four tracks recorded by Watson at Triple Zed and sent to community radio stations around the country – brought Carmody to national attention, and painted a remarkably lyrical image of black life in Brisbane:

Well Job and me and Jesus, sitting underneath that Indooroopilly Bridge
Watchin' that blazing sun go down behind the tall-treed mountain ridge
   The land's our heritage and spirit here, the rightful culture's black
And we're sittin' here just wondering, when we gonna get that land back

It quickly became clear at Triple Zed that a solitary, pre-recorded Murri 'Hour' was inadequate to cater to the Aboriginal community's needs. Just as Radio Skid Row had been forced to scale up its black airtime, after 12 months Murri Hour was expanded to eight live-to-air hours a week. So keen was the community to become involved that, during evening shows, busloads of up to 80 people would turn up at the station's campus studios. The program soon expanded again, to 16 hours a week. The show was attracting upwards of 120 phone calls per shift, putting pressure on a range of other interest groups at the station.[7]

Louise Butt: As Murri Radio developed – and obviously out of respect for the self-determination issues that are involved in Indigenous politics – the collective took a bit of a hands-off approach, and that could have caused a few problems . . . It was difficult, because the Murri Hour program was obviously so needed that as it grew it became a focal point for the Indigenous community, and it started to have its own independent life.

Tensions were rising on several fronts. The slow drift back towards a higher percentage of block programming meant that Triple Zed was moving ever further away from its original mass-minority audience aspirations. The confrontational politics of Murri Hour was alienating listeners the station could ill afford to lose.

Ross Watson: We would have people ringing up saying we were being outrageous and we were being racist, that sort of thing. Sometimes we'd try talking to them, and other times we'd end up telling them to get fucked. We got a lot of that sort of stuff.

Tiga Bayles, then working at Radio Redfern, would later learn to temper his approach.

Tiga Bayles: We called things as they were. We identified the racist businesses, the racist police. We spoke openly about the racist policies and practices that were taking place on a daily basis. And so a lot of non-Indigenous people found us offensive.

The occasional abrasiveness of the on-air content was matched by an increased militancy in Aboriginal music, a trend that was entirely in keeping with the era. While Midnight Oil went on their own fact-finding tour of Aboriginal communities with the Warumpi Band, Kev Carmody was stockpiling a number of songs dedicated to the upcoming 1988 Bicentenary. Even more than the Commonwealth Games, the planned celebrations of the country's colonisation represented an opportunity for Aboriginal people to contradict white Australia's sunny view of its own history.

Kev Carmody: My mother said you've got so many songs about this Bicentennial stuff, why don't we put an album out and see if we can counteract it, to the best of our ability. And so

that's what I did; my family put together enough money to do a
little eight-track recording; I went to Sydney, and I recorded at
Megaphon Studios . . . Most of the stuff is one take.

The resulting album, *Pillars Of Society*, was relentless.
The songs fairly glowed with anger; the truths they spoke
so unbearable, they still await official acknowledgment.
Bruce Elder's review for *Rolling Stone* – 'The best album ever
released by an Aboriginal musician and arguably the best
protest album ever made in Australia' – was incorporated
into the album's cover art upon its release by Larrikin
Records. One song, Black Deaths In Custody, anticipated a
royal commission into the issue:

I say, show me the justice, to be had here in this land
Show us blacks the justice, for every black human being
Show us blacks the justice, in this white democracy
When you can execute us without a trial, while we're held in custody

Where Midnight Oil's Beds Are Burning spoke of 'we',
and Archie Roach limited his own accounts of personal
tragedy mainly to 'I', it is perhaps unsurprising that
Carmody's accusatory 'you' would prove too difficult for
white audiences to swallow.

While Triple Zed continued to provide a platform for the
Murri Show, diverging interests made a split inevitable.
Ross Watson spent most of the latter half of the '80s
jumping through the necessary hoops to win the Brisbane
Aboriginal community its own radio licence, eventually
granted by the then Australian Broadcasting Authority
in 1991.[8] The debut of 4AAA Murri Country in April 1993
represented the culmination of his work. Operating out
of well-resourced studios in the south-west suburb of
Fairfield, 4AAA is Brisbane's only country music-format
broadcaster.

Under the management of Tiga Bayles, the station is careful in how it delivers its message.

Tiga Bayles: If we wanted to reach people, if we wanted to be a station that anyone could listen to and not be offended, if we really wanted to make changes within the society, if we wanted more people to tune in and not less people, we had to change the way we delivered the message . . . Also, because we're funded, we're not volunteer-based or dependent, [so] we're able to place demands on our staff!

CHAPTER TEN

too much acid

Those whom the gods wish to destroy, they first make mad.
— Euripides

Punk never really died in Brisbane. There was always something to complain about, and an anti-authoritarian streak – fomented so effectively by the police – ran deep in the city's youth culture. During the long years from 1981 to 1989, by which time the alternative music explosion was just around the corner, new bands continued to spring forth, thrashing out minor variations on a sound most believed exhausted.

There were still a few gems. The Vampire Lovers' Buzzsaw Popstar was one: derivative but fabulous in spite of itself, it sounded like a lost Damned single, and inadvertently prefigured that band's Gothic period. (The Screaming Tribesmen's classic 1984 EP *Date With A Vampyre* pursued a similar theme and was huge in the band's home town: despite the heat, the Goth subculture has proven mysteriously enduring up north.)

The majority of witnesses to the second-generation punk explosion in Brisbane, however, were searching for fresh musical avenues, most of them south of the border. This was understandable. The Go-Betweens were going from strength to strength internationally; Died Pretty and the Tribesmen were blazing trails of their own; Mark Callaghan's new band GANGgajang was a mainstream hit. There was simply no precedent for bands achieving any kind of commercial profile while remaining in Brisbane.

Those who stayed behind – or came back – were free to make music chiefly for their own amusement, a different kind of recognition that achieving any kind of commercial success from Brisbane was impossible. While groups like Xero and Lovs é Blur balanced their eccentricities with sufficient concessions to structure and melody to remain alluring, dire acts like the Pits and Pork eschewed any attempts at popularity for the sake of being as annoying as musically possible. They had their adherents, though:

Tex Perkins: Pork were quite groundbreaking, actually! When I was first going out and looking for some rock & roll, most of the bands that were getting about were like Xero and Pork, and they were very un-rock & roll. Pork would play in their underpants, or their cricket gear or something like that, and their music was completely experimental, but with a good deal of humour.

Born in 1965 in Darwin, Greg Perkins grew up in Sandgate. His older brother Robert had been a roadie for the Leftovers, and Tex, as he would soon be known, was initiated into Brisbane's punk scene from an early age. His potential was first spotted at the bottom of a flight of stairs by the Pits' Ian Wadley, during a gig at a hall in Fortitude Valley that was owned by the Communist Party.

Tex Perkins: I was a punter, and I'd taken some sort of inebriant and I was *particularly* out of it, shall we say. And I made a complete buffoon of myself . . . I actually fell down this very large, long staircase. A month later I was at a nightclub and these two guys came up to me and said, 'Aren't you that

guy who was causing havoc at the communist hall?' And I
went, er, yeah.
'You want to form a band with us?'

Although the influence of the Pits was apparent in the
performance-art approach of one of Perkins' countless
later bands, Thug, his tastes lay mainly in traditional rock
& roll. Formed in late 1981, his first band the Dum Dums
was completed by Greg Gilbert and brothers Greg and Ian
Wadley. 'We could have been Ian and the Gregs,' Perkins
says dryly. 'That was another reason for me to become Tex.'

As Tex Deadly, Perkins had a ready-made role to walk
into. With songs like This Here Country and Cheap
Funerals, the Dum Dums were very much an early
version of the hillbilly swamp-rock he perfected later
with Sydney's Beasts of Bourbon. Rangy and photogenic,
with a precociously deep, growling voice, Tex fitted the
gunslinger part perfectly, but his band was too ramshackle
to pack much of a wallop.

The recruitment of Mark C 'Marko' Halstead in late 1982
gave the Dum Dums some much-needed muscularity. Some
years older than the rest of the band, Halstead had already
achieved small-time notoriety with the Disposable Fits. The
name was not just an in-joke: the collective bad habits of the
group could have killed a horse. Some of the members later
formed the Fuji Angels, named after a brand of syringe.

Mark Halstead: I'm sure the drug squad kept our posters on
the wall . . . 'Anyone here play bass? Our guy's just turned blue
in the gutter outside . . . Is anyone pumping him up, that'd be
a good idea, good, OK. Oh fuck, he's throwing up, I don't want
to give him mouth to mouth . . . Oh all right, I'll do it! Jesus . . .'

Halstead suited the Dum Dums' approach. Schooled on
rockabilly and the outlaw country of Merle Haggard and
Waylon Jennings as much as punk, he possessed a wider
grasp of musical structure, and vocabulary of chords, than

most of his peers. With a new line-up including another ex-Fit and former Swell Guy, Cyril Culley, and additional guitarist Clem Lukey, the group – but mainly Perkins – was spotted by manager Roger Grierson after a gig supporting ska band the Allniters.

The Dum Dums moved to Sydney in early 1983, where the attention lavished on their charismatic frontman helped ensure they didn't last long. Perkins was at the beginning of a slow climb to household-name status.

Tex Perkins: Cyril and Marko left because I wasn't helping load out enough. They just got the shits and went back to Brisbane in the dead of night. Without saying anything! That was pretty funny. That was the main reason the Dum Dums broke up, because I wasn't helping to lug enough gear. Well, you know, I've got a microphone! It's one of the reasons you *become* a singer!

Mark Halstead: I thought at the time, if he sticks at it, he'll be a star, this guy. There was no two ways about it – just through sheer force of will and this irresistible craziness. I don't think it entered his head that he wouldn't somehow be able to make a living out of it.

Halstead and Perkins were not alone in their interest in the rural roots of rock & roll. Another songwriter was creating his own brand of self-described 'urban and western' under the unlikely name of John F Kennedy.

John Kennedy: My dad's name's John Kennedy, so I've never thought twice about it, although I was always aware from a very early age of President Kennedy, and can recall seeing the images on television when he was assassinated. But I did take it one step further – being from a Catholic background, you can take a confirmation name when you're about 10 or 12, and I picked a name that started with F. I thought it was a good joke at the time and have since lived to find the joke's not funny anymore. It's a double-edged sword – once people know you, they never forget your name, and the other side of it is, once people know you, they never forget your name.

Born in Liverpool, where he spent his early childhood, Kennedy nursed an understandable Beatles fixation, but after his parents settled in the industrial southern suburban wasteland of Acacia Ridge in the late '60s, he found himself drawn to the occasional country tune that would cross over to the local AM radio. A decade later the only punk or new wave artist of substance allowing any country leanings to filter through his work was Elvis Costello. Kennedy latched onto Costello's debut *My Aim Is True* like a drowning man.

In 1980 Kennedy met guitarist Graham Lee, then playing with Mark Halstead in pop band the Gasmen. Lee – whose nickname 'Evil' was a playful twist on his choirboy features – had earlier played on folk singer Eric Bogle's original version of And The Band Played Waltzing Matilda, appearing on the album cover wearing a fetching set of white flares. After assisting on some four-track recording, Lee helped Kennedy recruit the rhythm section of bassist John Downie and drummer Steven Pritchard.

Dubbed JFK and the Cuban Crisis by Kennedy's school friend and guitarist James Paterson, the band quickly became a fixture at the 279 Club. Kennedy was, by his own admission, something of an honorary member of the local scene – he actually had a job – and as one of the few bands able to put together not one but two full 45-minute sets of mainly original music without falling over, the Cuban Crisis played several prestigious support slots, notably to the Pretenders and Ian Dury.

John Kennedy: Looking back on it, that was one of the benefits of being a band in Brisbane. Most bands on a similar level in Sydney wouldn't have been getting that type of access to larger audiences, because there was a lot more of them, so there was much stronger competition for support slots.

Of course, the high profile the band enjoyed made a move to Sydney all the more inevitable. After two cassette releases and the Paterson-penned first single Am I A Pagan? (written, allegedly, about the relationship between Paterson and Mark Halstead), the Cuban Crisis' name was made by a jaunty, keyboard-driven song originally titled Take Something.

> **John Kennedy:** After Am I A Pagan? was sent off to be pressed, James said, 'I think the next single definitely should be Texan Thing.' And I thought, that's a bit rude, because he'd already had the A-side of the first single, and now he was mentioning this song I'd never heard of to be the next single. Unbeknownst to me, when I played him this song called Take Something, he'd misheard it as Texan Thing. So I had to go back and rewrite the lyrics for the song.

Released in December 1982, the four-track EP *Careless Talk Costs Lives* (featuring The Texan Thing) was the first release for Sydney independent label Waterfront Records, and gained Kennedy a wider audience. But Kennedy enjoyed precious little good fortune thereafter. Having left Downie and Pritchard back in Brisbane, momentum was stalled by constant line-up changes. After Paterson's departure in 1983, Kennedy was joined by the gifted Lee, only to lose him to Perth band the Triffids, then cutting a swathe through Europe and the UK.

In a later song originally titled Hicksville – its title underlined by a sawing fiddle and plunking banjo – Kennedy bade a not-so-fond farewell to his old home. The song was eventually released as Brisbane '82.

> I come from a little town that they call Brisbane
> Where the government wants progress at all costs

Repression's a small price to pay, and corruption's going to
pave the way
To a future where innocence is lost

In June 1984 Joh Bjelke-Petersen was knighted for his services to Queensland. The source of his nomination is actually something of a mystery: the *Courier-Mail*, in one of its more breathless moments, suggested that perhaps Buckingham Palace had initiated the honour itself. Author Evan Whitton later wrote: 'If that were the case, it would be difficult to know whether to condemn Palace minions for not making proper inquiry, or to applaud Her Majesty for a tour de force of sustained and sleepless irony.' Bjelke-Petersen's citation read, in part:

> In the high and responsible office of premier for 15 years, Mr Bjelke-Petersen has been not only an inspiration and a guiding light, but also a living embodiment of the spirit of self-sacrifice and service . . . Mr Bjelke-Petersen is a strong believer in the historic tradition of parliamentary democracy and he has had implemented many improvements in the parliamentary process.[1]

When more than 1000 employees of the South East Queensland Electricity Board went on strike in early 1985, protesting against the government's bid to break the Electrical Trades Union through the introduction of contract labour, Bjelke-Petersen's response could hardly have been more emphatic: he sacked the lot. Peter de Hesse, of punk band La Fetts, was one of them, and wrote the scathing SEQEB Scabs in response.

I'll tell you what Joh did to the electricity workers
For expressing their rights, he put 'em on the dole!

The unionists were eventually offered back their jobs on the condition of signing new contracts with punitive anti-strike clauses. A little over half buckled. The rest lost their positions and their superannuation.

It was a bitter time. Bjelke-Petersen had previously hinted that Queensland might be better off seceding from Australia, complete with its own currency (coins could potentially have featured two heads, with Bjelke-Petersen's opposite the Queen's). The sense of unreality that was becoming a part of living in the state – the feeling that, at times, one really was living in a foreign country or perhaps on another planet – deepened when the newly knighted premier was awarded an honorary doctorate of law by the University of Queensland in May 1985, an occasion that prompted outraged protests by staff and students alike.

Even more curious was the awarding of another knighthood later the same year, this time to Terry Lewis. It was the first and last such honour accorded to a police commissioner and, as Lewis' diaries later showed, came after considerable agitation on his own part. (Shamelessly, Lewis let it be known he would prefer to be addressed as 'Sir Terence' henceforth.) According to self-confessed bagman of the force, the late Jack Herbert, Lewis was receiving as much as $11,451 a week in corrupt payments at the time.[2]

It was against this surreal backdrop that the most deliriously weird album ever to emerge from Brisbane surfaced. The Pineapples From the Dawn of Time were an odd hybrid, initially a three-piece featuring former Dum Dum Clem Lukey (aka Big John Featherduster), singer Michael Gilmore (King Farouk) and Rod McLeod (Vance Astro). McLeod was a veteran of the Brisbane scene, notorious for two primitive EPs cut with underage punks the Young Identities, the band he had formed with his brothers Clayton and Gavin in 1978. Inspired by the Leftovers – McLeod had helped cover the manufacturing costs of Cigarettes And Alcohol – the Young Identities' disdain for anything that

smacked of professionalism was the common thread of
McLeod's many bands right through to the Pineapples.

> **Rod McLeod:** I think music had become too serious in
> Brisbane, the whole scene had become dour and self-
> important by that stage . . . Everything had started slowing
> down, people were getting methodical and self-absorbed, so
> we decided to speed it up a bit.

The group's drum-machine augmented demo Too Much
Acid was seized upon by Triple Zed, and injected a welcome
dose of levity onto the scene:

> Taking acid made me aware
> Bent my mind, lost my hair
> Lived my life to the full
> Now I am a vegetable

The band quickly expanded to include like-minded
spirits Peter Kroll and Mark Halstead. Both were playing
in country combo the Kingswoods, who in 1983 recorded a
cover of the Sex Pistols' Pretty Vacant (as Purty Vacant) for
Sydney label Green Records. On the 'straight' single version
of Too Much Acid, released in 1986, Kroll's faux-Hendrix
guitar playing established the Pineapples' blueprint as, in
McLeod's words, a 'joke hippie psychedelic band'. Live, the
group put a more tuneful spin on their inspirations, the Pits
and the Leftovers.

> **Mark Halstead:** You weren't allowed to perform or for that
> matter record sober, but despite all the psychedelic bullshit,
> I don't think anyone took any drugs at the time, other than
> Victoria Bitter.

Crediting ex-Leftover Warren Lamond for spiritual
guidance, the band's sole album *Shocker* spiked the punch of
many a local party. Recorded on an eight-track machine used

to capture an Engelbert Humperdinck gig the night before, it featured a sleeve worthy of the album's hallucinogenic content.

> **Rod McLeod:** There's an infamous episode of *Star Trek* where these space hippies take over the *Enterprise*. That's the space hippies on the cover; Spock ends up jamming with them and he's actually playing this thing that looks like a spare tyre from a bicycle . . . I suppose it comes back to a trash aesthetic, I think most rock & roll definitely comes from that.

The paucity of venues available in Brisbane by the mid '80s meant that it helped one's cause greatly to create a sound acceptable, and preferably familiar, to punters. If the country crowd were looking backwards for inspiration, and the experimentalists were glancing sideways, then the Ups and Downs were very much the band of the moment.

The core of the band, rhythm section Greg and Darren Atkinson, had played together in 42nd Street since 1979 and had already tried their luck in Sydney. Making no secret of their commercial aspirations, 42nd Street was straight guitar pop, and had been included on a compilation album (the appalling *That's Queensland!*) put together by local AM station 4IP.

> **Darren Atkinson:** Rather than play the Triple Zed circuit we got ourselves involved in the Hutchinson booking agency, which looked after all the cover bands and booked all the places on the Gold Coast like the Jet Club and the Paradise Room, places that all the big mainstream bands played.

Unsurprisingly, 42nd Street was unable to gain a foothold in the Detroit-obsessed Sydney scene. Returning to Brisbane, the two brothers recruited guitarists John Flade and Peter Shaw. The Ups and Downs plied a slightly edgier trade

than 42nd Street, drawing heavily on the jangling sounds
of early R.E.M. and American 'paisley underground' bands
such as the dB's and the Rain Parade. The most obvious
reference point was the Church, an influence some members
took rather too close to heart: Shaw even hyphenated his
surname to Hamilton-Shaw in homage to Church guitarist
Marty Willson-Piper.

Ultimately, the Ups and Downs stood out on the Triple
Zed circuit almost as much as 42nd Street had in Sydney.

Greg Atkinson: I think we were considered to be fairly
squeaky-clean pop, although we got a little bit darker as we
went along. We didn't even do drugs, apart from a little bit of
pot. Actually we didn't smoke pot until we got to Sydney, most
of us! We were just good Brisbane boys. I remember seeing
Lovs é Blur once, and Wendy [Seary, singer] blew me away
when she said it was as dry as a nun's cunt up on stage. I
remember thinking, wow, that's an expression I haven't heard
before! I may never hear it again!

The band's first single, Living Inside My Head, had
little impact on its release in December 1984, but the next,
Perfect Crime, transformed the Ups and Downs into
next big things. With the single reissued by Waterfront
in the spring of 1985, the group were again caught in
Sydney's gravitational pull. This time, they found the city
considerably more accommodating, despite groups like
the Lime Spiders and the Celibate Rifles having usurped
Radio Birdman's crown.

Greg Atkinson: The press was starting to get on to us,
because I suppose they needed something to align with the
new music that was happening in America, like R.E.M., and
Ups and Downs fitted into that perfectly . . . We weren't a
part of that Detroit thing happening in Sydney, which was why
some journalists jumped on us. We got hyped to death.

After a third single, In The Shadows, gained them a deal with Polygram subsidiary True Tone, the sublime The Living Kind, released in August 1986, saw the Ups and Downs on the edge of the mainstream Top 40. The accompanying mini-album *Sleepless* showcased a deeper sound, albeit still a derivative one, with the group in thrall to British groups the Cure and Cocteau Twins (and wearing black instead of paisley). But the band peaked too early: when their management tried to capitalise on The Living Kind's commercial promise by prising more money out of True Tone, the Ups and Downs spent two years in limbo before crossing to Mushroom. They never recaptured their momentum.

> **Greg Atkinson:** In retrospect it's easy to say we shouldn't have done that; that was a decision our management made and we could have said no. But of course we didn't want to know about that stuff; we just wanted to play in a band. What we should have done was go overseas and follow that up while nothing was happening for us here, because we were making the college charts [in America], and we made a dent in the European independent charts with *Sleepless*.

The story of the Ups and Downs was emblematic in many respects. Countless other Brisbane bands were ground under the wheels of the music industry machine after developing in relative isolation, especially those yet to develop a strong sense of musical identity. Had the Ups and Downs surfaced at the tail end of the '80s, when the rapid rise of Sydney's the Hummingbirds pre-empted the incorporation of independent bands into the mainstream, the band's fate might have been different.

Of course, in the mid '80s Australian music was ruled by pub rock, and the fact that musicians with higher artistic aspirations were achieving greater recognition overseas than at home was hardly unique to Brisbane artists. This applied not only to the better known likes of Nick Cave and the Triffids, but also those working in what were then marginal musical genres. Dance music, in particular, was viewed as something sung primarily by soap stars. The appearance of Boxcar – who, as a non-touring electronic band, had their greatest successes in America while remaining in Brisbane – was a genuine anomaly.

> **David Corazza:** We were kind of like the ugly pig stuck in the middle. We were viewed with cock-eyed suspicion by a lot of indie bands in Brisbane because we didn't have street cred. We weren't playing thrash or indie pop or anything, we were trying to be this electronic band, and they thought we were just this hilarious rip-off of New Order, which I think is grossly unfair in retrospect.

If accusations of plagiarism were inevitable after Boxcar supported New Order on their Australian tour in 1986, they also highlighted a wider ignorance of dance culture in Australia. The band – songwriter and producer-engineer Corazza, singer David Smith, keyboard player Carol Rohde and, later, drummer Crispin Trist and additional keyboardist Brett Mitchell – was as much a product of the increasing availability of music technology locally as it was a response to the breakthroughs in electronic music in Europe and the UK. 'If we'd been where we were in the late '70s,' Corazza says, 'we couldn't have done what we did.'

Corazza had assembled a small eight-track recording studio in the city called Music Systems, in the vain hope that the equipment on offer would prove a magnet for aspiring electronic performers in Brisbane. He was at the wrong party, but found in Smith a creative partner who shared an eye for the future. Unfortunately, an electronic group in Brisbane was always going to be a novelty greeted by raised eyebrows at best and bottles at worst, especially during the band's rare live performances, where Boxcar was unafraid to challenge visual as well as musical expectations.

David Corazza: I look back with a wry smile, because promoters used to put us in places like the [outer suburban] Calamvale Hotel. I was doing front-of-house that night and there must have been 2000 people there, it was pretty packed. There were maybe 100 to 120 Boxcar fans, who were up against the stage waiting for the band to come on, and I was down the back nervously prepping the mixer and making sure everything was OK. And as you can imagine, the night wears on, the beer gets consumed in more copious quantities, and the natives are getting restless. And then the band walks on stage wearing gas masks, and this wave of howls just came up around me.

Picked up by Sydney label Volition, the band's debut 12-inch single Freemason, released in November 1988, cruised to number eight on the American Billboard dance charts when it was issued in the US by Arista, an extraordinary feat. The band remained almost unknown in Australia, but working in a genre where live work was incidental rather than essential meant that Boxcar had the rare luxury of staying put long after their commercial breakthrough.

In late 1986, shortly before the state election, a Hong Kong businessman dropped by Joh Bjelke-Petersen's office. He left the premier a donation of $100,000 cash in a brown paper bag. The premier claimed not to remember exactly who the businessman was. Perhaps this was understandable: he later remarked that such gifts were not at all uncommon. After some further refinements to the state's electoral boundaries, the government won the poll handsomely.[3]

What happened next can only be put down to a case of acute megalomania and, perhaps, the advancing years of Bjelke-Petersen, by then well into his 70s. Three months after his victory in the state election, he announced that he would stand for a seat in the federal parliament. 'Joh for Canberra' quickly became 'Joh for PM', the public relations campaign kicked off by the distribution of thousands of bumper stickers through Queensland newspapers.

Exactly how Bjelke-Petersen aimed to achieve his goal remained opaque: he did not resign as premier, nor did he give any indication of his intention to do so. But his fantasy of remaking the country in his own image would prove fatal. As he hit the hustings and his government looked on aghast, a young journalist from the *Courier-Mail* and an ABC film crew were busy combing the streets of Fortitude Valley. What they found there would turn the state on its head.

The Saints behind bars, 1976. Left to right: Kym Bradshaw, Ed Kuepper, Chris Bailey and Ivor Hay. *Photo Joe Borkowski*

The Saints ripping it up at Paddington Town Hall in Sydney, April 1977, shortly before their departure for England. Ivor Hay's T-shirt reads 'It's better to be a Saint than a Sap!' *Photo Jorge Munoz*

Author Clinton Walker (centre) fronts the 'pseudo Saints', 1977. Many musicians and fans had their photos taken in the Petrie Terrace house immortalised on the cover of the Saints' debut album. *Photo Joe Borkowski*

The Go-Betweens. Rough Trade promo shot for the *Before Hollywood* album, 1983: Grant McLennan (left), Lindy Morrison and Robert Forster. *Photo Tom Sheehan*

Another classic Go-Betweens pose, this time with bass player Robert Vickers, 1985. Beggars Banquet promo shot for *Liberty Belle And The Black Diamond Express*. *Photo Richard Mann*

The Survivors in rehearsal, 1977. Left to right: Jim Dickson, Bruce Anthon and Greg Williamson.
Photo Doug Spowart

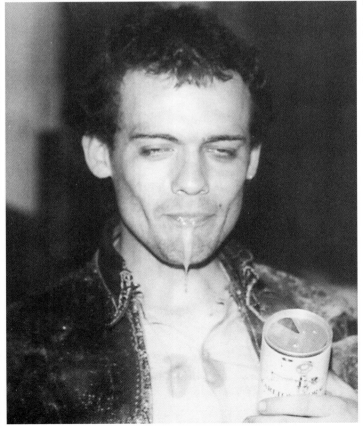

Leftovers singer Warren Lamond — 'The end product of rock & roll.'
Photographer unknown

Original three-quarter sleeve for Razar's Task Force (Undercover Cops) single, 1978.

The Apartments' Peter Milton Walsh. *Photo Judi Dransfield Kuepper*

The Riptides, circa Tomorrow's Tears. Left to right: Andrew Leitch, Dennis Cantwell, Scott Matheson and Mark Callaghan. *Photo Barbara Willoughby-Thomas*

The only known picture of the Fun Things, a band who built their legend on one single and a dozen gigs. Left to right: Graeme Beavis, Brad Shepherd, Murray Shepherd and John Hartley. *Photo Matt Mawson*

The classic three piece line-up of the Screaming Tribesmen, left to right: John Hartley, Murray Shepherd and Mick Medew. *Photo Liz Taylor*

Cloudland: high camp on the hill. 'Had the sails of the Sydney Opera House flown atop Bowen Hills, they would scarcely have appeared any more anomalous than Cloudland.' *Photo courtesy Queensland Newspapers*

Cloudland's interior. No building better symbolised the contradictions at the heart of Brisbane. *Photo courtesy John Oxley Library*

Dennis (Mop) Conlon performing in
Musgrave Park, 1988. *Photo Michael Aird*

Kev Carmody in King George Square,
1987. *Photo Michael Aird*

Black man's burden: Joh Bjelke-Petersen gets a ride, Torres Strait, 1973. This image was reproduced in the inner sleeve for Pig City (below).
Photo © The Courier-Mail

Outer sleeve for the Parameters' Pig City. Written for the 1983 state election, the single was not officially released until 1984.

Sleeve for the Various Artists compilation *At The Fuhrer's Request*, released by Rubber Records in 1985. The title was later amended under legal duress to *At The Solicitor's Request*. Artwork by Paul Curtis.

Sleeve from the Pineapples from the Dawn of Time's only album *Shocker*, featuring the *Star Trek* Space Hippies.

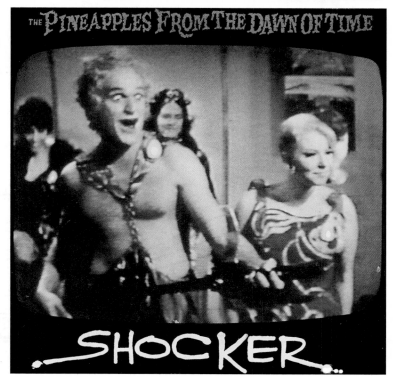

How *Courier-Mail* cartoonist Sean Leahy saw the attempted eviction of Triple Zed from its studios at the University of Queensland, 15 December 1988.

Leahy again, this time commenting on the Rocking Horse Records bust, 15 February 1989.

A 1989 handbill advertising the inaugural Livid Festival at the University of Queensland. The whimsical 'head' designs became a Livid signature.
Courtesy Peter Walsh

Screamfeeder, left to right: original drummer Tony Blades, Kellie Lloyd and Tim Steward. 'We all had long hair and our gym boots on, and we looked at each other and went, "Man, we all look the same — we should form a band!"' *Photo Cedric Ingra*

Custard, riding the wave of fashion at the Campbelltown Riding School, Sydney, 1994. Left to right: Matthew Strong, Paul Medew, David McCormack and Danny Plant. *Photo Jonathan Clabburn*

A meeting of the minds: David McCormack with Joh Bjelke-Petersen, at Bethany for Bob Ellis' *J-Mag* piece (Wahooti not pictured). *Photo Jonathan Clabburn*

Regurgitator, in Thailand for the recording of *Tu-Plang*. Left to right: Quan Yeomans, Ben Ely and Martin Lee. Yeomans' shirt reads 'Enslave me'. *Photo Dominic O'Brien*

Savage Garden, living the dream on the Superstars and Cannonballs tour, 2000: Darren Hayes (left) and Daniel Jones. *Photo Tony Mott*

Powderfinger. 'The overall effect was of a rather laddish bunch of Queenslanders who didn't take themselves too seriously.' Left to right: Darren Middleton, John Collins, Bernard Fanning, Ian Haug and Jon Coghill. *Photo Ian Jennings*

CHAPTER ELEVEN

ss brigade

I remembered one night seeing a strange man stalking about in the shadows of one of our places. Narrow faced, with square glasses that had eggshell-thin lenses, a man not drinking, not using the women, not gambling – just watching, seeming to observe everything and everyone . . .

Fool. I was so far beyond genuine newspaper work that I couldn't even spot an investigative journalist when he was jotting down notes right next to me at the bar.

That's all it took, in the end. The serious elements in the media shook off their 30-year lethargy and almost casually, certainly with no belief that anything serious would happen, they began to report what everyone already knew.

– Andrew McGahan, *Last Drinks*[1]

The *Courier-Mail* had not been known for its vigour in its pursuit of political and police corruption allegations; indeed, it had regularly taken advertisements from establishments euphemistically offering massage and escort services. Following a change in editorship in early 1987, however, journalist Phil Dickie was given enough rope to follow up an earlier piece that had tentatively prised open the lid on police protection of Queensland's sex industry. It was like lifting a piece of corrugated iron in the forest. Vermin scattered blindly from the sudden burst of light.

Cleverly, Dickie avoided naming potential scapegoats, concentrating instead on exposing a network of illegal vice and gaming so prolific that only corruption or incompetence at the highest level could fail to detect it. On the evening of 22 April, Dickie watched an illegal casino shift its premises from the Roxy on Brunswick Street to Wickham Street around the corner. The move took place in full view of gathered police and amused drivers on the adjoining Alfred Street cab rank.[2] Police baldly labelled Dickie's resulting article a fabrication.

As Dickie continued to build his case, however, the official denials began to look decidedly comical. Police minister and Deputy Premier Bill Gunn, interviewed on *A Current Affair* by Mike Willesee, was made to look foolish when he refused an invitation to take a filmed tour of the brothels he claimed did not exist.

Willesee later interviewed Bjelke-Petersen, who had already announced he would stand for a House of Representatives seat at the next federal election. After a particularly excruciating response to one question, Willesee paused for a moment. 'Sir Joh,' he eventually asked, 'do you think senility may be affecting you?'

Enormous public interest preceded the ABC's airing of *Four Corners'* The Moonlight State on 11 May. The hour-long documentary spliced Queensland's Puritan image – of the strict Lutheran premier singing hymns at church in Kingaroy while wife and federal senator Flo played the organ – with scenes of strippers, gambling and red-lit brothel shopfronts. In between, a succession of informants provided the hard data. Following Dickie's approach, presenter Chris Masters was careful in identifying mainly crime syndicates rather than police, making it obvious that the industry was protected without naming anyone who could be turned into a convenient fall guy.

With Bjelke-Petersen interstate, drumming up support for

his doomed Canberra campaign, Bill Gunn was the acting premier. The stolid Gunn was marked by a will matching his artlessness: without consulting his absent superior, he made the remarkable decision to hold an independent inquiry, with the words, 'A series of police ministers have had these types of allegations hanging over their heads. They are not going to hang over mine.' When an alarmed Bjelke-Petersen later told him he had 'a tiger by the tail', Gunn was unperturbed. 'I'm not worried about that, Joh,' he said. 'It'll end up eating you, if anything.'[3]

The distracted Bjelke-Petersen was too late. Gunn's swift reaction to the outpouring of revulsion that greeted The Moonlight State had set the wheels of his promised inquiry moving at a pace no one could contain. Although inquiries had been held previously to appease earlier allegations, all had been buried by tight terms of reference and a dozing mainstream media. The scale and publicity of the new revelations meant that, for the first time, the political damage of suppressing information – at least in Gunn's mind – outweighed the danger of taking action.

The next six months was the most turbulent period of Queensland's political history. The appointment of Gerald 'Tony' Fitzgerald QC to head the inquiry – and the granting of some critical indemnities from prosecution – ensured that the focus remained not on securing as many convictions as possible, but on pulling the rug out from the whole rotten system. The media and public gorged on the daily diet of increasingly gross revelations. The inquiry took on a life of its own: Fitzgerald's frequent requests for wider terms of reference were meekly granted, to the point where, in the end, there were virtually no terms of reference at all.[4]

Two days after leaving on a business trip to the US, Bjelke-Petersen was caught off guard on another front. Capitalising on the disarray in federal coalition ranks, Prime Minister Bob Hawke called an early election. Bjelke-Petersen had already engineered the coalition's destruction with his

Canberra push, declaring that he alone would now lead the National Party. But when Hawke played his ace, Bjelke-Petersen – marooned in, of all places, Disneyland – had not even nominated for a seat, much less resigned his premiership. Labor won the election easily, winning four extra seats in Queensland alone; then opposition leader John Howard's ambitions were set back a decade, and the Nationals were decimated.

Formal hearings for the Fitzgerald Inquiry began two weeks later. They would continue for another 18 months. In the end, a system that had looked invulnerable unravelled remarkably quickly, as a cornered police force and government turned first upon themselves, then each other. The first witness, Sir Terence Lewis, suggested that the state government – the same one that had based its electoral agenda on law, order and family values – had an unofficial policy of toleration towards prostitution. In fact, this was strictly police policy, and the chain of command was pointing straight to the top.[5]

The desertions mounted along with the evidence; by September, Lewis' deputy Graeme Parker had rolled over, pleading for an indemnity and absolution. Days later, the heavily implicated Lewis was suspended from his position, initially on full pay. Two cabinet ministers, Russ Hinze and Don 'Shady' Lane, were also adversely named in the inquiry's hearings.

Bjelke-Petersen had lost control of Queensland's political agenda and with it his party. Mike Ahern, the relatively youthful health minister, wanted to see the introduction of condom vending machines to counter the spread of HIV/AIDS; Bjelke-Petersen was having nothing of it.[6] When university campuses went ahead and installed the vending machines anyway, police were sent on pre-dawn raids to remove them.

This otherwise marginal issue ironically became central to Bjelke-Petersen's demise. As the Nationals' fortunes plummeted, Ahern was viewed as the only voice in the party remotely in touch with reality. When Bjelke-Petersen threatened a snap election to bring his enemies to heel in October, the party finally moved against him. His bluff called, the premier backed off, declaring in a press conference that he would resign the following year, allowing him to preside over the forthcoming World Expo and see out his 20th anniversary in office.

The stalling tactic wouldn't last long. On 23 November, as the inquiry began to engulf one of Bjelke-Petersen's closest advisors, Sir Edward Lyons, the premier attempted to sack five of his ministers, including Ahern and Gunn, in what both regarded as a transparent attempt to take over the police portfolio and shut down the inquiry. Mayhem ensued. Ahern challenged for and easily won the leadership of the party; Gunn remained as deputy.

Bjelke-Petersen wasn't finished. Refusing to resign, he locked himself in his office, phoning Buckingham Palace in an attempt to hold onto his job. When the Queen declined to intervene, Bjelke-Petersen then attempted to broker a bizarre deal with the Labor and Liberal parties, which he hoped would see them uphold a motion of confidence in his premiership on the floor of the parliament. When this last, desperate move failed, Bjelke-Petersen buckled. He resigned from parliament on 1 December 1987.

Many years later, Andrew McGahan, writing in the voice of the fictitious composite Marvin McNulty, summed it up this way:

> It was a cataclysm. That was the only word for it . . . Like we'd flown too high and challenged the gods. It started out so small, just a whisper, but someone lost their nerve, someone let it slip, and suddenly it was the end.[7]

The Bjelke-Petersen era – in name at least – was finally over.

* *

While the rest of Queensland emerged from its long slumber, students at the University of Queensland, the traditional hotbed of political agitation, had fallen asleep at the wheel.

Triple Zed was in serious decay, so poor it had been forced to cancel the local newspaper delivery. The station was hit on several fronts: as venues and gig promotions around town dwindled, so too the station's lifeblood of subscriptions began to dry up. With the station relying on a core group of mostly inexperienced volunteers, it became harder to turn the broadcaster's fortunes around. David Lennon was one forced to sink or swim.

> **David Lennon:** That last six months before the eviction, there were only a very small handful of us running the station. The main core of staff before then just floated off and never came back, basically.

For more than a decade Triple Zed's sheer necessity had been enough to justify its existence, and for much of that time the station had repaid its listeners with much more besides. But by 1988, with economic rationalism in the ascendant and the state government on the skids, selling the 'warm inner glow' of being part of the station was no longer going to be enough. Triple Zed's great mistake was of the kind so common to the left: it took its righteousness for granted. While this was understandable in the face of Bjelke-Petersen, it meant that when the inevitable challenge arrived, the station was thoroughly unprepared.

> **David Lennon:** Andy Nehl came up with the idea of the warm inner glow at a radiothon in 1986 and I think that line was used as a cliché ever since. We used to be able to say give us money because we need it and we're on your side, but it doesn't work now. You have to show that you're giving people value for money.

Jim Beatson: There's a great episode of *The Simpsons* about community television, where it just shows one person in a room, begging people to give him money. Well, people give money because they like something; they don't give money because somebody's jangling a tin.

Triple Zed had another crucial benefactor underwriting its survival: the student union. The close links between the union and station founders in 1975 had resulted in a start-up loan (never expected to be repaid) of $250,000, while the station paid a peppercorn rent of $2 per month for its use of the premises. Ongoing administrative costs were funded by the union too: around $17,000 per year. The dominance of the left in student politics had kept the arrangement cosy long after the union ceased to have any effective representation or influence on the station's direction.

The first shot across the bows came in March 1988, when a union council meeting refused to approve the station's quarterly administrative budget. The response was immediate, with hundreds of station supporters picketing the union building in response. But the union president of that year, Dirk Moses, had fingered the station's weak link: Triple Zed had no formal links to the student body, and its right to ongoing student funds was dubious at best. Sensing danger, the station quickly introduced a campus news program, but the rumblings continued.

Union elections are a colourful annual feature of campus life, engaged in passionately by a small minority of the most politicised students and studiously ignored by the rest. For weeks the campus is strewn with flyers and graffiti; lectures are invariably preceded by electoral hopefuls stating their case. Previously, the right had never much threatened the left's control, seemingly content to contain their representation to the traditionally conservative faculties of law, medicine and engineering.

In September 1988, however, a well-drilled and ambitious

group led by a 19-year-old medical student and National Party member, Victoria Brazil, was elected under the banner of The Better Alternative. The treasurer was Julian Sheezel, a first-year commerce student and a member of the Liberal Party.

Julian Sheezel: We were motivated to run because of a great frustration with what we saw as waste and mismanagement in the union . . . We formed a team around like-minded people, people who believed that the union should be accountable to its members, people who believed that the union should not be charging excessive fees for its services, and that all money the union did collect should go into student services. We ran on the basis that we believed we represented the average student at the time.

On TBA's election, Triple Zed's station coordinator, Gordon Fletcher, wrote to Brazil seeking clarification of the union executive's plans with respect to the station, following an on-air interview in which she inferred that she would be seeking unspecified changes. Brazil, who had seen the ALP-aligned Moses caricatured as a conservative puppet by the station, replied:

I hasten to add that I am not a right-wing fascist interested only in axing 4ZZZ. My policy has always been that 4ZZZ is a valuable student and community resource. My reservations in supporting the current structure and programming of 4ZZZ are the result of students' comments . . . With this in mind, I would very much like to discuss our plans and yours for 1989. I look forward to contacting you early in December when we take office.[8]

But the discussion never happened.

* *

The new executive had been in office less than a week when it made its move. At 4.17am on 14 December, Brazil, along with other executive members and four security guards, entered the Triple Zed studios, serving an eviction notice – effective immediately – to the two graveyard announcers on duty, Mark Solway and Stefan Armbruster.

David Lennon: I got a call at about 4.30 saying they'd just been evicted, so I told them to stay outside and I turned up there post-haste. They wouldn't let me in, but they let Mark in for some reason, so I told him to go into the newsroom and get a tape recorder and microphone, which he did. I called Gordon Fletcher and Anita [Earl, announcing coordinator] and we drove up to the transmitter site on Mt Coot-tha, and on the way up we recorded an emergency broadcast explaining what happened. We plugged the Superscope directly into the transmitter and started broadcasting the message over and over.

Brazil's team had hardly been encouraged in its actions. In a file note dated 21 February 1989, the university registrar, Douglas Porter, confirms that a meeting was held on 12 December with executive members Cameron Spenceley and Alastair Furnival, who requested an opinion on whether the university would support action by the union to 'deal with' Triple Zed. Porter advised that this was not a matter for the university to decide, counselling the union only to remain within the law.[9]

The following day, the executive received a three-page legal briefing from solicitors Litster Mann and Ffrench. This strongly advised the union to give a 'reasonable' period of notice (classified as three to four weeks) in order to evict Triple Zed with legal certainty. It also made the point, however, that the station was unlikely to possess the financial means to challenge any eviction in the courts.

Julian Sheezel: I don't believe that Triple Zed would have

moved off campus after one or two months and I don't
believe the university would have moved them off campus
either . . . They would have used every means available to them
to frustrate an eviction order, from legal challenges to calls for
special elections and, failing that, occupation of the student
union's premises. Anything to buy time! They only had to hold
out until the next elections and they probably would have been
safe.

Sheezel rejects suggestions the executive had no student
mandate to evict the station, insisting that its actions were
consistent with its policy platform of sound financial
management. But there was, naturally, more to it than that.
Commerce representative James Gifford, who was not a
party to the decision, argues the executive was driven at
least in part by its overwhelming ideological conviction:
Brazil herself hung a photograph of then British Prime
Minister Margaret Thatcher on her office wall.

James Gifford: I suspect that they felt, here's a really big leftie
target – let's attack [it], defeat them on their domain. They
fundamentally believed that the left was bad and it needed
to be undermined and fought, and that was a good way of
fighting it: to shut down their main source of communication.

Julian Sheezel: What we had to decide was whether it was
appropriate for an organisation that was not associated with
the student body, and that the students had not agreed or
endorsed to give money to, to continue to receive student
money . . . [We decided] that we had a fiduciary responsibility,
consistent with good corporate governance, to sever our
relationship with Triple Zed.

Regardless of the executive's motives, they failed to
appreciate the level of residual support still attached to
Triple Zed, or to anticipate the vehemence with which
its action would be greeted. Within half an hour of the

emergency broadcast going to air from Mt Coot-tha, hundreds of enraged supporters were massing outside the station headquarters. The result was inevitable: shortly after 1pm, supporters poured into the station, sweeping security aside. They weren't met with great resistance.

Douglas Porter: They reoccupied the premises and kicked young Cameron [Spenceley] out. I asked him why he didn't stay – possession being nine-tenths of the law – and he basically said there was a howling mob outside and he was in fear of his life, so he left.

A young writer, John Birmingham, was commissioned to cover the demonstration for *Rolling Stone* magazine. Then 24, Birmingham was in the period of personal itinerancy that he would later document in the celebrated *He Died With A Felafel In His Hand*, and was thus well placed to cover what developed into a rolling series of occupations of the union premises.

John Birmingham: I tended to take a different approach to most reporters who'd just turn up and do a stock-standard violent student demo story. I decided I was going to be there for the long haul, and if it took a week of hanging around with these crusty motherfuckers that was what I was going to do.

About an hour or so after I got there, people had begun to work out how they were going to get back into the station . . . [Triple Zed] was in the basement of the union building and it was like a rat's maze down there; there were any number of ways of getting in.

By this stage the union's offices were being occupied along with the radio station. The police were not long in arriving. And in true gonzo tradition, Birmingham had no problem with involving himself in the action he was supposed to be reporting on.

John Birmingham: Triple Zed by this stage was broadcasting the whole thing over the airwaves, but also over the loudspeakers, and continually looping the song Pig City over and over again. This of course was getting on the nerves of the cops, to the point where one of them ended up banging her car into a railing with a big crunch, which caused a huge cheer among the protesters and even more consternation among the cops, which probably resulted in an extra half a dozen heads getting broken later on that afternoon.

Anyway, it went on for a couple of hours. The cops eventually decided that they were going to kick everybody out. I went upstairs to watch them break into the union offices. It was quite interesting; I knew enough not to stand in front of the cops as they came in the door, because they get the blood up and just mow everybody down. So I went outside and stood with the 30 or 40 police who were going in. They tried to tell me to fuck off but I showed them my press pass – which was completely bogus, I'd just put it together myself with a bit of cardboard and laminate and colour-photocopied *Rolling Stone* letterhead on top – and they grudgingly agreed I had a right to be there.

So they went in, slammed the shit out of everybody, and I went in with them. It was quite funny, because the last two blokes in the line were probationary constables who had been whipped into quite a state by their mates. By the time I got in on the tail of these two probationary guys, they'd got themselves worked up for nothing, because there was nobody left for them to hit; everybody had been subdued.

One of them was literally fucking mad, foaming at the mouth, looking left-right, left-right, left-right . . . I was standing on a desk by this stage with my tape recorder running to get the whole thing. He came at me, I showed him the pass, he veered off, ran to a wall and there was a telephone on the wall. And he ripped the telephone off the wall, threw it on the ground and kicked it across the room. I wish I'd had a video camera! It was all good fun.

But the police were unwilling to risk the possible legal consequences of re-evicting Triple Zed themselves. None of those who occupied the station can remember very much about the days that followed.

> **David Lennon:** It was just a big long party; there was lots of running around, skinny-dipping in the vice-chancellor's pool . . . Yeah, that was the most enjoyable week of my life.

Triple Zed was not the only communications outlet in the union's sights. Curiously, despite the election of an ultra-conservative union executive, *Semper* had remained in the hands of the radical left: editors Jeff Cheverton and Bree McKilligan had run on a socialist gay and lesbian ticket. Cheverton guesses the anomaly was probably a result of the ticket's name – *Semper* Extraordinaire – being shortened to SEX on ballot sheets, a quirk that saw them across the line despite being subjected to a malevolent smear campaign.

> **Jeff Cheverton:** They tried to be a bit clever. The campaign flyers had something like, 'Jeff is a caring, idealistic sort of guy, the fact that he's gay doesn't enter into it,' and they put it out all over campus with a little photograph of me. It was pretty amazing.

Two days prior to the attempted eviction of Triple Zed, Cheverton received notice of a Student Representative Council meeting scheduled for 21 January. The agenda included the demotion of the *Semper* editors to part-time roles and the appointment of Cameron Spenceley (who had stood unsuccessfully against the pair in the preceding election) as editorial supervisor. In addition, it was proposed that Spenceley be charged with producing the handbook for the upcoming campus orientation week for new students, traditionally the province of the *Semper* editors.

For Brazil and her executive, the political platform
Semper embodied was, like Triple Zed, unrepresentative
of the mainstream student population. This was entirely
true, but ignored the fact that the students who had elected
the *Semper* editors were, by accident or design, the same
students that had appointed Brazil president. In the end,
Cheverton and McKilligan held onto their jobs, but the
attack furthered suspicions that the executive was more
concerned with silencing their opposition on campus than
it was with financial accountability.

There were reasonable grounds for suspecting that
at least some members of Brazil's group boasted strong
connections at government level, especially as the state
government (which was in the process of preparing a bill
outlawing compulsory student unionism) repeatedly came
out in support of the executive's actions. After issuing
a second eviction order giving the station notice to quit
by 19 January, Brazil set the scene for another almighty
showdown when, in a meeting with Douglas Porter and
the vice-chancellor, Brian Wilson, she requested written
confirmation of the union's occupancy and control of
their buildings.

Porter writes that, on questioning, Brazil revealed police
had requested the confirmation as a basis for taking action
against the station. Disturbed, Wilson refused. Less than an
hour after the meeting with Brazil, Wilson took a call from
the state director-general of education on the request of
the minister, Brian Littleproud, in which he was pressured
to provide the written confirmation Brazil required.[10] With
hundreds of students continuing to occupy the station, the
second eviction was forestalled.

In fact, the university administration was as keen as
the union executive to be rid of Triple Zed. Porter's note
records that the station 'has not been a comfortable tenant
and creates occasional problems for the union and the
university through irresponsible actions and sometimes
through its broadcasts'.[11] The station's position on campus

had become untenable. The occupation had resulted in a string of well-founded complaints: the station had never been designed to house 100 or more hard-partying defenders of the faith.

In a meeting attended by Porter, Brazil, Cameron Spenceley, Gordon Fletcher and station director Charles Scandrett, the station eventually agreed to vacate its premises by 8 July 1989. Ironically, the union's ham-fisted actions had probably improved Triple Zed's bargaining position with the long-suffering administration.

First semester arrived in late February, the university ankle-deep in flyers.

Under the terms of the student union constitution, the executive could be forced to hold a referendum to determine whether fresh elections should be held in the event of a petition gathering the support of more than 10 per cent of the student body. After a pre-dawn eviction and a violent counter-occupation, the high moral ground of due process remained available to anyone willing to seize it. A law student, Jane Lye, waded into the murk after a friendly offer of assistance from an unexpected quarter.

> **Jane Lye:** That's the role that I thought I could play some part in, because it was the boring stuff that no one really wanted to get into. And there were actually a couple of law lecturers who came and offered support – they just said look, we're happy to look into where you stand constitutionally, and I thought well, that's the logical thing that I can help with.

Lye, whose eminently reasonable public manner belied a mind like a cobra, contrasted effectively against Brazil's shrill defensiveness. The executive was losing the PR battle to its more media-savvy opponents. Above all, their timing was lousy: as Sheezel admits, storming a radio station before dawn during summer holidays was easily depicted as being 'consistent with the hallmarks of the National Party during the '70s and '80s'. The day after the eviction *Courier-Mail* cartoonist Sean Leahy portrayed Brazil and her well-dressed supporters as a convoy of jackbooted Joh clones. Their next move would do nothing to dispel this impression.

On 23 February a petition consisting of 2200 signatures (400 more than required, and well over the approximately 1300 votes that had elected the executive) was handed to Brazil, who, amid uproar, dismissed it as a forgery. It was a fatal error.

Julian Sheezel: Politically the executive's mistake was not accepting the petition when it first came in, because at that stage we had significant student support for what had occurred. Where we made a mistake was trying to avoid a referendum, which certainly weakened our position with the student population.

John Birmingham: I always contended that if those guys had actually gone to the student body and asked for an endorsement of what they'd done in kicking Triple Zed off campus, they would have got it. Because by that stage it had become pretty much completely divorced from the middle-class mainstream population. Realistically they had no reason and no right to be there any more.

With Triple Zed now locked into moving, the executive's actions ensured that its own legitimacy became the central issue on campus. The demonstrations that followed – a rolling series of occupations of the union premises, intermittently broken up by police, hired security and Brazil supporters – were some of the most violent in memory. Short of a constant police presence, however, there was no way of keeping the mob at bay. John Birmingham, a self-confessed 'enthusiastic member of that mob', was one who took up residence over the Easter break.

John Birmingham: I had no permanent address at that point; I was supposed to be house-sitting for a couple of friends in Auchenflower, but I was hardly ever there. They had a cat I was supposed to feed. They were vegans and this thing was completely malnourished, so I'd pop around every couple of days with a carton of chocolate milk and a meat lover's pizza, throw the pizza on the ground, pour the milk into a bowl and go back to the occupation for another 48 hours.

It was funny, because you had a lot of weedy, underfed, often vegetarian students going up against these big, blocky, steroid-abusing nightclub bouncers who would just hammer on them like machines. You'd get four or five students on two or three nightclub bouncers, and the bouncers would just bash and bash and bash. But eventually there were so many students that their arms would get tired, and the tide would just roll over them.

Eventually we all ended up outside the president's office. There was myself and a guy called Bill Ferguson, a pillar of the community these days. Bill was a long stringy character who looked like a cowboy junkie. There were a couple of hundred of us beating on the doors of Victoria's office. Finally Bill looked up and said, 'Look at the roof, it's all tiles – we can push up and get into the ceiling space and go down.'

I dropped onto the floor of the office and the next thing I remember was Bill pouring through the roof like a liquid metal terminator. It was fantastic. It's very rare in modern life that you get to whale on people you really don't like very much and we were all lashing out at each other. Of course as soon as they had to start beating up the people who were coming through the ceiling, they lost control of the door, and hundreds of people poured in.

Whereupon, of course, the party started all over again.

John Birmingham: It was quite marvellous actually. The right made a lot of accusations about people having sex on desks and stuff like that, which at the time I just dismissed completely out of hand. I didn't realise it was true until I spoke to the culprits years later! But it was a huge party. There were a lot of people like me, who didn't have a place to live, who just took over the building for a couple of weeks, and I was there for all of it, except for the occasional trip back to Auchenflower to give the cat a pizza.

We got a TV in and hired videos. Every night there was a big party with lots of drugs and booze and probably quite a bit of unauthorised rumpy-pumpy on the president's desk. But what are you gonna do? Everybody was full of piss and bad manners and savage righteousness. Looking back on it now, that sort of bad behaviour was completely fucking infantile, but everybody was infantile, in their late teens. I was one of the oldest ones there! So the protesters, myself included, didn't cover themselves in glory, but we had a fucking good time. I don't resile from any of it.

While the 'unauthorised rumpy-pumpy' carried on in the union building, the university administration had accepted a certified copy of the petition against the union executive, which it declared valid after a careful count. The executive, however, was unmoved. It preferred the verdict of its own hand-picked appointee, law student Anthony Ryan, who found sufficient irregularities in the signatures to pronounce the petition null and void.

Brazil's own rhetoric was contradictory. Although several members of her executive were members of the Liberal Party and Brazil was a card-carrying National, the 'real students', she claimed, were not interested in politics at all. While insisting she would complete the job she had been elected to do, her favourite strategy was to claim the tacit support of the 15,000 students that hadn't bothered to vote at all. 'It's not trendy to be idealistic,' she said. 'It's trendy to get out on the stock market to get money for that BMW, to listen to FM-104 [Triple M] and drink Powers.'[12]

In fact, Brazil (who lived in a St Lucia apartment owned by her parents) represented the constituency that had elected her rather well. Almost all of her executive were based on the campus colleges, overwhelmingly the preserve of the wealthiest sector of the student population. During her year in office, funds for college activities enjoyed a healthy increase, while the budget for the Aboriginal and Torres Strait Islander students was slashed.[13]

The stalemate over the petition and continued chaos on campus had wearied the university administration, with the deputy vice-chancellor, Professor Ralph Parsons, calling publicly on the union to submit to fresh elections in accordance with its own constitution.

Douglas Porter: Ralph was a very, very proper person. He was as straight as a die, and he could not bring his mind to bear on the way in which the student union executive attempted to manipulate the situation. Whether they were correct or not in law, he clearly had a problem with their ethics.

Julian Sheezel: The university clearly buckled to most of the demands of Triple Zed and the left-wing members of the student union council. The university wanted a very quiet life; they made it well known that as long as peace was maintained on campus they didn't really care what happened to student funds.

By the middle of May the petition had wound its way to the Supreme Court. Although finding no serious problem with the signatures, Justice Paul de Jersey nevertheless struck the document down on the basis of its wording. Fortunately, the kindly judge took the time to draw up his preferred sentence construction before sending the plaintiffs on their way. Within days of submitting the re-worded question to the student body, a second petition had gathered over 3000 signatures. Finally bowing to the inevitable, the executive resigned on 14 July.

The week earlier Triple Zed had made its scheduled move to new studios in the adjoining suburb of Toowong. The location would quickly prove unsuitable, but for the moment the station was riding a tremendous wave of support.

David Lennon: Gordon Fletcher and myself had been keeping the financial side of the station afloat. And then the eviction happened, and within two weeks we had some astronomical amount of money donated to us. Really, I think Victoria Brazil did the station a huge favour; it could have very well died a dribbly death at that stage if something like that didn't happen.

Students were suddenly more interested in politics than ever before. The union elections of September 1989 were the biggest ever: more than 5000 students turned out to vote, more than a quarter of the campus at that time. Jane Lye's group, Reform, won a landslide victory, while the *Semper* editorship was claimed by a group calling themselves the Doug Porter All Stars, a pun on then-popular comedy trio the Doug Anthony All Stars. John Birmingham – now married to Lye – was a frequent contributor, occasionally in the guise of his alter ego, Harrison Biscuit.

Most of the members of the 1989 executive have gone on to successful legal, medical and commercial careers. Julian Sheezel has maintained his political interests: a former president of the Australian Liberal Students Federation and advisor to the iron-plated Bronwyn Bishop MP, in 2003 he was appointed state director of the Victorian division of the Liberal Party. While comfortable that Triple Zed's eventual departure from campus was for the long-term benefit of the student population, Sheezel suggests in hindsight that the battle that followed was a product of the political and moral certainty typical of the transition from adolescence to adulthood.

Julian Sheezel: At the age of 18 you have the advantage of being more pure in your motives, be that on the conservative side of politics or on the left. You tend to think, well, this is the right thing to do. I passionately believed that this was correct, that Triple Zed had no place on campus, and if I was castigated publicly for upholding that view, I was quite happy to wear that at the time.

Victoria Brazil, for her part, steadfastly refuses to discuss the events surrounding her union presidency. While the university claims her security was never in danger while on campus, she was certainly the victim of sustained harassment and vilification for years afterwards. Refusing an offer of a safe seat from the National Party in the lead-up to the 1989 state election, she retreated entirely from view following her graduation. While some former allies and opponents suggest she was manipulated by her more astute peers, not all are so forgiving.

Jane Lye: I think Victoria was very naive about the whole thing . . . Of course unfortunately for her, all of the people around her were far more politically savvy and had different agendas, so suddenly this shy country girl who'd never had her head out of a book found herself at the centre of this enormous fight.

James Gifford: She was never a political animal. There was so much infamy involved in the whole thing, she just wanted to get on with life, and become a normal person and not some right-wing freak. She was totally demonised; she was made out to be a really evil wicked witch, which she wasn't.

Jeff Cheverton: I think she'd be about as innocent as Pauline Hanson, actually.

CHAPTER TWELVE

cyclone hits expo

The Fitzgerald Inquiry was in recess when the world came to Brisbane on 31 March 1988. This was just as well. The suffocating internal paroxysm Queensland was enduring was entirely at odds with the tourist-brochure marketing of Expo. If Brisbane was growing up, it was a painfully self-conscious metamorphosis.

There was an irony in this. More so than the Commonwealth Games, Expo '88 continues to enjoy its status as the symbolic turning point for its host city, the moment wherein the most insular of Australian capitals threw open its doors to the world. But such openness contained hidden dangers for the ageing junta that queued up to bathe in the afterglow.

Anne Jones: When Brisbane was smaller, they could shut things down without too much difficulty, but as it developed and became a real city – which the Bjelke-Petersen regime wanted, because of the economic benefits – with that came a demand for a lifestyle that was something more than what you might find in Kingaroy. Brisbane was turning into a big city, which was making it culturally more diverse, and that was something the Nationals couldn't control.

Like most gigantic public events, Expo brought with it a darker side that few cared to acknowledge. The huge sails that shaded much of the South Brisbane site also helped cover up the monstrous redevelopment that had turned one of inner Brisbane's oldest and poorest areas inside out. The suburbs of South Brisbane and West End were dominated by students, migrants, Aboriginal people, the elderly and the alone. Almost all of them rented their accommodation.

As Expo approached, hundreds were forced to leave as landlords raised rents or evicted tenants with a view to either refurbishment or attracting higher-paying Expo staff and tourists. Boarding houses were torn down and crisp new apartment blocks erected. No one was prepared for the housing crisis: while the state and federal governments blamed each other, welfare agencies did their best to cope with the human spillage.

In a live-to-air gig at Triple Zed, Choo Dikka Dikka (named after the sound made by traffic lights at pedestrian crossings) made their wistful protest after a severe thunderstorm in November 1987 tore the Expo sails apart:

> Cyclone hits Expo, hits the very spot
> Cyclone hits Expo and destroys the fuckin' lot!

The event itself was, it must be said, hugely successful. Few Brisbane residents could possibly have missed it; millions of visitors poured in from interstate and overseas. All that grated was the enormity of the contrast between the Brisbane being sold to the world and the real Brisbane sweating it out in the witness box. Even the vice money doled out to Terry Lewis and the Licensing Branch by bagman Jack Herbert was referred to in-house as 'The Joke': something you were either in on, or you weren't. There was nothing terribly sophisticated about corruption Queensland-style.

Peter Walsh: I was living in a warehouse in Fortitude Valley when the cops shut off three lanes in Ann Street so a crane could lower a roulette wheel into the building opposite mine.

They shut off three lanes to do it, and there they were saying there were no illegal casinos!

Then a 19-year-old student, Peter Walsh (no relation to the Apartments' Peter Milton Walsh, who humorously refers to his namesake as 'The Lesser') created the Livid Festival with his then partner, artist Natalie Jeremijenko, as a kind of anti-Expo. The initial idea, to attract an all-Brisbane line-up of artists that had been forced to leave the city to find an audience, served as both a tribute to and condemnation of the city that spawned them. Originally intended as a one-off, the first bill, for 21 January 1989, featured the Go-Betweens, Chris Bailey, Died Pretty and the Ups and Downs.

Peter Walsh: I just hated the way that everyone said that Expo was the turning point for Brisbane and that this was the thing that was going to put Brisbane on the map, because there was so much out there that had already put Brisbane on the map . . . Some of the greatest bands in the world had come from here, and they weren't getting any recognition.

The establishment of the festival itself was little short of a miracle. Walsh knew so little about event promotion at the time that, when someone later asked him if he was the promoter, he said no; he didn't know what a promoter was.

Peter Walsh: We were both university students. We had some obvious problems – we had no money, we had no idea how to organise it, and we had no idea how to get in contact with bands. We got around the money bit when I went to a credit union one day and said I wanted to borrow $4000 to buy a car, then Natalie went the next day and said she wanted $4000 to buy a car. So we had $8000, which was enough to get the tickets and the posters printed. That certainly wasn't enough to run a festival, but no one asked us [how much money we had]. It was a wing and a prayer; we just didn't care, you know.

We were so into the idea of meeting the Go-Betweens that we didn't give a fuck!

The Go-Betweens were brought to the festival via their manager, Roger Grierson, who years earlier had brought Tex Perkins to Sydney. A friend of Walsh's happened to work at Grierson's favoured local in Sydney. Walsh's friend asked Grierson; Grierson said yes; and Grierson liked Walsh's idea enough to be of critical assistance in helping get the show off the ground.

For the Go-Betweens themselves, much had changed. After several years in London, the group had been signed to Mushroom Records, and had based themselves in Sydney. Two years earlier the band had become a five-piece with the recruitment of multi-instrumentalist Amanda Brown; later, bass player Robert Vickers departed, to be replaced by former Xero guitarist John Willsteed. Adding to an already volatile internal chemistry, Brown and Grant McLennan were romantically linked, long after the relationship between Robert Forster and Lindy Morrison had ended. The group would split a year later.

Musically, however, the band was at its peak. With the release of their most commercial and in many ways their best album, *16 Lovers Lane*, the Go-Betweens' profile had never been higher.

Robert Forster: It was our juggernaut phase, where we could say to a record company, this is what we want to do, and they'd push a lot of money across the table. None of it would go into our pockets; it would go into making records and touring . . . It was a fairly typical major-label situation, where you're earning $300 a week but there's hundreds of thousands of dollars flying around you.

The lead single was Streets Of Your Town, the closest the Go-Betweens ever came to a hit. John Willsteed – who played the heavenly acoustic solo at the song's centre – describes it, perfectly, as 'like summer coming out of the stereo'. As instantly appealing as anything from Crowded House's *Temple Of Low Men* (also released in August 1988), the song gained the band its first commercial airplay, only to inexplicably stall just outside the top 40.

Ironically, with the attempted eviction of Triple Zed still fresh in the minds of students, and the union buildings under siege, the first Livid Festival was held on the grounds of the University of Queensland, where Forster and McLennan had met more than a decade before. With Forster dressed in a bright orange flared bodysuit, the Go-Betweens' performance that night ranked among their most memorable.

> **Peter Walsh:** People often ask me what was the best show you ever saw at a Livid Festival; I always say the Go-Betweens. They played Karen, which they hardly ever did, and broke halfway through that into Patti Smith's version of Gloria. Then they broke halfway through that while Robert lay on his back reciting poetry, then they went back into Gloria, then back into Karen . . . Grant and Robert have both said to me at various times that it was one of the best, if not the best, Go-Betweens shows ever. And to me, it was the greatest thing I'd ever seen.

After succeeding Joh Bjelke-Petersen as premier in late 1987, Mike Ahern had attempted to distance himself and his party from its tainted past with a promise to implement the recommendations of the Fitzgerald Inquiry 'lock, stock and barrel'. But the government could not hold the line with any credibility: Ahern's ministry was dominated by his predecessor's faithful servants, and he himself had been a part of Bjelke-Petersen's cabinet since 1980. As Fitzgerald prepared his report, the Nationals were nervous and divided.

With the party's support in freefall, even in its Bible-Belt heartland, some members clearly felt that a campaign against sin in all its forms would help light their path to political salvation. Claiming that ordinary Queenslanders were less concerned with allegations of political corruption than with the decline of so-called family values, however, was a complete misreading of the fundamental shift of consciousness among the state's mainstream middle class. No incident illustrated this misinterpretation more than the police raid on Rocking Horse Records on 14 February 1989.

Rocking Horse was, by then, one of the country's oldest independent record stores. After moving from its tiny original shop under the stairwell of Rowes Arcade in 1979, it was well established in slightly roomier surroundings at 158 Adelaide Street. In a typical police entrapment operation, an undercover officer from the Licensing Branch cased the shop, seeking out rude records for, according to Warwick Vere, 'a wild Valentine's Day party'. Later that morning, four uniformed police raided the store, seizing around $500 worth of stock and charging Vere under the Vagrants, Gaming and Other Offences Act for exhibiting and selling obscene material.

The origin of the raid itself was a curiosity. Cosmic Records in Ipswich, west of Brisbane, had already incurred the attention of the Licensing Branch following a complaint by a local fundamentalist preacher, the Reverend John Pasterkamp. (Cosmic, keen to avoid litigation costs, meekly withdrew the offending items from sale.) Pasterkamp claimed to have made his original complaint to then federal Labor member and later governor-general, Bill Hayden, who in turn referred the matter to the state attorney-general, Paul Clauson. A political neophyte, Clauson then wrote to Pasterkamp pledging the government's full support, pre-empting the city raid.

Warwick Vere: The police basically admitted to me that it was a ministerial thing; that they didn't want to pursue it. [The government] was on the ropes by then, they were trying the

old Rona Joyner kind of fire and brimstone rubbish. They were
clutching at straws, basically, and they grabbed the wrong straw.

The records and cassettes seized were indicative of the
investigative powers of a police force that was officially
unable to find brothels and casinos. Titles included Do
The Shag (an instrumental number by early '60s band the
Champs); the Sonic Youth EP *Master Dik*; and *Dickcheese*, by
Sydney favourites the Hard-Ons. Also taken were items by
New York provocateur Lydia Lunch and the huge-selling
Guns n' Roses album *Appetite For Destruction*, which already
carried a sticker warning its contents may offend.

More revealing, however, was the seizure of records by
the Dead Kennedys, whose Festival Hall show in 1983 had
prompted such outlandish police attention. In the US, the
San Francisco group had long been a target of the religious
right: singer Jello Biafra had earlier been driven close to
bankruptcy after being forced to defend himself against
similar charges of obscenity.[1] The Dead Kennedys' albums
Give Me Convenience Or Give Me Death (which included the
earlier single Too Drunk To Fuck) and *Fresh Fruit For Rotting
Vegetables* (specifically, the album track I Kill Children)
would form the centre of the police case against Rocking
Horse and Vere.

One week after the raid R.E.M. played an extraordinary
show at Festival Hall. On their final tour as a support band,
the Go-Betweens dedicated their song The Clarke Sisters to
the staff at Rocking Horse. Michael Stipe ended the evening
by repeatedly singing the Velvet Underground's After
Hours, refusing to leave the stage until the crowd dispersed.

Queensland had long boasted its own Film and Literature
Boards of Review: the year before, *The Last Temptation
Of Christ* had been banned from screening in the state's
cinemas. Several years earlier, Triple Zed had fallen foul
of the Australian Broadcasting Tribunal for broadcasting

(among other items) the Dead Kennedys' Too Drunk To Fuck. Station journalist Linden Woodward responded by preparing a deliberately scholarly program on the social history of bad language; shortly after, Woodward and then station coordinator Haydn Thompson were hauled before the tribunal to explain themselves.

Linden Woodward: Language was a significant issue in Queensland at that time. If you got arrested in Queensland in those days, as likely as not you'd get charged with resisting arrest, possibly with assaulting police and certainly with indecent language. And I used to think, well, who exactly was offended by this language – the police?

I think Haydn was immensely amused, because I sounded terribly meek and mild, and here I was standing before the tribunal and explaining to David Jones, who was the head of the tribunal, why 'cunt' was really an important word. It was tripping off his tongue by the end.

When the tribunal praised Triple Zed and Woodward for producing such a fine and responsible piece of radio, it effectively gave the green light for the contextual use of bad language in future Australian broadcasting and public performance. Queensland law, however, had yet to catch up. Three months before the Rocking Horse bust, Stipendiary Magistrate Don Fardon had found comedian Rodney Rude guilty of obscenity for uttering the word 'cocksucker' on stage. Fardon was thus hand-picked by the prosecution to preside over the case against Warwick Vere.

After initially ruling that Vere had a prima facie case to answer (despite the fact that the recordings under discussion were readily available in most other major chain stores, none of which had received the attention of the Licensing Branch), Fardon set aside three days in May for the case. The hearings were predictably surreal. Prosecuting Sergeant Geoff Cartner opened proceedings by playing a cassette of

Give Me Convenience Or Give Me Death to the courtroom. He assured the magistrate he would only need to listen to the first side to get the effect.

'I'm very grateful,' Fardon replied.

After patiently sitting through Too Drunk To Fuck, Fardon complained of the 'dreadful' and 'garbled' sound, but agreed he could detect the word that was the subject of the charge.[2] From that point, the case rested almost entirely on whether or not 'fuck' could still be regarded as obscene to the average Queenslander.

> **Warwick Vere:** Fortunately I was privy to some good advice. I had a QC living next door, [the late] Shane Herbert, and we basically had to prove that community standards had changed. We gave evidence that the word 'fuck' had long ceased to shock and amaze people, and that in fact it occurred 17 times in the Academy Award-winning film of that year, which was *Rain Man*. It occurred in a book for 12-year-old kids that had been named children's book of the year! The prosecution tried to make out that tracks like I Kill Children were just unbelievably outrageous; they seemed to miss the irony of what the song was all about. We compared it to the Jonathan Swift essay 'A Modest Proposal', where he describes how to cook up an Irish baby for the delectation of the English table. But that was all lost on them.

In the end, however, the crusty old magistrate was painted into a corner. After a painfully wordy preamble, Fardon eventually turned his attention to the matter at hand:

> The titles of these songs are I Kill Children and Too Drunk To Fuck. The latter song repeats those same words monotonously, over and over, concluding with a sound I think intended to imitate vomiting. If the defendant is to be believed, there is a considerable market for these items and that is an interesting comment, but not unexpected, upon the taste of the general community . . .

The use of the word 'fuck' or its derivatives is quite common . . . I am well aware that amongst men in men-only situations its use is such that it is quite a common word, sometimes it amounts to every second word, and little or no objection seems to arise to it. It may well be the same at women's-only gatherings, but I don't know about that . . .

In this community today, I think the word itself has well and truly ceased to shock or alarm even the tenderest of feelings if it is used with some circumspection . . . The community in general could not care less if Joe Blow bought one or all of these things and took them home. It would be dramatically different if Joe Blow then turned up the volume of his player to the extent that all his neighbours for a hundred yards in all directions could hear the delightful strains of Too Drunk To Fuck. There would be an immediate outcry, and not just about the noise . . .

On the balance I come to the conclusion that merely selling these things, all of them, or having them for sale without public performance and without undue public display, is not something which is offensive to current community standards. Both complaints are dismissed . . . [3]

The delivery of Tony Fitzgerald's report on 3 July 1989 saw the government's final descent from crisis into collapse. True to his inquiry's intentions, Fitzgerald focused not on apportioning blame but on rebuilding public institutions in a way that would protect the state from again falling into the hands of a criminal and political elite. His most central recommendation to this effect – the abolition of the perverted electoral system that had entrenched the Nationals in power – drove a stake through the heart of the government, by then facing a resurgent Labor led by former lawyer Wayne Goss. Fitzgerald wrote:

A government in our political system which achieves office by means other than free and fair elections lacks legitimate

political authority over that system. This must affect the ability
of parliament to play its proper role in a way referred to in this
report . . . The institutional culture of public administration
risks degeneration if, for any reason, a government's activities
ceased to be moderated by concern at the possibility of losing
power.[4]

But the National Party had lost the stomach for Ahern's
'lock, stock and barrel' approach to reform. Perceived as
weak and indecisive by a party used to authoritarianism, he
was ousted two months later by his police minister, Russell
Cooper. In just his second term of office, Cooper was a
National in the orthodox mould, a conservative grazier and
grain-grower, attractive to the party's old guard. His first
day in office was hardly promising.

As the final witness to appear before the Fitzgerald
Inquiry, Joh Bjelke-Petersen had been quizzed about
his knowledge of the conventions of parliamentary
democracy. Asked what he understood by the doctrine of
the separation of powers – which provides that the various
arms of authority (that is, the executive, the parliament,
and the enforcement arms, including the judiciary and
police) be kept separate, in order to avoid the potential
for tyranny – Bjelke-Petersen was stumped. After lengthy
attempts to evade the question, he eventually managed,
amid laughter: 'Well, you tell me, and I'll tell you whether
you're right or not. Why – don't you know?'[5]

Just 10 months later, Russell Cooper accepted an
invitation to appear on the ABC's *7.30 Report* on the day of
his promotion. Host Quentin Dempster's first question hit
the new premier flush between the eyes.

Dempster: What do you understand by the doctrine of the
separation of powers under the Westminster system?

Cooper: Is this a trick question, Quentin?

An election, employing the existing electoral boundaries, was announced weeks later. Queensland would go to the polls on 2 December. Cooper, with no time to prepare an agenda of his own, relied on a flamboyant scare campaign. Television advertisements depicted a curtain of blood descending over the screen: such was to be Queensland's fate should it elect a Labor government. Cooper claimed the state would be overrun by drug-pushers, gays and lesbians. Undeterred by the ruling in the Rocking Horse case, Cooper also promised that 'pornographic' rock music would be made subject to the state's censorship laws.[6]

In a marvellous quirk of history, the election date coincided with the holding of the second Livid Festival. This time the venue was the RNA showgrounds in Bowen Hills, the same venue where, 18 years earlier, a South African football team had taken the field under police protection.

Peter Walsh: The election date was announced after we announced ours, and we subsequently advertised that we would have a wall of TVs so you could watch the results come in. Five minutes before we opened someone said, 'Peter, where are the TVs?'

So I went, oops, and I ran home and I got my 12-inch portable black and white. It must have been a record for the most people watching a portable black and white TV! I got up on stage half an hour before Wayne Goss claimed victory for the Labor Party, and announced that the National Party had been kicked out.

The quote was, 'No more fascism!', which looking back on I'm very embarrassed about. But there was certainly that feeling in the air at the time.

affirmation

(1990–2000)

CHAPTER THIRTEEN

rock against work!

Graham Don was keeping his head low. During the mid 1980s, he had been resident DJ at the Love Inn, located at the top of Ann Street in Fortitude Valley. The venue was owned by vice king Hector Hapeta, an overweight, unlovely man who for years had paid off the Licensing Branch in exchange for police protection of his prostitution interests.

The Love Inn, however, was not a brothel. Instead, it was one of the few music venues in town regularly putting on interstate and occasionally overseas bands during Brisbane's darkest years. In July 1986 legendary garage rockers the Flamin' Groovies played there. When the venue was unable to meet the band's guarantee, Hapeta was called. In a jam, he despatched some girls and pot to keep the group happy while he came up with the cash. The Groovies thought Brisbane was the best place they'd played since their native San Francisco in 1969.

Hapeta's world was about to fall apart. Fingered as (literally) Brisbane's biggest underworld figure by Phil Dickie and *Four Corners*, he was summoned before the Fitzgerald Inquiry in August 1987. There he refused to answer 164 questions on the grounds of certain self-incrimination. The following year he was arrested and charged with heroin trafficking; in June 1989 he was sentenced to life imprisonment.

Before his death behind bars in 1999, Hapeta was in

good company. He was joined by four former government ministers, along with many of the police he had bought off. The biggest casualty was the former commissioner. In August 1991, Terry Lewis – the man who would be Sir Terence – was sentenced to the maximum 14 years jail for official corruption and stripped of his knighthood.

Also facing trial in 1991 was the former premier. Joh Bjelke-Petersen had originally been charged with one count of official corruption and another two counts of perjury before the Fitzgerald Inquiry. The special prosecutor, Doug Drummond QC, reduced this to a single charge of perjury in the belief that this would address the issue of corruption, given the allegation pertained to the former premier's knowledge of a $100,000 political donation by a Singaporean businessman.

The trial itself was stranger than fiction. After the first jury panel was mysteriously dismissed, the second was unable to reach a verdict after days of acrimonious deliberations. The deadlock – 10–2 in favour of a guilty verdict – had been forced by the jury foreman, Luke Shaw, later revealed to be a branch secretary of the Young Nationals with connections to the Friends of Joh group. The debacle resulted in an official inquiry into the jury's selection process and an ABC docudrama, *Joh's Jury*. But Bjelke-Petersen was never retried.

As one of Hector Hapeta's employees, Graham Don had come under heavy scrutiny. On one occasion he was dragged out of bed at six in the morning and down to the watch-house for questioning. For more than a year after the inquiry, he stayed away from nightclubs, doing labouring jobs and waiting for the purge to subside. A peripheral player in the old Brisbane scene, he would soon become a significant force in the new one. As a DJ he was aware of Brisbane's unusual club culture.

Graham Don: Brisbane was one of the only cities in Australia where you could actually go to a dance club and dance to rock & roll. When I was in my teens and going out underage, I'd go to nightclubs and I'd be dancing to the Stranglers, the Birthday Party, the Saints; Iggy Pop's Lust For Life was huge on the dance floor. Whereas in Sydney it was all dance music.

It would take much more than a change of government to change Brisbane. Even as the new Labor regime instigated a vigorous round of criminal justice and electoral reforms in line with Fitzgerald's recommendations, the city was in something of a lull for the first year after the changing of the guard.

The complacent administration of the lord mayor, Sallyanne Atkinson, exemplified the sense of stasis. A ludicrous bid to bring the 1992 Olympic Games to the city, coupled with Atkinson's showy style and overweening personal ambition, were at odds with the fact that you still couldn't get a decent meal after hours in Brisbane, and even if you could, you had to eat it indoors. In many ways Brisbane remained the big country town its detractors had always claimed.

The music scene, too, was close to dormant. Part of it was simply generational. The Go-Betweens were gone; Ed Kuepper and Chris Bailey had settled into respectable solo careers. Occasional reformations by the Riptides were viewed with cynicism by the music press. Most of those whose late-'70s adolescence had been defined by the punk movement and its fraternal twin, radical politics, had grown up and got out.

David Corazza: There are Brisbane mafias all around the world. The litmus test of that was when I left I had a going-away party and about 90 people rocked up, and it was a who's who of our little coterie of the music and arts scene. And then I remember coming back about two years later and there were only two people out of that 90 who were left. It was a real wake-up when I realised that.

By early 1991 Graham Don was ready to break back into clubs. The local scene wasn't strong enough to support another live venue, but there was plenty of new music to play from elsewhere. From England came the Happy Mondays and the Stone Roses, playing euphoric guitar rock over a funky, shuffling beat that was impossible not to dance to. And the American underground was exploding. In the previous two years, Sonic Youth, Mudhoney and Dinosaur Jr had all undertaken successful tours of Australia, verifying the existence of a fresh young audience hungry for new sounds. Budding writer Simon McKenzie, later the editor of street paper *Time Off*, saw Mudhoney in March 1990, at Easts Leagues Club in suburban Coorparoo.

> **Simon McKenzie:** There were loads of people stage-diving, and one guy took it a hell of a lot further by getting up on top of the main speaker stacks and vaulting into space from about seven feet higher than everyone else. In mid-arc a flash went off – he had a camera and was taking a picture in the air. Mark Arm stopped singing and said, 'Man, whoever that was, send that photo to Sub Pop! I gotta see it!'

With Fitzgerald's men having torn through the Valley like a cyclone, Don decided to relocate to the city centre. On 1 March he opened a new club in the Lands Office Hotel on George Street. Although it lasted barely 18 months, the Funkyard would become the hub for a new generation of music fans.

> **Graham Don:** The idea behind the Funkyard was to take junk culture and chuck it all together and spew it back out. The name came from looking through my records – I had a James Brown record next to the Birthday Party's *Junkyard*, and I came up with Funkyard. It was just like everything mashed into one.

Don was assisted by a former artist for the Love Inn, Paul

Curtis. Wiry, hyperactive and, according to Don, 'a total acid casualty, running up the walls, you couldn't make sense of him', Curtis was also something of an ideologue in his quest to do things independently.

Paul Curtis: When I was at the Love Inn I had this naive concept that I was never going to take money for the art I did, so I refused to take payment from anyone. I would do it all off my own back, cover all the costs. If the costs were exorbitant I would try to get them to cover those costs, but I wouldn't actually take any payment for the art itself, because I thought it would corrupt it. Of course the ridiculous thing is I was doing it for advertising, for other people to make money!

A stint working for the Murdoch press in the late '80s helped convince Curtis that being paid for his artwork wasn't so bad after all, and his psychedelia-meets-splatter-movie imagery captured the Funkyard aesthetic perfectly. It also unwittingly tapped into another visual trend: the modern primitive look of rising Los Angeles bands such as Jane's Addiction and the Red Hot Chili Peppers. Within two weeks the Funkyard was attracting 800 payers through its doors.

By August the club had relocated to the more spacious Bertie's Tavern on Elizabeth Street, under the Myer Centre. There the Funkyard went through the roof, with up to 1400 kids jamming into the room on Friday nights. When six police entered the venue one Friday evening – alarmed, perhaps, by the sudden proliferation of tattoos and dreadlocks – they found themselves hopelessly outnumbered.

Graham Don: They walked through the middle of the crowd, and I turned off the music, jumped on the microphone and said, 'Warning, warning, police are in the house, if you've got anything they can bust you for, drop it.' The place went nuts. Everyone started throwing their cans of beer at the cops; they

pulled their hats off and were throwing them around . . . They'd
never seen that many weirdos in one place at one time!

Other factors were at play. As Triple Zed struggled to
adjust to life in its new Toowong studios – and to establish
an identity for itself in the post-Fitzgerald era – the newly
nationalised Triple J began broadcasting into Brisbane.
Triple J's near wholesale appropriation of both the music
and the listeners of public radio stations around the
country suddenly gave previously marginal musical forms
tremendous commercial impetus.

In September 1991 Jane's Addiction played Festival Hall.
The gig sold out on the night, and the 850 fans turned away
walked the block to the Funkyard instead. But when the
band stepped off stage a few hours later, everyone who *had*
seen the show tried to join the party. The resulting queue
extended up Elizabeth Street all the way to the Treasury-On-
George. Placing a speaker box outside, Graham Don cued the
band's hit Been Caught Stealing and cranked the volume up.
And suddenly, just like the old song went, there was dancing
in the street.

Then came the Big Bang. An old Survivor, Bruce Anthon,
had managed to import a few platters of Nirvana's second
album *Nevermind* into Kent Records more than a month
before the album's Australian release. Curtis and Don were
the first in. Don played the single, Smells Like Teen Spirit,
three times a night: 'The place would just erupt every time.'

At the crest of their fame, the band was booked to play
Festival Hall – second-billed to the Violent Femmes – in
January 1992. Nirvana's set was short, with Kurt Cobain
battling heroin addiction, a chronic stomach complaint and
a sound mix that turned the first half of the show into mud.
Until the band hit the chorus of Come As You Are: suddenly,
the sound snapped into focus, the band blazed away, and a
wall of beautiful noise sent the room into orbit.

Nevermind was, from the name down, the *Never Mind The
Bollocks* of its era: as divisive as it was defiant, at the very

least it set the agenda and the benchmark for much of the decade to come. And for the first time in years – even if only for a moment – popular music felt like a genuine popular movement again.

In the mid '70s, before anyone had heard of punk, bands sprung up all over the world, working off the same basic template handed down by the Stooges, the MC5 and countless garage bands. Similarly in the late '80s, before grunge had a name, there were countless groups exploring the possibilities of introspective lyrics, soft/loud dynamics and melodies drenched in distortion. These were the musical descendents not just of the Ramones and the Sex Pistols, but '80s icons the Replacements, Hüsker Dü and the Pixies.

By 1990 a new crop of bands was surfacing in Brisbane, the direct influences of almost all of whom could be traced to immediate American antecedents. Formed in Townsville in 1988, the Madmen were the first of many local bands attempting to unearth hooks from a bottomless pit of noise, and their second single, Tower, confirmed the melodic sense of songwriter Tim Steward, a stringy Londoner who had begun playing in bands after his family emigrated to north Queensland in 1983. By the turn of the decade, the Madmen had relocated to Brisbane. It didn't take them long to fall in with a like-minded crowd.

Tim Steward: There were bands like Noose, Krud, Budd and Midget . . . I remember me, Kellie and Jeremy and John from Budd were all at the Funkyard one night. We all had long hair and our gym boots on, and we looked at each other and went, 'Man, we all look the same – we should form a band!' So we formed this covers band called Slugfest, and we'd do songs by Mudhoney and Tad and all that Sub Pop stuff. This was all pre-*Nevermind*.

Kellie Lloyd was already playing bass in Krud. A second-year film student and fan of the Madmen, she wrote to Steward offering to make a film clip for the band. She got more than she bargained for.

> **Kellie Lloyd:** My practice room was actually my house; I lived in a flat above a barbecue shop with this other girl. Bands in Brisbane were always on this never-ending search for a practice room that you could stay in for more than six months. And Tim wrote to me saying yeah, we'd love you to make a clip for us, can we share your practice room, and I said well, actually it's my living room, but why not? So they basically moved into my living room! They practised there for about a year.

The Madmen had already released three singles and a mini-album by the time Lloyd joined the band in early 1992, replacing Cam Hurst. Changing their name to Screamfeeder, the group inked a deal with Sydney's Survival Records. A promising debut album, *Flour*, quickly followed, and Screamfeeder were soon playing to packed houses in Sydney and Melbourne. For almost any Brisbane band before them, it would have been time to move on. But Screamfeeder set a precedent in being content to remain at home.

> **Tim Steward:** I guess we didn't need to leave. We could always go on tour. We were comfy in Brisbane, Tony [Blades, drums] and I had girlfriends and we just didn't want to move.

Screamfeeder's inner-city sound and musical alignment with the American underground saw them attract early press and some devoted admirers. But their shows were erratic, and the gap between Steward's best and weakest material was still wide. Out in the suburbs, heavy metal ruled: if a group could play well enough and put on a show, the strength of the songs barely mattered. The other rising tide was rap, then being mainlined to white kids by funk-metal bands Faith No More and the aforementioned Chili Peppers.

The unlikely birthplace for this new musical force in Brisbane was Cleveland, more than half an hour from the city on the southern shores of Moreton Bay. Cleveland High School boasted an exceptionally strong music department, and three of its pupils would form arguably the most potent and influential new combination on the scene. The first of them, Ben Ely, had excelled on trumpet at school after being forbidden the drums by his parents. Like most adolescents, Ely wanted to make as much noise as possible, and he took up bass after a friend reminded him that fire-breathing hero Gene Simmons played the instrument for Kiss.

Ben Ely: I've always liked bass because you could feel the vibrations in your body. It's a caveman's axe!

Ely had finished high school and was playing in punk and metal covers bands when he met drummer Martin Lee. Lee had just returned from Los Angeles with Simon Gardner, a graduate of the city's Guitar Institute of Technology. Gardner was, unsurprisingly, an extremely technical player in the Joe Satriani mould. Completed by singer Andy McDonell, Brasilia's trad-metal indulgences impressed some, but Ely didn't last long, sacked by the demanding Gardner. Ely was heartbroken, until he remembered two younger high school chums, Dave Atkins and Jim Sinclair, were also playing the covers circuit.

Ben Ely: I remember them being phenomenal players, they were really studying their jazz stuff and playing different time signatures and scales. I was also doing a bit of acid at the time, so we were kind of trying to make the music as freaky as possible. Those guys were still in their school uniforms when we were going and doing our first shows.

Dave Atkins, a stocky young man of South American heritage with massive forearms, had been spotted as a natural drummer in his first year of high school. At home, his dad would spin records: everything from Mozart to *Led Zeppelin IV*. Television in the early '80s was *Countdown*, breakdancing (Atkins' older brother was a regional champion), and early hip-hop: Malcolm McLaren's Buffalo Girls, Grandmaster Flash's The Message, Sugar Hill Gang's Rapper's Delight. But jazz was Atkins' first love.

> **Dave Atkins:** I could play classical, I found it really easy, and I did it really to prove to my father that I could cut it in that scene, but jazz was like, wow, that's the free area, that's the punk, you know, that's the rock & roll! You can be outrageous, you can be like Animal in the Muppets; you can be whatever you want.

Sinclair, for his part, was a guitar shredder to rival Simon Gardner.

> **Dave Atkins:** I met Jim in the music block at school . . . He was a year older than me, and he was sitting there playing some classical piece of music at lightning speed, and I was totally blown away. It was like he was Eddie Van Halen; there was no one like him around.

Sinclair and Atkins played in a variety of covers bands through school, performing underage around the suburban pubs. Sinclair dropped out, convinced he was a career musician. He bumped into Ely soon after the latter's ejection from Brasilia.

> **Dave Atkins:** I was finishing high school, and right at the last month of term, Jim rings me up and says, 'I've just hooked up with Ben again, he's really changed, he's writing some really crazy stuff.' They came around and we had a jam. Ben had dreads, you know, it was like, 'What happened?' I'm pretty sure

he told me there was a whole year there where he ended up just eating mushies and taking acid.

Taking their name from Miles Davis' 1975 jazz-rock fusion album, Pangaea's debut in January 1992 made an immediate impact. Ely's feral energy (and appearance) next to Sinclair and Atkins' virtuosity – the band could stretch out and improvise on stage like no other in town – covered for the rudimentary songs. Brisbane had a long history of punk bands that prided enthusiasm over ability, but Pangaea's sets were showcases of groove, volume and instrumental prowess.

Dave Atkins: We wrote a song called The Power Of Three; it was all about uniting and becoming one force. That was the whole concept of the three of us coming together to make this sort of supergroup, you know, a dominating group that could outplay any other band.

Playing alongside Screamfeeder and Pangaea in 1992 were two other bands whose burgeoning reputations were forcing venues to open their doors again to original music. The first were the Dreamkillers, formed from the ashes of earlier hardcore groups Mystery of Sixes and Insane Hombres. Fronted by former Mystery of Sixes lead screamer Les Jobson, the Dreamkillers brand of punk-metal mayhem was made for the alcohol-fuelled frenzy of live performance. Paul Curtis took on the daunting role of managing the band.

Paul Curtis: I think I was amused by the intensity of their image. I did all the graphics for them as well, and I found that worked really well. I liked to draw things that were very kind of dark and horror in a cartoonish kind of manner, and there was a certain cartoon element to them, a larger-than-life thing.

The second band was far more traditional, looking past punk to the classic rock of the Rolling Stones, David Bowie, and the mellow early '70s folk of Rodriguez. They even took their name from a Neil Young classic: Powderfinger.

The success of the Funkyard made it inevitable that the management of Bertie's Tavern would agree to put on live shows. It was still a substantial risk. When Livid mastermind Peter Walsh began staging shows on Thursday nights under the name Alive She Cried, the midweek timeslot did neither the bands nor the venue any favours. It wasn't until Walsh's assistant Jessica Astrid (then known as John Darcey) came up with the idea of reviving the shopworn concept of Rock Against Work on Friday afternoons that things really started to happen.

Australia was in the middle of a devastating recession, with more than 10 per cent of the population unemployed in every state. Youth unemployment was closer to 25 per cent. There was plenty of time for seeing bands, or forming them. The Rock Against Work shows were free, and the drinks cheap.

> **Kellie Lloyd:** We were all rocking against work! I don't know whether it was how old we were, but everyone was doing the same sorts of things. Everyone was mixing and going out, no one was married or having kids or any of that kind of thing. Everyone was finishing a degree or starting a degree or just on the dole.

The Funkyard, too, started putting on shows. When the club hosted the launch of the Dreamkillers' debut CD in April 1992, 560 people came. While it wasn't the numbers the club pulled when Graham Don's DJ skills were the primary attraction, it was more than any local band had ever attracted without first making a name for itself interstate or overseas.

Graham Don: Before that, local bands were getting 60 people, you know. I remember going to see Ups and Downs when they were the hippest things around and they'd get 50 people, 60 people. Same with the Headstones, who had a record out on Waterfront.

The Rock Against Work concept was extended further on public holidays, with Astrid staging mini-festivals of up to 10 local bands in the venue. For these shows, Rock Against Work moved from Bertie's to Metropolis, a 1500-capacity venue deep in the bowels of the Myer Centre. The results were revelatory. Putting local bands on a big stage with a decent lighting and sound system – sometimes even head-lining over interstate visitors – gave them a status they hadn't previously enjoyed. Hundreds came to Rock Against The Queen (on the Queen's Birthday) or the Ekka (on Exhibition Day in August).

The Dreamkillers began tearing the roof off Metropolis, attracting more than 1000 punters to their shows, prompting Paul Curtis and Graham Don to set up a record label catering solely to Brisbane artists. The Dreamkillers' live popularity made them the obvious first signing to Velvet Urge, but the inexperienced duo failed to heed the warning signs: a shortage of genuine quality material, compounded by internal strife and personal problems dating back to the troubled Mystery of Sixes.

Graham Don: They looked like they were going to sell. They scared people enough; they were going to get noticed no matter what. But the wheels fell off in the end, because they had the addictions.

Curtis later fell out with the band and, more bitterly, with Don, after the demise of the Funkyard in August 1992. At the same time Pangaea had split with their Elvis-impersonator manager. Curtis, who had sidestepped earlier advances from the band to concentrate on the

Dreamkillers, stepped into the breach.

Pangaea's blistering live shows had attracted the attention of Michael Parisi, then working in A&R for Imago Records. When Imago folded in 1992, Parisi returned to his former employer, Warner Music, working on the tougher end of the label's American roster including Helmet and Nine Inch Nails. At the time, no Australian bands had ever been signed directly to the label. Parisi thought Pangaea might be the first.

Fortitude Valley was slowly coming back to life. Paradoxically, the exodus of business – compounded by the recession and the precinct's tarnished reputation – helped create the necessary space for music to filter back into its natural environment.

Once run by another Fitzgerald Inquiry star, Tony Bellino, the reclamation of the Roxy as a medium-sized venue by Paul Curtis and Livid Festival co-producer Paul Campbell-Ryder was critical. Only a few doors down from the Brunswick Street railway station, the venue's capacity of 1500 proved the ideal substitute for Metropolis, after the Myer Centre's management quietly decided a shopping precinct was no longer an appropriate place for an alternative nightclub.

Even more important was the December 1992 opening of the Zoo, on Ann Street. Beginning as a gallery-cum-café-cum-pool hall, the Zoo boasted a rare combination of atmosphere and conviviality (ghosts, apparently friendly ones, were claimed to be regular after-hours patrons). After experimenting with acoustic shows on a makeshift stage, the venue's owners, Joc Curran and her business partner, known only as C, threw open the 450-capacity room to bands. Curran and C had made the decision to open a venue after the demise of their own group, Creatures Downstairs.

Joc Curran: We were looking for somewhere that was quite cheap in terms of rent, and we didn't want to come to the

Valley at all. It had a really bad reputation; it was really rough; people didn't go there. And we looked at rental prices in the city and they were astronomical and beyond our budget.

C: We were looking for about nine months, and in that nine months the concept of how people viewed the Valley began to change. It just had the tiniest seed that was going to develop into something kind of groovy and a bit more offbeat.

Even the practice room situation had been solved. Bands had begun renting out the deserted offices above an old Target warehouse in the Brunswick Street Mall. Built in the '50s, the themed floor plan of the offices – three floors individually carpeted in blue, red and yellow; porthole-like windows; toilet doors more like submarine hatches – gave the Target building the spooky ambience of an abandoned film set.

Kellie Lloyd: There were bad vibes in certain places; in a lot of the rooms the lights didn't work. We used to break in there before it was a practice space and go looking, and you'd find places where people had been squatting, with needles everywhere and human faeces and stuff . . . A couple of the rooms were used by prostitutes, like dens.

The offices were carved into rehearsal and studio spaces. Bands played and sometimes lived there, honing their craft, mingling, sharing ideas. Not all of it was healthy: sometimes rooms would get broken into and gear stolen. For one skinny, charismatic young singer, however, it marked a convergence of common interests.

Bernard Fanning: The combination of Rock Against Work and the Target building were the catalyst for it becoming a real scene, I reckon, where everyone started to get to know each other and did gigs together . . . That's when that group of people all started hanging out together a lot more, and that

kind of fostered things. And there was a certain amount of
pride after a couple of years of that, which got people thinking,
we've got some really fucking good bands here.

Powderfinger were rising fast. Accusations of the group
being musical followers were of no consequence to those
flocking to their shows. The launch of their debut CD in
August 1992 – a self-titled seven-tracker generally known
as the Blue EP – had seen lines form around the block
of their original stomping ground, the Orient Hotel. For
their second effort, the *Transfusion* EP, the five-piece sold
out Metropolis in September 1993.

The gig was a watershed in more ways than one.
The launch attracted 1100 people, more even than the
Dreamkillers had managed. Moreover, one song, Reap
What You Sow, was receiving heavy rotation on Triple J.

At the *Transfusion* launch was Polydor's Tim Prescott.
Prescott went out drinking with the band after the
show, and the band appreciated his earthy demeanour.
Ambitious and driven, Powderfinger were all in their early
20s and had no qualms about jumping in the deep end
with a major label. Like Screamfeeder, though, they had no
intention of leaving home to do it.

Ben Ely's music may have united punk and metal fans
across town, but he was something of a hippie at heart,
and he was a regular attendee at the Full Moon parties
hosted by a friend on the Sunshine Coast hinterland at the
end of each month. Jam sessions were always held, and one
night, through the fog of smoke and booze, he recognised
the guitarist of heavy funk-fusion band Zooerastia sitting
in on drums. Aloof and mysterious, Quan Yeomans liked
to keep himself in reserve. On this night, however, the
usually abstemious Yeomans was under the influence.

Ben Ely: I remember hanging out with him afterwards. He walked off into the bushes, I followed him and said, 'What are you doing?', and he said, 'Oh, I'm just going to lick the leaves on the trees.' I think that was the moment I thought, this guy's good fun.

With up to 10 bands occupying the Target building, it was not uncommon for musicians – especially rhythm players – to moonlight in several groups at once. When Martin Lee told Ely of Brasilia's breakup, the bass player didn't hesitate before suggesting they form another band with Yeomans. Ely quickly became more enthusiastic about his new combination than he was about Pangaea.

Ben Ely: I think we wrote She's Got A Hangup in our first practice, and we went straight on to talking about trying to get signed . . . We'd all been on the dole for about three or four years by then, we were just scraping through, trying to pay rent and get food every day.

Regurgitator took to new extremes the Funkyard's original concept of mashing styles together and spewing the results back out. The band quickly recorded a demo, which Ely passed on to Paul Curtis. The first song on the tape was the lumbering, metallic Like It Like That. But in Quan Yeomans' lyrics, Curtis sensed a kindred spirit.

Paul Curtis: I could totally relate to it . . . It echoed the political concepts I had in my mind about punk rock versus the corporate way of doing things. Which was ironic, because it became embroiled in the big corporate world.

Live, the group's impact was immediate. Within three months of their debut in March 1994, Regurgitator had notched a string of impressive support slots.

Peter Walsh: I gave Regurgitator their third gig, supporting
Primus at the Roxy, and I couldn't believe the crowd reaction,
because no one had ever seen the band, and the crowd went
nuts. And I thought fuck, we've got something going on here.

In August 1993 Screamfeeder's second album was released.
Burn Out Your Name was Brisbane's singular contribution
to the Seattle sound, the songs carried on a tidal wave of
distortion. On the heavier numbers, the group sank under
the weight of their own ennui. But when Tim Steward
allowed his melodic gifts to shine, the results transcended
his band's generic limitations. Wrote You Off and Around A
Pole melded speed and sweetness like the very best Hüsker
Dü songs; Button was compact and explosive; while the
agonised loneliness of Kellie Lloyd's contribution, Sushi
Bowl, was a clear highlight.

But Screamfeeder enjoyed little luck thereafter. After a
successful tour through Europe, broken promises on the part
of US independent label Taang! saw a planned American
jaunt fall through. Replacing original drummer Tony Blades
with the dynamic Dean Shwereb in 1995, the band matured
into an accomplished outfit, trading some excitement for
consistency in the process. Despite a loyal following and
increasing radio exposure, Screamfeeder never caught fire
commercially.

Powderfinger were a different story, although the band
almost came dreadfully unstuck following the July 1994
release of their first album for Polydor, *Parables For Wooden
Ears*. If the pedantic title implied lessons being learned,
those lessons were entirely the group's to absorb. Produced
at great expense by Tony Cohen (then riding on the success
of his work with the Cruel Sea, whose lean sound was
perfectly suited to his signature atmospherics), every song
on *Parables* was overburdened as songwriting took a back
seat to technique. Jack Marx's review in *Rolling Stone* typified
the album's reception.

> [Powderfinger] write, construct and execute themselves rigid: their songs are meticulously planned feats of engineering . . . This is not necessarily a compliment. Sometimes it's a certified jerk-off.[1]

Curiously, Marx claimed to like the band. He even entered into the spirit of his own critique, playfully signing off his review as Jackson G Marx. But his point was not lost on the group.

> **Bernard Fanning:** A lot of it was really a product of being influenced by bands like Soundgarden and also on a local level Pangaea, where it was all very technical. But that wasn't our strength at all, and that's why our first album was so misguided and strange. As someone said at the time, it disappeared up its own arse![2]

Shortly before *Parables'* release, Paul Curtis drove down to Sydney. His intentions were twofold: to negotiate a deal with Warner for Pangaea, and to seek a manufacturing and distribution deal for his new label, Valve. As part of his pitch, he handed Michael Parisi a tape of what would become Pangaea's *Raggacore* EP, with the Regurgitator demo on the other side. His excitement was tempered by unease: as a vocal champion of DIY enterprise, Curtis felt he was dancing with the devil. After a fitful night's sleep in his car, he drove back to Brisbane the next day. Parisi was not long in calling.

> **Paul Curtis:** Parisi said, 'You've got a problem, Paul. You have to make a choice.' I said, 'What do you mean?' And he said, 'I don't want to sign Pangaea anymore. I want to sign Regurgitator.'
> I just thought, oh my god, this is going to be so messy.

CHAPTER FOURTEEN

spring hill fair

I've got a little melody, and it hangs in the air – there!
I've got a little melody – there it is again!
And again, and again, and again, and again
Melody is my friend
– Custard, Melody

While Screamfeeder smothered their best tunes in distortion and Pangaea eschewed song craft in favour of the extended jam, another emerging group of musicians was looking in the opposite direction. Rising from late 1980s incarnation Who's Gerald?, Custard's influences cut a clear line through classic American college rock from the Modern Lovers to the Pixies. Moreover, the band's leader, David McCormack, held a healthy regard for Brisbane's musical past: his favourite Australian band was the Go-Betweens. Custard would provide as bracing a challenge to rock orthodoxy post-*Nevermind* as Robert Forster and Grant McLennan had to punk, circa 1977.

McCormack had grown up in the upwardly mobile western suburb of Kenmore, completing his secondary education at Ipswich Grammar. In 1986 he was accepted into the University of Queensland, eventually graduating with a double major in psychology. He could not have cared less: 'The idea of having people tell me all their problems for hours on end was not my idea of a good time.' For McCormack, tertiary education's appeal lay in its social and recreational benefits:

David McCormack: The whole reason I was at uni was because it sounded like a really cool thing to do. By the time I went to uni I was listening to Triple Zed and I heard the Go-Betweens, the Saints . . . Everything I learnt about Brisbane music was from Triple Zed, because there was no other way to hear it, unless you were already in the scene, or you had an older brother who knew what records to listen to. I think the Go-Betweens were like the key in the lock and from there it was like, the Saints, Know Your Product, hey, that's a pretty good song. Stranded, that's pretty good. And then the Riptides, nice one!

McCormack had formed Who's Gerald? – a name purpose-built for a mass graffiti campaign – with fellow Ipswich Grammar boy Paul Medew after leaving school. The band's drummer, Cathy Atthow, earned her place at least partly through McCormack's obsession with the Go-Betweens and Lindy Morrison. By his own admission, Who's Gerald? had no redeeming features: Wrestle Wrestle, the band's sole seven-inch single, is so poorly recorded that when played at its correct speed of 45 rpm, the group sound like they're on helium.

David McCormack: That's when the drugs really came into play, around that time . . . In 1988–89 it was all speed, acid, ecstasy had just hit. And because we had nothing to do – we'd basically finished our degrees and were on the dole, and we were white middle-class kids from Kenmore – we could just get out of it forever. That's why Who's Gerald? broke up. We'd be speeding for days on end.

When Who's Gerald? mercifully folded in 1989, McCormack formed a new band, Custard Gun. Retaining Medew on bass, he was joined by drummer Shane Bruun and, briefly, another Ipswich Grammar alumnus, James

Straker. A junk-culture obsessive, Straker's uncanny likeness to his hero, Dinosaur Jr frontman J Mascis, was unfortunately not matched by his guitar prowess.

> **James Straker:** I was then, and am now, a shithouse guitarist, terrible, I'm close to retarded . . . I lasted a grand total of about four shows, I think, and I got a phone call from David saying that they were having band practice the next night and I didn't have to come, and as a 16-year-old, that hurt!

But the energetic Straker would not be denied his place in Brisbane's musical pantheon so easily. In late 1990 he opened a shop in the Toowong Arcade, the same location where, in 1978, original Go-Betweens manager Damian Nelson had attempted to establish his own record store. Though Straker was no more successful in private enterprise than Nelson had been, Silver Rocket – named after a track off Sonic Youth's milestone album *Daydream Nation* – represented the beginnings of a new angle on the trash aesthetic in Brisbane.

> **James Straker:** Silver Rocket started as a record store, and it got burgled three times in one week, everything got stolen. I had to find something to put in the windows to display, so I brought in some toys that I had at home, and the toys started doing heaps better than the records. There weren't a lot of people selling anything like that in Brisbane at the time.

After moving Silver Rocket from Toowong to Elizabeth Arcade in the city, Straker experienced a lifetime thrill when Sonic Youth dropped by the store while on tour in January 1992. Avid toy collectors themselves, the band's Festival Hall show climaxed with a seething encore of Silver Rocket, guitarist Thurston Moore sporting a T-shirt bearing the name of Straker's new band, the Melniks.

* *

Custard's debut EP, the sprightly *Rockfish Anna*, was released in December 1990. The B-side included a cover of C Is For Cookie, the signature song of *Sesame Street*'s resident glutton, Cookie Monster. It served notice of a group never in danger of taking itself too seriously. Like Robert Forster, David McCormack had drawn considerable early inspiration from the suburban obsessions of Jonathan Richman.

> **David McCormack:** I was at John Swingle's house, he was in the Melniks, and he said you've got to hear this . . . He played me Roadrunner and Government Centre and it just blew my mind, it was one of those life-changing experiences. Because up until then I was listening to Devo and Kraftwerk, stuff like that, which is all very alienated, but it's not really Brisbane. Brisbane's too hot for that!

By then McCormack had also met artist Glenn Thompson through a mutual friend, Who's Gerald? keyboard player Glen Donald. Originally from Toowoomba, Thompson had played stand-up drums with his friend Bob Moore in a busking trio called Tumblin' Tumbleweeds. True to their name, the band exploited country music's clichés to the hilt, playing material from Johnny Cash to the Violent Femmes.

> **Glenn Thompson:** We used to get really dressed up. I was the Indian Scout, Robert was the Gambler and Troy [Skewes, guitarist] was some kind of renegade cavalry runaway or something. It was that kind of vibe.

Country music had long been the two dirtiest words in independent rock circles, but McCormack loved the idea of the Tumblin' Tumbleweeds, prompting Glenn Thompson to call up Bob Moore. Several years older, Moore had recently married and had retired from music to concentrate on his own blossoming art career.

Bob Moore: Thommo rang up and said, 'I've met this kid, he's just learning to play guitar, but he's got something, Bob. We should have a jam with him.' This was Dave McCormack. And I said, 'Glenn, I don't want to be in a band anymore, I'm sick of being in a band.'

And he said, 'But he's really good, Bob, he's really good!' And then he said, 'I've got the idea for the band. It's a country *or* western band, and it's called COW.'

COW was far more than the in-joke their name suggested. Intending to score a hotel residency where they could have some fun, a few drinks and pick up a little extra cash at the end of the night, the band could indeed play country 'or' western, albeit with a knowing smirk. But such was the improvisational flair and natural showmanship of the musicians – McCormack in particular was becoming a formidable guitarist, distilling influences from Tom Waits' sideman Marc Ribot to the Pixies' Joey Santiago – that COW's scope was almost limitless.

McCormack, meanwhile, had moved into an old artist's studio annexed to the rear of his father's advertising business on Boundary Street, Spring Hill. Along with the Target offices in the Valley, the room became Brisbane's most fertile practice space, and as the house band, COW became the fulcrum for a dizzying number of new outfits, all seemingly under the faux-naïf spell of Jonathan Richman. (COW's timing was spooky: little more than a year after the band's live debut, Richman released *Jonathan Goes Country*, exploring an uncannily similar sideways-glancing take on the genre.)

Bob Moore: The reason that whole Spring Hill scene happened was because Dave's mum and dad, Jude and Ian, allowed that place to exist. None of us paid any rent! . . . If you took that practice room away, none of it would have happened, it would have all gone back to bedrooms in Toowong, St Lucia and Kenmore.

But McCormack's ambitions lay firmly with Custard. Rockfish Anna had been included on the third *Youngblood* compilation by Sydney label rooArt, and the band boasted two shiny new recruits in guitarist Matthew Strong and manager Adine Barton, then editing the *BUMS* (Brisbane Underground Music Scene) fanzine with Screamfeeder's Kellie Lloyd. The strictly local focus of *BUMS* catered to a niche only partially fulfilled by a mushrooming street press.[1]

> **Adine Barton:** I think it certainly helped tie the music community together a little bit, especially the younger bands . . . There's heaps of music management courses now, but back then, nobody had managers, nobody, it was all a big mystery. We used to get lots of phone calls from venues saying I want to put such and such band on, what local bands would suit playing with them, to bands ringing up saying I want to send my tape to a few record companies, how do I do it, can you give me any names. And even just seeing your friends' bands in print was a bit of a boost and an encouragement. It was needed then. Something like that wouldn't be anywhere near as important today.

After winning eight hours of recording time in an encouragement award from the Australian Academy of Music, Custard decided they were ready to make their first album. The result, *Buttercup/Bedford* – the dual title a result of McCormack accidentally asking both Moore and Thompson to design a cover for the release, giving both artists different names to work with – was enough for rooArt, who signed the band immediately after the CD's launch in May 1992. Released in a pressing of 500 once reserved for vinyl singles, *Buttercup*'s lightness of touch could hardly have been more refreshing. It was the striped sunlight sound all over again.

> **David McCormack:** We hated all that [post-Seattle] music.

> We'd say 'Oh, this is crap,' and put on our little jangly
> Go-Betweens record or They Might Be Giants' first album or
> something like that.

Following Shane Bruun's defection to form Hugbubble (to be replaced briefly by Gavin Herrenberg, later by Danny Plant), Custard's debut EP for rooArt was released in October. Including *Buttercup*'s standout title-track-of-sorts, Bedford, *Gastanked!* showcased McCormack's rapid growth as a songwriter and, especially, as a performer. Listening to the band was becoming a game: lyrics would be pilfered from unexpected sources (Satellite, for one, cherry-picked the Electric Prunes' acid classic I Had Too Much To Dream Last Night); riffs recycled in unfamiliar contexts. And although Custard wore their influences as openly as Screamfeeder, the band could not be contained by a single genre.

There was something else about Custard, too, underlined by the band's next EP, *Brisbane*, and its childlike cityscape artwork by Glenn Thompson: a mixture of self-deprecation and whimsy, born of a hick city that had somehow managed to host a Commonwealth Games and a World Expo, that before the recession had featured its own brand of white-shoe entrepreneurs, that was only just emerging from the shadows of a corrupt government. Out of such contradictions, somewhere in the early '90s, the term Brisvegas came into popular usage. The term gave many of the city's occupants a chance to feel they truly owned their town for the first time.

Adine Barton: Everyone expected Custard to move once they signed, everyone assumed it was just going to happen. And they considered it, they talked about it a lot, but decided that they'd probably break up within a week of all being poor, away from girlfriends and family and living in a house together . . . Plus I don't think David really wanted to leave, I think that was it more than anything – he liked living in Brisbane, he felt secure.

He's very family-oriented; he loves his mum and dad and his brother, and Brisbane was home, he didn't feel he needed to go anywhere.

Robert Forster returned to Brisbane in the winter of 1992, after three years secluded in the south of Germany with his new wife, Karin Baümler. His first solo album, *Danger In The Past*, had been recorded in Berlin with ring-ins from Nick Cave's band, the Bad Seeds. With a swag full of lighter-sounding songs that leaned naturally towards country, he wanted to make a 'smaller, boxier Brisbane record'.

Forster had felt uncomfortable on previous visits to his home town, finding little he could relate to. This time the atmosphere seemed more sympathetic, and he tested the waters with a few acoustic performances at the Zoo.

Robert Forster: The Zoo had only just started. I can't think of anything over the last 10 years, including Livid, that has done so much for Brisbane music as the Zoo, there's just no two ways about it . . . It's a venue run by really nice people; there's no greasy 50-year-old publican cruising around the room, no thugs in tuxedos . . . You'd just walk in there and relax.

Forster had made up his mind to record at Sunshine (formerly Window) Studios, where the Go-Betweens had cut their first singles. All he needed was a new set of musicians to play his songs. An old acquaintance, Rocking Horse's Warwick Vere, steered Forster down to the Queen's Arms Hotel in the Valley where COW had a residency. Moore, McCormack and Thompson were in a position to offer Forster more than just equipment and a rehearsal space.

Robert Forster: When we went over to practise they'd immediately get the bat and ball out and start playing backyard cricket, which Grant and I used to do with the Riptides! They

were all into Jonathan Richman . . . It was a little bit eerie,
how much it superimposed back on an earlier time. I felt like
phoning up Grant and saying, there are guys here who are just
like we were back in the late '70s.[2]

But Forster was not to be distracted. According to Glenn
Thompson, COW's rehearsals with Forster at Spring Hill
were 'relentless – he had a real holistic idea of what he
wanted'. Essentially, what Forster wanted was a genuine
band record: while COW's loose feel allowed his songs
plenty of room to breathe, the group had little previous
studio experience, and Forster needed them locked tight
behind him before venturing into Sunshine.

Released in June 1993, the resulting album was perhaps
Robert Forster's most fully realised work. Where *Danger In
The Past* was brooding, even solemn, *Calling From A Country
Phone* was bright and optimistic. And while McCormack's
impish guitar style highlighted the frequently droll lyrics,
the addition of boogie-woogie piano, violin and pedal steel
also lent the music a certain grandeur. On one song, I Want
To Be Quiet, Forster's domestic bliss became a sly comment
on a musical era:

> I want to be quiet
> That's what I need
> Not this constant volume that brings me to my knees

Robert Moore had imagined COW as a musical collective
similar to the Wild Bunch behind the first Massive Attack
album, where a virtual reserve bench of musicians would
be on call to play gigs or recordings. Often the band would
be joined on stage by backing vocalists the Sirloin Sisters,
twins Maureen and Suzie Hansen; at other times, former
Go-Between John Willsteed and occasional Queensland
Symphony Orchestra violinist John Bone would jump up
to add their own flourishes.[3] But while the shows were

magical, Custard's rising profile meant COW remained a distant second in McCormack's priorities.

> **David McCormack:** There was always resentment from the other bands, because Custard had the record deal and the marketing dollars and the touring revenue, but I always defaulted to that, because that was completely my baby. I came up with the name, I was singing, writing the songs, and it had this big industry machine behind it.

> **Bob Moore:** Custard were going down that very traditional four-piece band route, where they'd hop in a Tarago and drive to Sydney every weekend and drive back . . . They were starting to put records out, people were starting to throw some serious money at them.

There was some suspicion between the two bands: the older members of COW looked down on Custard as, in McCormack's words, 'kiddies' music', while Custard fretted about their leader becoming distracted. They need not have worried: as he admits, 'I'd just steal all the best ideas and put them in Custard.' McCormack's muse was freed by COW and *Country Phone,* and his assimilation of influences was crucial to the recording of Custard's first full-length album for rooArt, *Wahooti Fandango.*

Adine Barton left Brisbane, *BUMS* and Custard in early 1993. The band's new manager, the genial, slow-talking north Queenslander Dave Brown, was something of a father figure to the band. Having just lost a job in a tiling business, he had time on his hands, and he liked a smoke. 'Wahooti' was actually McCormack's pet name for pot; as manager, Brown was christened Big Chief Wahooti. He was fortunate to arrive as the band neared its peak.

Dave Brown: I just thought David was an amazing talent, and even though Custard weren't playing music that I was really into, they were the most consistent live band I'd ever seen in my life. I travelled around with them for two years and they would just do it every night, they were a superb live band. And the smaller the crowd was, the better the show they did.

The gigs had certainly become colourful affairs. Boys followed the band's penchant for Hawaiian shirts; girls dressed in day-glo and carried lunchboxes in place of handbags. Custard's sense of playfulness could not have been further removed from ripped denim and flannels. On the cover of *Wahooti Fandango,* the band's name is spelt out by a flamenco dancer twirling a lasso; on the back, the band appears on horseback, guitarist Matthew Strong in cowboy gear. The inner sleeve, however, contains a more telling clue to the musical contents within: lurking in the background of each portrait of the individual band members is a bottle of nitrous oxide.

Wahooti Fandango saw Custard's transformation from an engaging but lightweight guitar band to something altogether more exotic. The album zigzagged from thrash pop to cocktail jazz on the whim of the group's eccentric leader: on Singlette, McCormack paid comic tribute to Muppeteer Jim Henson; on the closing title track, an outrageous scat section is followed by a mock public service announcement. 'People of Australia,' McCormack declares, 'I have an important message!' – and, with a final tinkling of ivory, the album is over.

For press commitments leading up to the album's release in October 1994, a bright spark at rooArt came up with the idea of sending Custard to Bethany to be photographed with another Queensland institution, the deposed Joh Bjelke-Petersen. Mischievously informed that Custard played old-time country music, the then 84-year-old agreed with unexpected grace. The band was flanked by veteran writer Bob Ellis, hand-picked for the task of skewering the old enemy.

But Bjelke-Petersen called the party's bluff completely. After cheerfully posing for photos in front of his old peanut thrasher while at least one member discreetly held a bag of 'wahooti' over his head, he turned to the group. 'Tell me, tell me, you young fellows,' said the ageing warrior, talking straighter than he ever had during his 41 years in public office, 'did *you* think I was a fascist dictator?'

The band, astounded, was stumped for a reply. 'See, when a lot of these television people accuse me of that,' Joh continued blithely, 'I used to say to them well, if I am, I'm a very nice one.'[4]

> **David McCormack:** We were all armed to the teeth about how we were going to be super cool and give him hell, but it was like going to visit your grandparents. I found him funny. Bob Ellis was vehemently opposed and then when we were driving away he said, 'What a lovely old gentleman.'

Although not a major commercial success, *Wahooti Fandango* pushed Custard to the forefront of Australian music. Extensive Triple J support for two singles (the Casio-driven Pack Yr Suitcases and the more conventional Alone) boosted attendances dramatically at the band's rambunctious shows, where the group's force of personality usually won sceptics over. But the humour became a trap. A hair's breadth away from novelty, Pack Yr Suitcases (co-written, as were several of the band's singles, by McCormack's younger brother Dylan) saddled the band with a quirky image it never shook.

Like *Calling From A Country Phone*, *Wahooti Fandango* was recorded at Sunshine Studios, where producers Simon Holmes and Wayne Connolly had succeeded brilliantly in capturing Custard's essential joie de vivre. For the next album, however, rooArt's chequebook was open. The band responded like any other group of young men in their early 20s with a collectively short attention span. Custard's great rock & roll swindle was at hand.

> **David McCormack:** Someone said, 'Who do you want to record it?' I said, 'I like the first Frank Black album, let's get Eric Drew Feldman.' And they said, 'OK, Eric, where do you want to record?' And Eric said, 'I want to record in San Francisco, because I live there, let's do it at Hyde Street where Creedence Clearwater Revival recorded.' The whole thing cost $140,000. It was recoupable, but it didn't matter because we got out of our contract! My theory always was to spend every cent you can, and then just walk away from the flaming bridges afterwards.

Custard had met keyboard player and producer Eric Feldman while touring in support of another of McCormack's heroes, former Pixie Frank Black. Feldman had a long list of credits and contacts, and Frank Black himself had been impressed enough by Custard to loan McCormack three of his guitars for the recording of what was to become *Wisenheimer*. If the album lacked its predecessor's rambling charm, it also contained some brilliant material (the woozy, beautiful art-rock of Columbus is perhaps Custard's greatest moment).

The obvious standout, Apartment, was the first single. It was a disappointing choice for Dave Brown, who reasoned that by leading with their best punch, excellent follow-up singles such as Lucky Star and Sunset Strip were rendered anti-climactic after the album's release in late 1995.

> **Dave Brown:** It's always my bitch that they released Apartment at the wrong time, and that was the difference between *Wisenheimer* being a successful album versus a really successful album. It was the first single and it was too good for that, without a doubt in the world. It should have been released second or third; I think that gets proven every time.

The cost of *Wisenheimer*'s recording was not only financial. Drummer Danny Plant, who along with Matthew Strong had given Custard considerable sonic muscle, was sacked soon after the band's return home. Strong was lucky not to join Plant in exile.

David McCormack: Matthew and Danny went home two or three weeks before it was finished. We went to San Francisco to make a good record in Hyde Street Studios, and those guys were just out of it all the time . . . Green Day were recording upstairs, and they were doing bucket bongs all day and playing pool.

The rot was setting in. Dave Brown, who had cautioned the band against their American adventure and had not accompanied his charges to San Francisco, soon found himself on the outer too. Where he favoured a steady approach, the rest of the band was happy to take everything it was offered, albeit perhaps for different reasons: while McCormack was content to milk the machine while he could, the non-songwriting members had more to gain if Custard cracked the big time. When the band was wooed by better connected Sydney management, Brown's handshake deal counted for little.

Inevitably, friendships were strained. Although Bob Moore never held higher aspirations for COW than to play a few gigs, he understandably bridled at his band's relegation to second-string status. The band's sole album, *Beard* – recorded over two weekends in September 1995 – barely rated a footnote by the time of its independent release almost a year later. When Glenn Thompson was roped into Custard to replace Danny Plant, COW slowly faded away.

Bob Moore: We were quite dumb-arsed, I knew that. COW was important to what was happening in Spring Hill, but I was very aware that didn't mean it was relevant to the rest of Australia. Whereas Custard did have something to say to the rest of Australia, and they had the drive and the ambition to do it . . . COW got everything it deserved, both good and bad, and I don't regret anything about it.

Although the Spring Hill clubhouse had seen the birth of upwards of 20 bands, facilitating the growth of dozens of musicians, the scene had also become insular. Groups such as the Melniks and Adults Today traced ever-diminishing circles of twee humour and perfunctory songwriting. The title of the Melniks' debut, *Have You Ever Noticed That Gordon From Sesame Street Looks Exactly Like Errol From Hot Chocolate* – an attempt to qualify for *The Guinness Book Of Records* under the non-existent category of longest album title – reflected a movement running out of ideas. When the McCormacks sold the property in late 1996, many of the bands simply evaporated overnight.

At the same time, BMG had bought out rooArt, with a promise to take Custard to the next level. Sent on a 40-date American tour with the like-minded Presidents of the USA, the band reconvened with Feldman to cut their third album in Easley Studios, Memphis.

If BMG had hoped to capitalise on Custard's likeable public face, they had reckoned without the group's increasingly headstrong frontman. *We Have The Technology* caught McCormack in an ornery mood. Heavily under the influence of Pavement's *Wowee Zowee*, also made at Easley Studios, McCormack's songs were growing ever more tangential and self-referential. And consequently, the music – as a review of another Brisbane band had earlier suggested – 'disappeared up its own arse'.

David McCormack: I remember Eric Drew Feldman sitting me down in some diner saying, 'Look, you've got to have a radio single, you've just got to have one . . . Go as crazy as you want, but you need three or four radio songs so the band can keep going, you can't just ignore that stuff,' and he was right. But I was just like, 'No, man, we're fucking artists!' It's maturity . . . If I could go back, there would be a lot of decisions I would make differently.

The release of Thompson's Music Is Crap as a single in February 1998 painted the band into a corner. Although Custard's final album *Loverama* included their biggest hit, Girls Like That (Don't Go For Guys Like Us), both songs effectively drew the line under the band's career.

David McCormack: We were going around in circles. Everyone had this idea of what Custard was and there was no way to break out of that. Girls Like That was as far as you can take the ironic pop love song; you just can't go any further than that.

A best-of compilation, *Goodbye Cruel World*, was released by BMG in June 2000. It was a fitting tribute to a brilliant but maddening group who, for all their debt to the Go-Betweens, in the end more closely resembled a very different Australian band: Mental As Anything.

CHAPTER FIFTEEN

black ticket day

After its enforced exit stage right from the University of Queensland campus in July 1989, Triple Zed had relocated to a tiny office block opposite the local ABC headquarters on Coronation Drive, Toowong. Like a teenager leaving home for the first time, the station faced an uphill struggle to survive in the real world. Initially awash with funds in the wake of its struggle with the student union, the cash quickly dried up as Triple Zed confronted the monthly reality of a rental bill.

The office studios were still being constructed when Triple Zed took over the lease, meaning the station was initially forced to broadcast out of a caravan on Mt Coot-tha, next to the station's transmitter. The Caravan of Love, as it was sarcastically known, prefigured the cramped quarters on Coronation Drive. Worse, when the station began broadcasting from Toowong itself, on-air sound quality was noticeably diminished, with the Toowong Village shopping centre blocking the low-set building's line of sight to the Mt Coot-tha transmitter.

Dave Lennon: We were slogging our guts out and we didn't really know where the station was heading. We were in this really small office and it just felt claustrophobic. You'd think, I've got to get out of here, and you'd go out and there's

Coronation Drive, with this big blue beast of a shopping centre
behind you. At least at the uni you could step outside and walk
around the gardens.

Triple Zed's departure from campus contributed to a gradual
loss of identity on several fronts. Denied the resources and
ready pool of subscribers it had enjoyed at the university, the
defeat of the National Party had also inadvertently deprived
the station of its common enemy and, in many respects, its
reason for existence. With no warm inner glow left to sell,
meetings were held attempting to define Triple Zed's place in
the new order.[1]

As Triple J continued its roll-out during 1990, a power
struggle erupted over music programming. When bands
Triple Zed had broken were elevated to stardom by the
national broadcaster, the station looked to the more abrasive
end of the musical spectrum to shore up its alternative
credentials. Custard – arguably the most original of local
acts – was one band considered too poppy to qualify.
Typically, David McCormack made light of the situation
with these lines from Fantastic Plastic:

> I wish that Triple Zed would play us
> I know in their heart of hearts they could
> I think they used to like us
> But now they don't seem to like us
> And I can't figure what went wrong

At the core of Triple Zed's difficulties was its failure
to adapt to changing circumstances. It still clung to its
antiquarian collective model of consensus decision-making
and, since a consensus could almost never be achieved, the
station became paralysed. The poisonous atmosphere was
further destabilised by the infiltration of harder drugs. Phil
Parker, a long-term volunteer cajoled back to the station in
1990 after leaving in despair years earlier, remembers the
Toowong years as 'evil'.

Phil Parker: There was a lot of smack floating around . . . It went from pot to powders, and that's when things started getting dark. Triple Zed was a place where people went when there was nowhere else to go. There were people living at the station, forever going out to the toilets – there would be vomit in the basins, all those kind of giveaways.

Parker, however, was made of stern stuff. He had initially lobbed in from Melbourne in 1979, subscribing to Triple Zed at an equally difficult time in the station's history.

Phil Parker: They had a collective meeting to decide whether Triple Zed should continue, and I wanted to get involved. It was so ugly, this meeting; I was with a friend of mine and as we left I said, 'I don't know what I'll do if Triple Zed dies.' And this voice from the shadows said, 'Triple Zed will never die.'

I looked over, and it was this guy sitting on a Harley, one of those big chopper bikes. He had his feet up on the handlebars and his head on the backrest, just in repose – righto mate, whatever you say! So it has had that clemency all the way through, and by the grace of God it continues.

Triple Zed's financial saviour was right under its nose. While so-called Market Days had been an annual fundraising feature of the station since at least 1982 (complete with novelties including TV smashing and AM radio-throwing competitions), the events were otherwise little more than an adjunct to October radiothons, with merchandise stalls set up at the back of the station's headquarters. Bands did not feature regularly until 1988. The revitalisation of the live scene would change all that.

Triple Zed had not always fulfilled its obligations to local music over the years – at various times, announcers had needed to be coerced into playing music from their home town – and by 1992 contact with musicians was next to non-existent, despite the commencing of live-to-air

performances at the station and new bands such as the
Dreamkillers selling out venues in the city.

> **Phil Parker:** The earth must have passed through a photon
> belt or something. I hadn't seen such a level of musicianship in
> Brisbane bands up until then. I went to Rock Against Work one
> Friday afternoon and there was a band playing Led Zeppelin
> note for note, which sounds clichéd now, but to hear it at the
> time was phenomenal. It wasn't until years later I realised it
> was Powderfinger.

Having scratched around for a suitable Market Day
venue after falling out with the student union, Triple Zed
settled briefly on Captain Burke Park, under the Story
Bridge at Kangaroo Point. With promotions coordinator
Belinda McPherson taking it upon herself to rebuild the
station's links with local bands, the Promised Land Market
Day of 14 March 1992 proved a turning point. Boasting a
festival-sized line-up of 13 acts including Custard and the
Dreamkillers, the event attracted 3000 fans and turned
a miraculous $6000 profit, most of it through cheap beer
sales.[2]

The result was a watershed for Triple Zed, which was
behind in rent and facing the expiration of its two-year
lease on the Toowong studios in July. Desperately searching
for new premises, the station was saved by another
remarkable stroke of good fortune when it was invited to
move into run-down but relatively spacious premises at
291 St Pauls Terrace in downtown Fortitude Valley. The
building was owned by the Search Foundation, set up
by the Communist Party in order to divest its assets as it
wound down its Australian operations.

In April 1993 Parker was joined at Triple Zed by two more
voices from the past. Jim Beatson was at a loose end, and he
persuaded former station journalist Jon Baird to accompany

him back to the station, initially with the aim of restoring its proud but ailing newsroom. With not even a telephone recorder booth to conduct interviews, 'news' consisted of two weekday shifts with announcers reading chunks of newspaper text. It was the best the station could muster.

> **Jim Beatson:** When I arrived the station had 700 subscriptions and it was going down. It had seemingly no audience. One of the station's staff, and the person shall remain nameless, actually told me that the fact we had no listeners was proof that Triple Zed was on the cutting edge. I thought it was a scandal.

Dismayed by the 'scruffy, tacky mess' before them, Beatson and Baird persuaded the collective to lash out on the construction of two interview booths while recruiting a new team of volunteers, mainly university students, to inject some life into the station. There remained no shortage of material to occupy journalists in Queensland: the premier, Wayne Goss, had disappointed many with a conservative approach to social reform, and police corruption, though less brazen, had hardly vanished overnight. But Triple Zed by then was its own worst enemy.

> **Jim Beatson:** There was definitely dealing going on at the station. I remember on one occasion a teacher rang me – we had a number of high school students there on work placement – and quietly warned me that a student had been offered drugs for sale.

Realising the futility of trying to rebuild a functioning newsroom inside a broadcaster that had lost touch with its listeners, Beatson approached the Queensland University of Technology to undertake audience research. The results threatened to tear the station apart for good. In the end, a sanitised version of the report needed to be prepared.

Phil Parker: The QUT survey was very much kept under wraps. People left over that, saying, 'What's so bad about this bit of paper that you can't tell us exactly how it is?' In the end they did a summary of it, and people were given an overview of what the feedback was for each announcer, and a lot of the stuff was just devastating.

Jim Beatson: Clearly there were a lot of people that absolutely should not have been announcers, they didn't have the first clue, and training them wouldn't have done much for them. It was probably the wrong decision, but any radio station has to continue, and if you sack a third of your announcers – or a third of your announcers walk out on the spot – you need to be able to replace them.

While undergoing this painful self-examination, Triple Zed also found itself wrestling with the logistics of running what had become a biannual festival, financed on alcohol and powered by a skeleton of overworked volunteers. It was an increasingly unhappy equation. Although the station was making enough money from Market Day to stay afloat, it soon found itself at loggerheads with the Brisbane City Council over the state of the venues after the event. In March 1993 the event moved from Captain Burke to Albert Park in the city; by 1994 that too was off limits. While volunteers worked themselves into the ground to put the event on, too few had the energy or the inclination to deal with the aftermath the next day. Lord Mayor Jim Soorley had reason to feel especially aggrieved.

Jim Beatson: I discovered that Soorley hated Triple Zed because the year before, when Triple Zed had sought his permission to hold Market Day, he'd knocked them back on the grounds that the crowd had left broken glass everywhere, which they had, and damaged the gardens, which they had . . . The station regarded that as completely unreasonable and called on their listeners to ring Soorley and tell him what they thought

of him, and so Soorley received a whole lot of abusive phone
calls, which made him dislike Triple Zed intensely, and frankly
I could understand where he was coming from.

Along with conducting research into Triple Zed's
audience, the QUT group also surveyed 800 Market Day
patrons. The results were equally depressing. What the
station naively envisaged as a free show designed to reward
the loyalty of its subscribers was being overrun by what
Phil Parker, a teetotaller, dubbed 'the 16,000-legged lager
monster'.

Jim Beatson: I wrote Soorley a letter and apologised, went
and saw him and tried to patch up that problem. His line was
that we needed to fence off the event, and we knew that would
cost a lot of money, so the research was designed to find out
how people would feel about a cover charge. And the results
were quite shocking. The great majority of them didn't listen
to Triple Zed, and when asked the question 'Would you care
if Triple Zed closed down tomorrow?', the only thing that
concerned them was the end of Market Day, because it was
a great piss-up, a great atmosphere, and it was unbelievably
cheap.

Triple Zed gradually improved its position, progressively
replacing several announcers and recording a steady
rise in subscriptions. Most importantly, Beatson began
negotiating to buy the St Pauls Terrace premises from the
Search Foundation, a move that eventually gave Triple Zed
a previously undreamt-of financial asset.

Jim Beatson: A number of people from the Communist Party
or children of members of the Communist Party were very
much aware that Triple Zed had done a lot of work that [they]
largely approved of. So we persuaded them that the best
thing they could do was sell us the building . . . Of course
we had an enormous amount of fundraising to do. We had

to present books to the state government and the books hadn't been done for three years! So we had to put a huge amount of effort into getting Triple Zed's hopeless collection of shoeboxes full of papers into accounts that could be presented to an auditor.

Beatson's efforts to revive the station's fortunes were not universally appreciated. Some correctly saw their positions threatened. Others, in a throwback to the early years, viewed his attempts to modernise Triple Zed as a sell-out of its core values. Above all, his belief that he knew what was best for the station – a natural result, perhaps, of his decorated place in its history – alienated the collective, which he held in contempt.

Dave Lennon: There was tension, but I think Jim brought a lot of that on himself. Jim has this attitude where he feels that what he's doing is right and to hell with everyone else and their ideas, and in a collective environment that arrogance got a lot of people's backs up. In some ways Jim's conservative too, so there was tension there.

Jim Beatson: I'm committed to the progressive side of politics very strongly, but there were a lot of complaints that the politics at the station was truly infantile. It was the infantile left at its most embarrassing, and a lot of the audience disliked it intensely, because they felt they were being patronised by people who knew less about politics than themselves.

A few were motivated by nastier impulses. When Beatson moved a motion proposing those at the station with drug dependencies be relieved of positions handling money, he found the locks of his car jammed full of Super Glue. Exhausted and dispirited, he left the station to its fate in early 1995.

* *

In October 1994, Market Day shifted again, this time to Musgrave Park in South Brisbane. The survey results had made the decision to fence the event a relatively easy one, with non-subscribers charged a token $5. But the additional income failed to prevent costs from blowing out. Upwards of 30 bands were needed to satisfy a growing audience, whose thirst for alcohol was matched by a proportional need for more toilets and more security.

Triple Zed's fractious relationship with the council meant every Market Day was preceded by increasingly onerous negotiations, as each event became literally more eventful. When an extra Market Day was held at the University of Queensland to coincide with orientation week in February 1995, summer rains forced the intended homecoming party to relocate from the Great Court to a concrete multi-storey car park. And when the regular event was moved back from its usual March date to 29 April, the oncoming winter chill resulted in punters imperilling the station's bond money by lighting fires around Musgrave Park when the sun went down.

But most ominous of all was the steadily increasing police presence. On 28 October 1995 a weekend event intended to celebrate the Roxy nightclub's 10th birthday went awry. With the venue holding only 1500 people, Triple Zed had proposed the closure of the adjoining Alfred Street in order to accommodate a second stage. When the council decreed at the last minute that the street was to reopen at 6pm instead of the advertised time of 10pm, the station was faced with a hostile force intent on dispersing a large and inebriated crowd. But the 20 arrests that followed proved to be a mere precursor to the debacle of the following year.

In February 1996 Wayne Goss' Labor Government fell in extraordinary circumstances. After two terms in office, Goss had held onto a single-seat majority in the parliament following a stiff rebuke in the July 1995 state election. His fate was sealed when a fresh election was ordered in the disputed Townsville-based seat of Mundingburra. Sensitive to the whims of conservative Queenslanders, Goss had run his government like a machine, basing his campaign on economic management with a lash of law and order.

But law and order was an issue on which Labor could never win. In the run-up to the Mundingburra election, the opposition, led by the Nationals' Rob Borbidge, signed a secret pact with the police union in exchange for its support in the campaign. The so-called Memorandum of Understanding committed the coalition to winding back the powers of the Criminal Justice Commission, the anti-corruption body set up in the wake of the Fitzgerald Inquiry. It also gave the police union the right to veto the appointment of a police commissioner and named six assistant commissioners the union wanted removed from their posts.[3]

If there was nothing legally improper about the deal, it certainly flew in the face of the state's post-Fitzgerald reforms, which the coalition referred to as an experiment. When the Liberal Party won the Mundingburra election, the reformed conservative coalition unexpectedly found itself back in power, forming a minority government with the support of a conservative independent. Moreover, the pole position of the police in Queensland's political life had been restored: the police union revealed its 'understanding' with the coalition by trumpeting its victory in its members' newsletter.

Despite increasing difficulties staging Market Day, Musgrave Park seemed a natural home for the event. Utilised mainly by the Aboriginal community, with whom Triple Zed maintained a cordial relationship, the park had been neglected for years by the council. Peter Rohweder, who began coordinating Market Days for the station with the pleasantly uneventful Zed-O-Mitter event of 23 March

1996, found the council relatively amenable to Musgrave
Park's use after the station's barring from Albert Park in
the city.

> **Peter Rohweder:** It was a crappy park anyway – there was
> hardly any turf, they'd lay the turf once a year, there were lots
> of rocks. Usually when we went through it we'd pick up all the
> glass that was already there from broken beer bottles, so we'd
> be doing them a favour by cleaning it out.

Rohweder had also built a sound working relationship
with Sergeant John Vincent and Constable Mark Simpson
from the West End police station. Overseeing one of the
most cosmopolitan populations in the city, with a high
number of Aboriginal, homeless and mentally ill persons,
West End police were known for taking a somewhat more
discretionary approach to law enforcement than their city
counterparts. They were also no stranger to rock festivals:
for several years the Livid Festival had been held without
incident in Davies Park at the bottom of Jane Street.

With Vincent away on holiday, Simpson took over the
brief for the spring Market Day, Cybernana, set for 19
October. Having already liaised with Rohweder for Zed-O-
Mitter in March, Simpson foresaw nothing untoward in
the lead-up to the event. Subcontracted by Triple Zed to
oversee police operations on the day, he prepared his usual
operational order confirming arrangements. No one can
readily explain why, on the morning of the event, he had
matters taken abruptly out of his hands.

> **Mark Simpson:** The internal management of the police
> service . . . They have their own little empires. So I was
> there on the day, but not in the capacity I was supposed to
> be. They changed things, brought somebody in that hadn't
> been involved to run the event, with no experience of doing it
> previously.

Peter Rohweder: The police force is all about rank and file. So we had been dealing with Mark Simpson, a constable, and then suddenly we were dealing with someone else who was above him. We'd say, 'Oh, we're talking to Mark Simpson,' and he'd say, 'Yeah, but he's below me, you're talking to me now.'

The day dawned fine and hot. The crowd poured through the gates, more than Triple Zed had anticipated. The line-up of bands, featuring a young and raw Something For Kate, was tougher than Zed-O-Mitter, which had kept things mellow with headlining performances by rising local folk-based bands the Toothfaeries and Isis. As the heat began to rise and the beer consumption increased, queues formed for the porta-loos. A few who couldn't wait were charged with indecent exposure when they made the mistake of urinating up against a large Moreton Bay fig that happened to be next to the police command post.

The number of police initially present on the day is contested. Simpson is adamant his team was under-resourced to deal with the large crowd, beginning with just two mounted units and five members of the Public Safety Response Team, along with a few officers from the West End station, of which he was one. Others, however, noticed the police presence early on. Phil Parker, working behind the bar, claims never to have seen so many, including plain-clothed detectives. Tam Patton, whose band John Lee Spider had performed earlier in the afternoon, was also spooked.

Tam Patton: Everybody commented, and I myself noticed at the time, that there was a really unusually strong police presence. There's always a police presence at any kind of festival event, Market Days perhaps stronger than usual, but in this case it just seemed abnormal.

The discrepancy in accounts may be explained by the appearance of the PSRT. Effectively the riot squad, the PSRT are easily identified, distinguished by head-squeezing

baseball caps in place of hats. Far from providing
reassurance, the mere presence of the PSRT communicated
to both Market Day organisers and patrons that the police
were anticipating trouble or, at worst, intent on making
their own. Other witnesses reported seeing PSRT members
unloading helmets, shields and batons adjacent to the park
in Russell Street.[4]

Communications were breaking down. Terry O'Connor,
Triple Zed's security coordinator, was under the impression
the PSRT would only be called in the event of a major
incident. Rohweder was more sanguine, and although he
describes the police presence as 'really uncomfortable', he
remained preoccupied with keeping the event running.
Simpson's operational order states the PSRT would be on
site for the duration of the function.[5] Paranoia – always an
active ingredient in relations between police and Triple
Zed – rose like the stench of urine around the base of the
fig trees.

By late afternoon a monstrous anvil of cloud was
billowing in the west.

At the height of festivities, the crowd climbed to over 8000
people. Rubbish was ground into the weary turf; dust
kicked up from the mosh pit in front of the stages. The
16,000-legged lager monster was alive and well.

> **Mark Simpson:** There was a lady in a porta-loo and a couple
> of jokers decided it might be fun to tip it over while she was
> inside. When people make complaints of a certain nature, it
> doesn't leave a lot of options but to arrest people, take them
> away and speak to them about their behaviour, and if they're
> intoxicated as well you've got to wait until they sober up before
> you can do that.

Simpson claims another much more unpleasant element
had permeated the crowd: a group of skinheads were

harassing the small group of Aboriginal people who made the park their home. The skins had turned up at Market Day before, notably in 1993 at Albert Park where they found themselves on the wrong side of both the bands and the crowd, but their presence at Cybernana is disputed. John Birmingham, whose journalism had already made him persona non grata with the Queensland Police Service, later reported on the day's events for *Rolling Stone*.

> **John Birmingham:** Well, I interviewed 36 people and that's the first I've ever heard of [skinheads]. I did hear about arrests all the way through the afternoon, mostly for indecent exposure and drunkenness and basically bad attitude.

> **Mark Simpson:** The crowd only see two blue uniforms escorting somebody out who's screaming and yelling to get lost and other language . . . You can't stop and explain to a drunken crowd why you've done what you've just done, it doesn't work that way. So that turned the crowd [against us].

When station journalist Brendan Greenhill arrived for his bar shift in the gathering darkness shortly after 6.30pm, antagonism between the police and crowd was reaching critical mass. He was greeted by the sight of two burly officers frogmarching a reveller out of the gates and into a waiting van. Told to forget about his shift, he was sent home to pick up his tape recorder and wide-band receiver instead.

Thunder began rumbling across the field. With rain on the way, most of the crowd started to drift off.

It took 25 minutes for Greenhill to walk back to his Highgate Hill home. As the rain began to tumble down, he paused under an awning to gather his wits before making the return journey. Tuning his receiver into the police channel, he realised there was going to be no waiting out the approaching storm. The call for reinforcements had already gone out. From his position on the hill, Greenhill could see the red and blue strobes of police cars descending on the venue.

> **Brendan Greenhill:** I heard them saying things were getting rowdy, there was something going on, so I legged it back down there and as I got to the corner of the park, that was when the rain *really* came down . . . I had pulled out my tape recorder as soon as I got there and I was narrating what was going on, but unbeknownst to me at the time the water had inundated the tape recorder and snuffed it out. There was only about 20 seconds worth of material.

Alarmed by the rapid downturn of events, Triple Zed staff decided to close the bar. This caused a further complication. To circumvent public drinking laws, the station was selling tickets that were then exchanged for alcohol, and the beer tent was crammed with punters anxious to get what they'd paid for. Along with the doof tent – which throbbed to the constant pulse of techno away from the main stages – it was the only effective shelter in the park. When the storm hit, wet bodies piled in.

Others were happy to take advantage of the elements. As the rain hammered down, a few revellers began sliding gleefully through the mud. Perhaps less mindful of a festival tradition dating back to Woodstock, 1969, the police dived in after the culprits. In a later CJC report into the melee, police witnesses justified the arrests by saying the revellers' behaviour caused 'annoyance' to others in the crowd and 'frightened the horses'.[6]

> **Phil Parker:** This torrential rain started coming in on a really sharp angle under the flaps of the tent. And the next thing all these people started coming over the canteen, which is a big no-no. I was trying to push these people back, and there were people screaming and panicking. I thought they were just getting out of the rain . . . I looked out and the first thing I saw was this mounted police horse pig-rooting.

Tam Patton: At that point the police just waded in. People who were rolling around in the mud were being held in strangleholds. And there was a lot of water gathering by then; there was enough water on the ground for people to drown in.

To the police, however, *they* were the ones under attack. If the mudlarks didn't succeed in frightening the horses, the sudden hail of cans certainly did. According to Simpson, one of the steeds was deliberately gashed by torn aluminium as outnumbered police were set upon by enraged punters. With the bands having long since left the stages to avoid electrocution, the bar closed and reinforcements rushing from the city, Cybernana 1996 was all over bar the riot, regardless of who was actually doing the rioting.

And yet few were moving. In the confusion of darkness and teeming rain, most of the remaining crowd – probably no more than 1500 – failed to comprehend what was going on. Many were still waiting to redeem their beer tickets. The rain had made the public address system unsafe to use. Brendan Greenhill charged to the bar area, aware that more police in riot gear were on the way, intent on clearing the park.

Brendan Greenhill: The worst part about it, I must admit, was running around inside the tent and saying to people, it's time to go, the bar is shut, thanks for coming, the police are on the way. People were arguing, saying, 'How can they do this?' . . . They were getting upset with us, and we were saying, 'Look, come [to the station] later and Triple Zed will fix you up, we'll redeem your tickets in cash.' No one ever did present a beer ticket back to us, but that's what we were saying – 'The coppers are coming right behind you to get your skull cracked and you want to argue with me about 12 bucks? Get out and save your skin!'

It was now 8.20pm. Over voluminous rain, the thunder was echoed by the sound of batons drumming on riot shields. The reinforcements had arrived in all their fury. Pivoting from near the centre of the park, the police line swept through the beer tent first. Some – finally getting the full picture of what was going on – made their way hurriedly to the exits. Most of the younger members of the crowd had no experience of being caught in the middle of a major police action.

> **Tam Patton:** I was at the Livid Festival in December 1989, and I remember the great cheer when [Peter Walsh] walked onto the stage and said Wayne Goss was the new premier of Queensland, you know, that was a pretty powerful moment. And I think people after that probably had become a little complacent – this wasn't supposed to happen anymore.

Greenhill, savvy enough to stay behind the police line, was still attempting to document the action, barking the unfolding events into his useless tape recorder. As the police began a second sweep through the area, this time pushing through the doof tent with batons flying, he caught sight of something new.

> **Brendan Greenhill:** There were these two gentlemen in camouflage gear, and I thought, jeez, where have these guys come from, they've been doing bush survival techniques! Then I had another look and I could see clearly on their arms the letters MP – military police.

The presence of five military police among the reinforcements was largely a product of circumstance. With their flock out for a night on the town, the MPs had been cruising the city with civilian police officers, then standard procedure so as to deal in-house with any army personnel who got out of hand. But when the call went out from Musgrave Park, the MPs found themselves along for the ride.

According to Terry O'Gorman, President of the Australian Council for Civil Liberties, it marked the first time since the 1976 raid on the hippie commune at Cedar Bay that the military had been employed in a civilian operation.[7]

> **Brendan Greenhill:** There was this fellow, they had three uniformed blokes onto him and they couldn't get him, he obviously had a bit of fight in him . . . Anyway, the brawl kept happening, it got worse and worse, and they finally pinned him down. But the person who was in the best position to apply the handcuffs was the military policeman, and I saw him do that.

In the final wash-up, 72 people were arrested. Within two hours radio bulletins around Australia were buzzing with the news of the riot in West End. Triple Zed, as ever, had been quick to mobilise its resources while under attack. Greenhill, Jon Baird and ex-Parameter Tony Kneipp inundated the media, pushing the line that, once again, Triple Zed and its audience had been victimised and harassed by the police. The press corps fell on the claims with relish, unable to resist a story that seemed cut from the cloth of Queensland's past.

But times had changed. On 21 October, Queensland Police Service and Triple Zed representatives met with the former premier, Russell Cooper, back in his old job of police minister. Cooper – who not 12 months before had, as shadow minister, signed the aforementioned Memorandum of Understanding that was by then the subject of a protracted CJC inquiry – astounded everyone by pointing out at a press conference that he wanted to see Market Day happen again, asking his horrified force to work with Triple Zed to ensure the next event went smoothly.[8]

But Triple Zed received little joy when they made their own formal complaint to the CJC. The commission's investigation exonerated the police, dismissing the station's claims that they had been subjected to excessive force. Noting the police's counter-claims that they, too, had been the victims of assaults, the report added that the crowd's conduct fell under the legal definition of an 'unlawful assembly': a riotous one, in fact. Further, no substantial injuries had been documented by Triple Zed, the worst being a chipped tooth on the part of a station worker. Specific allegations of assault were dismissed on the grounds that complainants had been unable to identify their alleged attackers. The suggestion that some police officers had deliberately removed their name badges was a difficult one to substantiate, as the CJC report dryly acknowledged:

> In relation to other complainants who alleged that police officers refused to give their names, as they were unable to identify the officers in question, this matter could not be pursued any further.[9]

The military conducted its own investigation into the presence of its officers. Its report to the CJC inquiry remains confidential. While the army denied any suggestion its officers arrested citizens over whom they had no legal jurisdiction, spokesperson Lieutenant Colonel John Weiland confirmed two weeks after the event that his men had no purpose being where they were.

On 18 October 1997 Triple Zed hosted the Zed Bubble Market Day, this time back at Musgrave Park. Tightly controlled, the day went off without a hitch, and here the event stayed for the next three years, moving back to Davies Park in West End in late 2000 before spiralling production costs finally forced a hiatus. The last Market Day – Bananageddon – was held in October 2002.

CHAPTER SIXTEEN

the human jukebox

With the exception of Festival/Mushroom Records, the major record companies in Australia are Sydney-based branch offices of their overseas masters. Their Brisbane outposts are the suckers at the end of the tentacles. Charged mainly with looking after local promotions and distribution, the outposts can only recommend bands, not sign them. Consequently they had shown no interest in the city's underground scene during the 1970s and '80s. The serious groups all moved to Sydney anyway.

When the scene began to explode in the early '90s, however, the industry's antenna began to quiver. A&R men (and they were all men) began flying into Brisbane from Sydney. Warner Music's Michael Parisi was one of them. With a brief to tap into the alternative music boom, Parisi understood the DIY ethos that underpinned the hitherto overlooked Brisbane scene. His pitch to Regurgitator was simple: complete creative control.

Regurgitator were in the right place at the right time. Record companies are far more comfortable following trends than instigating them. When Nirvana's *Nevermind* ushered underground music into the mainstream, the music industry was caught further behind than usual. While most of the acts signed in the wake of the band's gargantuan success were pallid imitations, the majors also seemed happy to throw a few more adventurous artists against the wall, just to see what stuck.

> **Paul Curtis:** When we decided to sign to a major, the thing that was uppermost in our minds was that it had to stay somehow real; i.e., we wanted lots of room to do our own thing. What worked in the band's favour was, at the time, Warner didn't have an Australian roster, and [A&R head] Mark Pope and Michael Parisi had been brought in to get it working. So we were their first signing, and it was approached somewhat naively even on their part.

Parisi's bosses were certainly queasy. When he played the homemade video for I Like It Like That to Warner's annual conference, the initial response was horrified silence. The song was, on the surface, an ugly wall of noise. Parisi heard the noise all right, but also the killer hook that set Regurgitator apart from his earlier interest, Pangaea. Regurgitator matched Pangaea's stylistic and visual appeal with the added bonus of songs that, he hoped, could be translated onto radio.

It was the hook that Pangaea, for all the excitement they generated on stage, had lacked. When both Parisi and Ben Ely shifted their priorities to Regurgitator, Ely's old bandmates were gutted.

> **Dave Atkins:** It really hit Jim [Sinclair] hardest. He thought his only train was Pangaea, and when Ben said that's enough, Jim thought he'd taken his whole thing away from him. I felt that as well. I'd put seven years into the band – I'd left the [conservatorium] for it, left a whole lot of things that I wanted to do because I could see Pangaea going somewhere. But obviously Ben thought he could do better with Regurgitator. We didn't have that commercial edge.

Born to a Vietnamese mother and fifth-generation Australian

father in Sydney, 1973, Quan Yeomans' family relocated to Brisbane in 1986. Picking up the guitar, his early musical influences were traditional ones: Hendrix, Led Zeppelin, Cream. (One high school band was named the Crunge, after the heavy funk number on Zeppelin's *Houses Of The Holy*.) Around the house, though, it was straight pop: 'The only records I remember listening to are Fleetwood Mac and Abba.'

Politically indifferent in his teenage years, Yeomans' awakening came in 1992, when he travelled overseas for the first time, accompanying his academic father to the World Economic Forum in Rio de Janeiro. The experience was profoundly influential, shaping Yeomans' attitude towards the music industry as the mouthpiece of global capitalism.

> **Quan Yeomans:** I was quite negative towards signing with Warner, because it was so fast, and I was always a bit sceptical about that sort of thing. The Rio experience was what made it all click . . . I'd heard all this information about how the world works on a global economic level, stuff that no one told me about when I was living in Australia . . . I felt like a hypocrite.

Yeomans' concerns were not shared by his band-mates. Drummer Martin Lee, who had been playing in Brisbane bands for a decade, was an advocate of the great rock & roll swindle, happy to take whatever a record company was gullible enough to offer. And while Ely seemed content just to be playing music, he was certainly aware of Regurgitator's commercial potential. As manager, Paul Curtis found himself walking a tightrope between his band and Warner, all the while wrestling with his own conscience.

> **Paul Curtis:** I remember at one of the first meetings with Warner, I was sitting there quietly, taking it all in, and suddenly Mark Pope turns around and says, 'Hang on, what does Paul Curtis have to say about this? If he's so anti-corporate and

hates record labels so much, we'd like to know if he's going to stay involved.' Which put me right on the spot.

Regurgitator's signing to Warner was a logical extension of the contradictions inherent within the group. Working from within the belly of the corporate beast deepened the irony at the heart of a band that, from the name down, was designed as a reflection of popular culture devouring itself from the inside out. In Curtis' words, 'The band calling itself Regurgitator should have clearly stated that this was not going to be a normal kind of approach.'

> **Quan Yeomans:** I always think of the band as a tool for understanding pop music and understanding music in general. In that regard I think of it as more of an interpretive form of art than actually real art. It's like a dead form of art.

With the deal inked, Regurgitator decided to broadcast its affiliations to the world. Egged on by Lee, the band's debut self-titled EP featured the famous Warner Brothers' logo emblazoned on the back. 'They didn't let us use Bugs Bunny,' Ely says wryly. When the suits at the parent label in America saw the EP, they were not amused. The logo was removed from future pressings of the CD. The front cover illustration – a hamburger – made explicit the comparison between record company 'product' and fast food. But Warner drew the line at Paul Curtis' video concept for the EP's second track, Couldn't Do It.

> **Paul Curtis:** My idea for the video was to get this pristine-looking McDonald's hamburger and then time-lapse it rotting away, and that's the video. I was far more art-orientated than anything else at that stage!

The music itself was impossible to pin down. Essentially a power trio, Regurgitator played at industrial strength and volume. Live, the band was an awesome, intimidating force, with Yeomans' guitar and muttered vocals driving the scratchy, funk-based rhythms forward. But while the music was perfect for the macho heaven of the mosh pit, the lyrics mocked power and gender relations: Yeomans would occasionally take the stage in nothing but a baby-pink teddy; another choice item was a standard black T-shirt bearing the slogan MASTURBATE.

The band was helped immeasurably by tousle-haired producer Lachlan Goold, better known as Magoo. After completing an audio engineering course at Broken Toys Studio in the old Target building (where Powderfinger had recorded their first CD), Goold landed a role assisting Jeff Lovejoy at Red Zeds in Albion, earning his stripes working with Pangaea and the Dreamkillers. Goold's signature clattering, percussive sound also captured every instrument with brutal clarity.

> **Lachlan Goold:** I do like things to be loud. I started out as a live mixer, and I always knew it was good when the bass drum was moving your shirt. You could feel the music as much as you could hear it.

The EP was a success from the moment of its release in January 1995. Couldn't Do It and I Like It Like That both made the jump to high rotation on Triple J with ease, and the band proved an instant hit with festival crowds when it was invited to play the Big Day Out at the Gold Coast Parklands the same month. Of all the bands to emerge from Brisbane in the early '90s, Regurgitator would experience the sharpest rise and, arguably, swiftest fall.

For the band's next EP, *New*, Yeomans began matching a winsome, singsong melody to lyrics adapted from an old Eskimo legend. An Inuit woman, distraught at her lover's drowning, carves his likeness in whale blubber, rubbing him over her genitals to keep his memory alive. As repetitive as a mantra, the lyrics were reinforced by a soft/ loud musical dynamic that had become almost musically verboten after Nirvana's Smells Like Teen Spirit.

Blubber Boy was unabashed pop, instantly memorable, with a lyric as ribald as it was eccentric. If Ely and Lee were hesitant about this new direction, Yeoman's cheeky wordplay was enough to mollify their concerns. Amazingly, the naughtiness slipped by unnoticed when the song followed Couldn't Do It and I Like It Like That straight onto Triple J's playlist.

> **Ben Ely:** I remember Quan brought the song into practice and Martin and I were going, 'Are you sure you want to do this?' To us it was so uncool, you know, because it wasn't in 7/8 [time]! But it felt good. And he said the word 'cunt' in it *quite* a lot. So then we were like, he's swearing, it must be OK!

Yeomans had picked up the story from singer and performance artist Kiley Gaffney, who had given him a book of feminist fairytales: 'I used to tell Quan he looked more Inuit than Vietnamese.' After innocuous beginnings singing jingles in her teenage years, the striking, assertive Gaffney quickly cornered the non-existent Brisbane market for confrontational female performers.

> **Kiley Gaffney:** I was always compared to Nina Hagen by my friends, and she really appealed to me because I liked aggressive, opinionated women . . . I love Diamanda Galas still. I still like Poly Styrene from X-Ray Spex, that sort of stuff.

Paul Curtis was impressed, especially after witnessing a performance at the New Farm Powerhouse.[1] Cloaked in a wedding dress with an ox heart slung around her neck, Gaffney sang opera standing in a pit of putrid water, surrounded by writhing, naked dancers. The pair began dating, and Gaffney was brought into the Regurgitator fold, writing press releases that themselves became an important component in the marketing of the group.

Not that Regurgitator really needed the help. Few bands boasted a public image so perfectly in tune with their music. The artwork for the *New* EP urged the consumer to 'please dispose of package thoughtfully', even supplying a use-by date of 15 August 1995 – the same day as the CD's release. Any accusations of gimmickry, however, were easily defended: musically, Blubber Boy and the ferocious Track One represented an enormous advance for a band little more than a year old.

But Regurgitator was not above pushing the creative control clause in their contract to the limit. Coming after Blubber Boy, the band's next release, FSO – Fuck Shit Off – was more statement than single. Ninety-three seconds of blistering hardcore, the song was buried in the middle of 18 minutes of feedback. Edited for radio programmers, the single became the most recalled Regurgitator item ever: many fans returned or sold their copies, unsure what exactly they'd spent their money on.

> **Ben Ely:** We enjoyed pushing people's buttons. We weren't really popular with the record company when we started; they didn't really like us, except for Michael [Parisi]. So we kind of liked pissing them off. The noise bit was my idea.

Such was Regurgitator's popularity, however, that for the time being the group held the whip hand. Following a tour of Europe and Japan, the band began 1996 as a major drawcard for the Big Day Out, playing every date from Auckland to Perth, handling their transition to the main stage with ease. When the group told Warner they wanted to record their debut album in Thailand, no one turned a hair.

* *

Lee and Ely had scouted around for a cheap local studio while on holiday in Bangkok prior to the band's European tour. One month after finishing the Big Day Out shows, the band reconvened in Bangkok for three weeks of recording at Centre Stage Studios.

> **Ben Ely:** Martin always instilled this idea in us that [we should] keep the costs really low, so if the record company looked at their books and said, oh, these guys have only sold 20,000 records, but we'd only spent 1500 bucks, their profit margin was better. It was better for us, too, because we weren't pissing all our money up against a wall. So we went looking around some studios and found this crazy one out in the suburbs, which ended up being quite dodgy. It looked professional at first, but in the end we were holding the faders up by sticking toothpicks and matchsticks in the desk to hold it together.

The resulting album was named *Tu-Plang*, taken from the Thai word for jukebox. The conventional guitar pop introduction is immediately shot down by Yeomans: 'I sucked a lot of cock to get where I am / I only wanna be the best that I can.' The sarcasm was cheap, but so indelible was the melody, it logged hours more Triple J airplay for the band, to only minor outrage, even as radio announcers were forbidden to introduce the song by its full name.

The remainder was almost perversely eclectic. The first single, Kong Foo Sing, was monstrous funk-metal, Lee's drums miked to sound more like garbage pails. Blubber Boy and Couldn't Do It were both reprised – the latter in reggae form – as Riding The Wave Of Fashion and Happy Shopper remixes respectively. The highlight, though, was the West Coast-style hip-hop of Music Is Sport. Yeomans was a limited singer, and his voice was more effective when deployed as an extra percussive effect, allowing the skill and wit of his wordplay to shine.

What the hell we hitting for? Record companies keeping score
Trying to get those shiny-plaqued trophies for the office wall
Pumping out the hits to feed a media blitz
Now watch the champs blow the champers on bikini-clad tits

Being mercilessly lampooned by their star act was of no concern to Warner as long as they stayed in front on the scoreboard. Breaking into the national top 10 shortly after its release in early May, *Tu-Plang* went on to sell over 70,000 copies. As Craig Mathieson points out in his survey of the Australian music industry's incorporation of alternative rock, *The Sell-In*, it was 'Shiny platinum album plaques for all involved.'[2]

Promotional duties fell mainly to Ely and Lee. Yeomans was in retreat, bewildered by his band's runaway success. He was also hopelessly in love with Janet English, bass player with the Melbourne-based Spiderbait, with whom he had formed a relationship shortly before the recording of *Tu-Plang*. Already somewhat removed from his band-mates and the hard-living boys' club he was expected to embrace as the singer and guitarist of a leading rock band (a dilemma he addressed in *Tu-Plang*'s Social Disaster), Yeomans found it easier to withdraw.

In some ways, Yeomans' relationship with English can be seen as an extension of his friendship with Kiley Gaffney: evidently the singer's loathing for the trappings of rock culture went hand-in-glove with an attraction to women tough enough to exist within that culture on their own terms. Both Gaffney and English had no problem identifying themselves as feminists, and their influence was felt on a string of anti-sexist Yeomans songs, from FSO to Pop Porn. A talented graphic artist, English's bold, colourful 2D designs also had an obvious impact on a string of Regurgitator CD covers and videos.

But the biggest impact the relationship had on the band was commercial: the besotted Yeomans just wanted to stay home. The band was attracting notice overseas – I Sucked A

Lot Of Cock To Get Where I Am had already been released as a limited seven-inch single by the prestigious Sub Pop label – and American label Reprise were courting the band so heavily they were prepared to set up house for them in Los Angeles. The label released *Tu-Plang* for the American market in April 1997, but lost interest when Yeomans refused to tour overseas for more than three weeks at a time.

Quan Yeomans: When you're signed to a big American label, of course they want you to move over there for a year and crack it for them. And none of us were really into that. Maybe Martin was, and maybe Ben was more than I was, but I certainly held us back in that regard.

Paul Curtis: I actually think they made the right decision not going there. It's such a long shot whether those things are going to work, and we thought we shouldn't go away from Australia for too long anyway, because if we did that we might have sabotaged our market here.

While Regurgitator struggled to ride their own wave of fashion, similarly inspired acts floundered in their wake. Ely found enough time to return to Pangaea, recording an EP, *Smile*, and single, Boys, before the release of the band's only album *Freibentos* in August 1997. It lacked something – most obviously Jim Sinclair, who was ejected from the band halfway through the recording. When Sinclair's jazz-fusion combination Elevation also folded, the gifted guitarist disappeared from view.

Dave Atkins, though, was inexhaustible. Once, the drummer played five gigs in one night, with Pangaea, Elevation, Toothfaeries, folk singer Paddy Dempsey and heavy industrialists Soundsurgery. He also formed what became his most successful band, the hip-hop/dance crew Resin Dogs. While the interaction between musicians was incestuous, the activity kept the home fires burning while Regurgitator, Custard and Powderfinger focused their energies elsewhere.

> **Dave Atkins:** It felt really important that I played with all those bands at the time, just to keep that whole scene going – if you played in five different bands, you were helping venues keep going, if you did all the sessions you could, you were keeping studios like Red Zeds alive.

Not everyone was getting along, though. The signing of Kiley Gaffney to Warner immediately led to unfair gossip that, as Curtis' partner and Yeomans' friend, she was storming the castle on Regurgitator's coat tails. While it is true the label was fascinated by her contribution to Blubber Boy – 'I think they were waiting for me to whip some great hit out of my arse that never came,' she quips – the accusations were not borne out by commercial reality.

> **Kiley Gaffney:** There was a backlash at the time that I got signed, with people saying I got signed because of Paul. I actually took it up with Warner, and they said that's just ridiculous, that they would invest as much money in me as they did because of him.

In fact, Gaffney's projects ran on tiny budgets – and for good reason. Billed as the soundtrack to a non-existent film, *Bitter Fluff*, Gaffney's debut single Punk Rok Chik went over most listeners' heads upon its release in August 1996. The high-concept album was subsequently held over for a year. While Yeomans could swear to his heart's content without endangering Regurgitator's chances of airplay, Gaffney was not granted the same latitude, although she defends the chance the label gave her.

> **Kiley Gaffney:** It proved to be relatively fruitless, but it was good. The Warner folk were always really supportive. I don't think they understood a lot of what I was trying to do, but they were pretty good.

Warner had thrown Gaffney against the wall – and she hadn't stuck. But she was never, ever just a bit of fluff, and that almost certainly counted against her.

It's that whole, 'She's pretty, she's confronting, she's ballsy.' But if she's not pretty and she's confronting, she's a fucking ballbreaker. You know what I mean?[3]

By 1997 Fortitude Valley was a long way from the near-deserted dive of five years before. An inner-city urban renewal campaign was in full swing. New cafes and restaurants had flowered from the Brunswick Street Mall towards New Farm. Outdoor tables crowded the footpath. The mall itself was under extensive redevelopment, with the old Target building transformed into a split-level arcade of expensive specialty stores. By night, thousands of revellers began flocking to the once-feared precinct on the corner of Brunswick and Ann Streets.

Three blocks away, Regurgitator gathered to begin recording their second album in a condemned, crumbling warehouse they dubbed the Dirty Room. This time, there was no suggestion of relocating to a cheap studio in Bangkok, or an expensive one in Sydney. It made more sense for everyone to stay home: Yeomans and English had just bought a house in the suburbs, and were recording an album of their own under the working name the Shits.

After spending most of Warner's advance money on recording equipment – drum machines, old synthesisers, sampling gear – the group still had little clue what kind of album they wanted to make. The clues came in the early '80s pop records the band members were listening to: the Cars' *Candy-O*, Prince's *Controversy*, even the British new romantics Ultravox and Duran Duran. Two new pieces, Everyday Formula and Black Bugs (a breakthrough song for Ely) retained a punk edge, but were demonstrably lighter, almost airy in tone.

Anticipating a backlash against Regurgitator's early success, Ely came up with the perfect pre-emptive strike: I Like Your Old Stuff Better Than Your New Stuff. The song was originally recorded as a straight rock tune – fast-paced, guitar-driven and ready for the mosh pit.[4] But the treatment only obscured Ely's pungent lyric: musically, the song wasn't all that different from the old stuff.

> **Lachlan Goold:** The intention wasn't clear enough; it sounded a bit like a cover band. So that's when Martin said, 'Let's go fully Ultravox!' I think someone brought in the song Vienna, and we started going, let's record the drums without any cymbals, let's have the keyboards play the bass lines, let's put the vocals through the Vocoder.

But for once the reliance on technology – albeit old technology – did not equate to a lack of musical warmth. The songs breathed with life, humour and wholly unexpected poignancy, with Goold's retro-futurist production giving the vocals added depth and texture. Yeomans' Beatlesque epic Just Another Beautiful Story wrapped a truly sweet love song in an existential lament – 'There ain't no God, there's just me and you' – while the thick groove of I Will Lick Your Arsehole again showcased his facility as a rapper:

> Evidence irrefutable I'm squarer than a cubicle
> I hug the straight and narrow like a Julie Andrews musical
> I never liked it loud, and crowded places scare me
> I dig the rock & roll as much as Peter, Paul and Mary

While the lyrics were more razor-edged than ever (especially on The World Of Sleaze and the barbed tribute to trophy wives, Polyester Girl), this time they came complete with disarming falsetto harmonies. The final song recorded, bearing only an exclamation point for a title, was built around a belching keyboard fill and another

Yeomans paean to playing live – in his lounge room. With its uncanny resemblance to early Prince, it was subtitled The Song Formerly Known As.

> **Kiley Gaffney:** Quan's basically a plodder. He can write a song quickly, but then he'll sit there and work at it until it's perfect. He'll do four vocals in perfect harmony and build these beautiful three-dimensional songs. Like the Prince song, the layering on there, that's so fucking great.

With recording complete and their lease on the premises up, the band finally abandoned the Dirty Room. The warehouse was immediately demolished to make way for an extension to BMW's luxury caryard next door. It neatly symbolised the changing face of Fortitude Valley.

> **Ben Ely:** I drove past two days later and the whole building was gone except for this Coke machine that was left downstairs. They tore away the whole building around it, so all that was left was a vacant lot with a concrete slab and this Coke machine in the middle.

Unit crowned Regurgitator's commercial ascent. '*Unit*, with its bleeps and blips, is going to confuse people, at least initially,' predicted Andrew Humphreys in *Rolling Stone*. 'But its daring and vitality will win them over in the end because *Unit* is a brilliant pop album.'[5]

He couldn't have been more correct. After a solid but unremarkable start on its release in November 1997, *Unit* followed *Tu-Plang* to platinum status – three times over. Championed by the dedicated Michael Parisi, both Polyester Girl and The Song Formerly Known As crossed over from Triple J to commercial radio; in a supreme irony, the buoyant but loaded Polyester Girl even dented the teen market, climbing to 14 on the charts.

On the road, however, Regurgitator was travelling worse

than ever. Less than a week after the album's release, Martin Lee went MIA for an all-ages gig in Perth; the mystery was solved the next day when he was found unconscious and seriously injured, not far from the nightclub where he had last been seen after a show at the University of Western Australia the day before. No one knows exactly what happened: comatose for more than a week, Lee was unable to shed any light on what had happened when he came to. There were no witnesses.

The band was shaken, and the incident widened the cracks opening between the members. Lee was already deeply disenchanted. Yeomans, understandably, had decided to claim sole songwriting credit for his songs, forcing Ely (whose smart, hooky confections had become an inextricable part of Regurgitator's identity) to do the same. While the creative tension and competition spurred the pair on, Lee felt cut out, and not only of publishing royalties.

Quan Yeomans: We all seemed like aliens to each other, me especially. Ben and Martin were closer at the beginning of the band, and I certainly formed my relationship with Martin through Ben. I think if I had been closer to Martin I would have supported him a lot more than I did [after the accident] as a friend, but I don't think I was close enough to him to do that.

But the runaway success of *Unit* made it almost impossible for Regurgitator to step off the live treadmill. The band spent almost all of 1998 on tour – three times around Australia, twice through Japan, a prestigious date at the UK Reading Festival. Even Yeomans found himself being sucked into the vortex. When the Shits' home recordings were released by Polydor under the friendlier handle of Happyland, he found himself circumnavigating the continent all over again.

Quan Yeomans: The bigger the audience is, the more people you feel like you have to answer to. And you do get swept up in it. Once you're successful, it's something you want to maintain – in the world of economics, things grow, you don't want it to go backwards.

Martin Lee had rebuilt the Dirty Room in new premises in Fortitude Valley, with the assumption that the studio would be used to record *Unit*'s follow-up. Already feeling undervalued, he was taken aback when a clearly uncomfortable Yeomans made it clear he required a change of working environment. For Lee, it was the last straw: when Ely and Yeomans relocated to Byron Bay for five weeks, Lee refused to join them, venturing south only to record his parts – and sometimes only half of them.

Lachlan Goold: We'd just got Pro-Tools then, which meant we could edit everything up, and Martin wouldn't even finish a song – he'd play the first verse, chorus, he'd be halfway through the second verse and say, 'Oh, I'm just going to be repeating myself,' and stop. The house we were in, the drums were downstairs, so I'd go downstairs and say, 'Martin, what's wrong, is your headphone mix not right or something?', and he'd already be out of there, wouldn't even be around!

Lee's absence, however, was only a symptom of the band's internal divisions. Certainly no one blames him for the end result. Despite a bright, almost fastidious production from Magoo, . . . *Art* (the canary-yellow sleeve of which bore the warning 'actual product may not match expectations') was a strangely lifeless set. Where *Unit*'s stylistic mish-mash had been united by sounds and themes and *Tu-Plang* was energised chaos, . . . *Art* was merely diffuse. Not even Ely's terrific Surfin' Bird-style rave-up, I Wanna Be A Nudist, could get it over the line. The band was simply spent.

Quan Yeomans: I don't think my heart was in it, I don't think any of our hearts were in it . . . I really wonder what would have happened if we'd spent a bit more time in the wilderness and not put out a record for two or three years after *Unit*, just see what would have happened, but of course we can't tell.

Lee left the band shortly after . . . *Art*'s release in August 1999.

While Lee's departure was not surprising, the loss of Michael Parisi from Warner came as a serious blow. Parisi had relentlessly pushed Regurgitator, sometimes bringing himself into conflict with his employers, still smarting over Yeomans' refusal to take America. Regurgitator, like so many before them, soon found their creative freedom applied only as long as they were selling records, and . . . *Art*, by the band's earlier standards, sold poorly. When Yeomans penned an unofficial anthem for the Sydney 2000 Olympic Games, Crush The Losers, his lyric may as well have described Warner's hardening attitude towards the band.

In early 2001 Ely and Yeomans reconvened for the recording of Regurgitator's fourth album, *Eduardo And Rodriguez Wage War On T-Wrecks*. Produced by the duo with the assistance of ex-Gang of Four member Andy Gill, the more overtly hip-hop flavoured album opened up plenty of new ground for the band to explore, with new drummer Peter Kostic (of Sydney's Front End Loader) providing the necessary injection of new blood. But worrying signs abounded.

Ben Ely: All the guys that signed us had left by that stage, and [new A&R head] Dan Hennessy was dropping in on our sessions, trying to get us to add choruses and take out this and that. And we'd never, ever had anyone from a record company interrupt what we were doing before.

Paul Curtis: They just decided the band didn't want to bend over backwards for them, basically. It was worse for *Eduardo And Rodriguez*. I got called in for a meeting and rapped over the knuckles – 'Paul, you're a bad boy, you're not making the band do what we want them to do!'

Regurgitator are now an independent act for the first time in their career. To secure their release from Warner, the group really did have to bend over backwards, their liaison with the label ended by a greatest hits compilation of singles. Its title: *Jingles*.

CHAPTER SEVENTEEN

new suburban fables

Powderfinger gathered in Sydney's Q Studios to record their second album in early 1996. The quintet was on the rack. Support for the band within Polydor was less than unanimous. The label had seen little short-term return for its investment, with neither *Parables For Wooden Ears* nor the following EP, *Mr Kneebone*, capitalising on the excitement generated by the *Transfusion* EP. Inside the studio, however, a gradual metamorphosis was taking place. A band once clenched tight as a fist was unfurling within a song that beckoned instead of pummelled the listener.

John Zucco, Polydor's national promotions manager, was a long-time supporter of Powderfinger. An old friend of founding guitarist Ian Haug, he had moved to Sydney in 1991 after his promotion from the Brisbane office. When *Parables For Wooden Ears* was released in 1994, Zucco was saddled with the unenviable task of pitching the accompanying single, Tail – the same song critic Jack Marx had memorably described as 'disappearing up its own arse' – to Triple J. But when an excited Haug invited him back to the studio to listen to a new song, Pick You Up, he had no doubts.

John Zucco: From listening to it we knew we had something really special, and we went after it quite hard. We wanted to place it with Triple J and the community stations first, because that was particularly the wishes of the band; they wanted to be organic about what was happening. And luckily for us, they went with it, and then the commercial stations went with it.

Bernard Fanning: You always read about artists who say, 'And I *knew* at the time I had this enormous hit on my hands.' And it's just not like that! But for me, the clue to a good song is when you play it and you get some kind of natural physical response in your body, where it's stirring around in your stomach. I remember feeling that a little, at the initial stage of that song.

Powderfinger were a couple of years older than most of their contemporaries. The band began as a three-piece in late 1988, with Haug teaming up with bass player John Collins and drummer Steven Bishop shortly after leaving Brisbane Grammar. The members' tastes leant surprisingly towards the indie scene: Collins admired the malignant throb of Joy Division, while Haug was a psychobilly fan, addicted to the primal voodoo beat of the Cramps and the Gun Club.

Overriding these, however, was a love of classic '70s rock implied in the band's name. Alongside Neil Young were all the big names: Stones, Zeppelin, Black Sabbath and Kiss. Bernard Fanning – who joined Powderfinger in 1989 after meeting Haug in an economics class at the University of Queensland – added a variety of earnest singer-songwriters to the pot of influences, although it would be several years before these softer touches were allowed to filter through the band's music.

It was a streetwise combination for a young and hungry band in Brisbane. Although Powderfinger always included original songs in their repertoire, the dominant booking agency in town was more interested in cover and tribute bands, accounting in part for the lean years for original music in Brisbane in the late '80s. Playing the covers circuit honed Powderfinger's chops, but admitting the occasional

Neil Young number to the set (sometimes Powderfinger itself) also caused some early confusion.

> **Ian Haug:** That probably put us on the outer with Triple Zed, because they thought we were some kind of concept band. We were sort of doing grunge music before we knew what it was called, which a million bands around the world would have been doing at the time.

The band certainly had the look: long hair and ripped jeans all round. But Powderfinger needed to beef up its sound to be convincing. Steve Bishop left, to be replaced with the raw but hard-hitting Jon Coghill, while second guitarist Darren Middleton was recruited to add the requisite metallic flash after the band discovered him strutting his stuff in a glam-metal band called Pirate. Middleton, now probably the least showy member of Powderfinger, has never heard the end of it since.

> **Ian Haug:** He was doing the shred thing, dancing on the tables with a wireless guitar. He was into Dokken and all those terrible bands and we thought he was just the sort of idiot we needed! He was really funny.

In fact, the addition of Middleton allowed the spotlight to settle on Fanning. The fact that Powderfinger could play was one thing; having a singer who could actually sing was something else. A devotee of soul greats Sam Cooke and Otis Redding, Fanning's warm tone and elastic range was Powderfinger's most obvious ace, the first thing anyone who saw the band noticed. Freeing Fanning from guitar duties made him more than just another member of the band: it made him the star.

Powderfinger's line-up was completed by their sixth member, manager Paul Piticco. A former housemate of Haug's, Piticco was asked to take the reins shortly after Fanning's induction. Barely 21, Piticco had yet to find his direction, and was biding his time in an office job selling building materials.

> **Paul Piticco:** My direction found me! I didn't ever really plan. I liked music and I pottered with it, but at the risk of sounding like my parents, you think it's never going to be a real job; you're never going to make a living out of it. And even after I was committed to it, for quite a few years that didn't look likely. It wasn't until about 1995 that I thought, hang on . . .

> **John Zucco:** A lot of bands have potential, but they fall through the cracks because they don't have strong management. And that's what they get from Piticco – he can be a real hard-arse, but bands need that, because when they're going up against labels who can be incredibly intimidating, you need someone in your corner who can fight for you.

The band found its first regular home at the Orient Hotel, a triangular block at the junction of Ann and Queen Streets, midway between the city and Fortitude Valley. It wasn't long before patrons began spilling out into the street. Powderfinger simply didn't sound like a local band – clearly the five-piece was purpose-built for bigger stages than the corner of the Orient could accommodate. The question was how well they would handle the transition.

There was no shortage of sceptics. Initially the band was unfavourably compared to the Black Crowes, an understandable conclusion to draw: Fanning's wafer-thin visage wasn't entirely unlike the Crowes' Chris Robinson, and the two groups shared a common set of influences (most glaringly, both covered Otis Redding's Hard To Handle). By the time Middleton and Coghill joined the band, Powderfinger's imagination had been captured by the new music emanating from Seattle – especially Soundgarden, whose influence on Powderfinger's early recordings is undeniable.

But originality, or lack thereof, was hardly the point. Powderfinger were all young men in their early 20s, and their tastes were perfectly in tune with thousands of others like them in the summer of 1991–92. If they were to be the local standard-bearers of grunge, they were doing it more than well enough. Being ahead of the game was something for critics to worry about, not the band.

Bernard Fanning: We were always trying to get bigger, and trying to go on tour wherever and whenever we could, no question about that. We weren't interested in being the coolest band around, because that was never my motivation for being in a band. I never wanted to be cool. I wanted to make music.

Powderfinger had approached signing to Polydor with a level head, asking the label to invest in the band's long-term potential. 'We said to them, buy our third album,' says Fanning. 'We wanted two albums to develop before we were pushed by the record company.' Piticco concurs: 'There was a definite plan to not be successful immediately but to be successful for a long time.'

Once the deals were done, however, both parties forgot their good intentions. Subconsciously, perhaps, the band had begun to believe that major commercial success would be the inevitable result of major commercial backing. When the band went into the studio to make *Parables For Wooden Ears*, they were cocky. 'We believed we were better than we were at what we were doing,' Fanning says.

Polydor seemed to agree, sinking more money into the album's recording and promotion than Powderfinger was ready for. Somewhere along the line, as Powderfinger and Polydor set out to prove themselves to each other, the music became lost. The album sold just over 6000 copies in its first year.

Paul Piticco: We realised at that point that we had to take control and really work for something and focus on it, basically. There was a feeling that maybe the record company dropped the ball on the first album, and we'd allowed ourselves to be directed . . . We were very easygoing about it all. We weren't as analytical as we should have been, and definitely not as controlling as we've become.

The instrumental heroics that dominated *Parables* had been influenced in part by the bands dominating the local funk-fusion scene, particularly Pangaea and Brasilia. By 1995, a new crop of artists helped point Powderfinger in a more natural direction. The Toothfaeries were selling out shows with their light, summery folk-reggae; Isis began as a feminist vocal trio before expanding, morphing from acoustic to electronic pop in the process. When Ben Harper toured for the first time in late 1996, the Zoo was jammed beyond capacity.

The music resonated with Fanning in particular, whose biggest stated influence was the early '70s folkie Rodriguez. Over the course of two EPs, Powderfinger began to take apart their sound. Technique took a back seat to melody; Fanning's lyrics found a new directness. When the band began recording demos for their second album, *Double Allergic*, Pick You Up was the standout result. Anthemic but graceful, the stately ballad became both template and talisman for the band.

Bernard Fanning: It's in a really unusual tuning, that song, I had never written a song in that tuning before. Of course, I subsequently wrote the next 27 the same way! It was like opening the door to what you thought was just a hallway, and inside there's this huge mansion full of rooms that you can explore.

This time Polydor handled their charges more carefully. Presenting the song to Triple J ahead of commercial radio preserved Powderfinger's credibility in the youth market, while giving the broadcaster its biggest Australian success since silverchair. With its soft/loud dynamic and keening vocals, Pick You Up remained identifiably aligned to the post-Nirvana era, but the invitation at the song's core – and Fanning's delivery, from warm entreaty to final, desperate wail – was irresistible to anyone who heard it.

Pick You Up was already an alternative hit by the time Triple M adopted the song, and with it the band, as the acceptable new face of Australian rock. If the strategy cost Polydor a bigger hit – the song peaked at number 22 in June 1996, not a true reflection of its overall impact – it also gave Powderfinger tremendous commercial momentum leading up to *Double Allergic*'s release in September.[1]

The album debuted in the top 10, but more importantly it stayed there, peaking at number four in February following a dominant run of performances by the group at the Big Day Out. Within a year, *Double Allergic* had gone double platinum, selling over 140,000 copies. It was an extraordinary result for a band coming off such a low base. The doubters at Polydor were silenced: Powderfinger had saved their career with what may well have been their last throw of the dice.

> **Paul Piticco:** If you sign a record deal with a major label, you're a commercial rock band, whether you like it or not . . . The guys had set out to challenge themselves musically, not necessarily by writing songs that were populist, but by writing songs that would at least not discount them from having a future in the music business.

Although a major improvement on its predecessor, in truth *Double Allergic* was carried almost entirely on the strength of its singles. DAF (named after its chord structure) was an excellent follow-up to Pick You Up, while Living Type was only just good enough. From there, the album fell away, and the band knew it.

> **John Zucco:** I remember sitting with Bernard and Ian at the

Dolphin Hotel in Surry Hills, and they were being interviewed by a music journalist who said, 'There's a lot of fuss about your album, and it's not bad, but it's not that great.' And the guys said, 'Exactly! That's what we think, too – we can't understand what all the fuss is about it.' It showed they had a good perspective on things.

The honesty that characterised Powderfinger's approach – to themselves, their audience and their work – was a significant part of their appeal. While Custard never outgrew their reputation as merry pranksters and Regurgitator were too clever by half, Powderfinger didn't really have an image, beyond the fundamental ordinariness of its members. Neither ugly nor particularly good-looking, the group wore their street clothes on stage and off and hated photo sessions. (The group has never graced the cover of one of their own albums.)

Paul Piticco: They were very normal guys, and normal guys are much harder to sell in the beginning, but once you break through it's a blessing. No one cares what Bernard wears! If it worked – and it worked in a big way – Powderfinger was always going to be something that stuck in middle Australia.

Not that Powderfinger lacked personality. Fanning, generally quiet and astute, was also highly quotable, once engaging in a memorable slanging match – via the media – with precocious young singer-songwriter Ben Lee.[2] Drummer Jon Coghill was the natural extrovert and joker; happy to poke fun at himself, his band and (especially) any journalist assigned to interview him. With Haug, Collins and Middleton content mostly to remain in the background, the overall effect was of a rather laddish bunch of Queenslanders who didn't take themselves too seriously.

But the music was a different story. Powderfinger (again, unlike Custard and Regurgitator) found no place for irony in their songs. And just as the band had to learn to streamline its musical attack, Fanning gradually gained the confidence to express himself more openly. The more plain-spoken the lyrics became – as with Pick You Up – the better the overall results. The soulfulness of Fanning's voice left no room for ambivalence: if the words were obscure, the vocals tended to overcompensate, as if the singer was working himself up over nothing.

Powderfinger's sincerity resembled earlier, salt-of-the-earth Australian bands, accounting for the band's success on commercial radio: Triple M finally had a contemporary band to complement (if not replace) its Australian quota of Cold Chisel, Hunters & Collectors and Midnight Oil. Comparisons to the latter increased with the release of The Day You Come in August 1998, which appeared to address the rise of Pauline Hanson's One Nation party.

Bernard Fanning: That's kind of gone into myth, that that song was about Pauline Hanson. It wasn't. It was more about the mood of the time, and One Nation definitely contributed to that, but to me it was the first witnessing of a really obvious nastiness against minorities, where people were being overtly racist and discriminatory, and to me that was disturbing. And it wasn't just Pauline Hanson that was doing that.

Hanson was the public reincarnation of everything the Deep North once stood for. Carrying more chips on her padded shoulders than she ever sold in her famous shop, she had won the old Labor stronghold of Oxley as an independent after being disendorsed by the Liberal Party in the weeks leading up to the 1996 federal election.[3] When One Nation won 11 seats at the Queensland state election on 13 June 1998, Hanson asked the party's spiritual godfather, the 89-year-old Joh Bjelke-Petersen, to instruct her new members on parliamentary procedure. (Ironically, the result also split the conservative vote, handing power back to the Labor Party, led by Peter Beattie.)

The choice to release The Day You Come as a single

was opposed by Polydor. Although the song was sonically gorgeous – with its lilting verse refrain and explosive, shimmering chorus, the sound was closer to late-period Crowded House than Midnight Oil – the label feared its grim subject matter and bleak atmosphere would cost Powderfinger the support of the commercial networks that had embraced them. But with the label about to be swallowed up by Universal, the final decision was left to the band.

> **Paul Piticco:** Most record companies make the assumption that you don't really know what's best for you. So you have these fights, and at the end of the fight somebody gets the ball tossed to them – 'OK, it's all yours.' So we made a lot of big calls, and we were right, things went well for us. And suddenly it was like, 'Oh, maybe these kids know what they're doing.' It took years.

Powderfinger's third album, *Internationalist*, was released in September 1998. Qualitatively, it was an even greater leap forward from *Double Allergic* than that album had been from *Parables For Wooden Ears*. If *Internationalist* lacked cohesion overall, it showed the band exploring every room in the mansion Pick You Up unlocked. And in Passenger, the band had an even better song, starting slowly and adding piano, horns and backing vocals for a stunning emotional catharsis.

At first Polydor's concerns about leading with The Day You Come appeared well founded. After a major publicity push that saw the album enter the ARIA charts at number one, sales of *Internationalist* quickly dropped off. But the single, while not a major hit, was a sleeper, a consummate sucker-punch. As the band embarked on a relentless touring schedule in November, they followed up the song with a full-throttle rocker, Don't Wanna Be Left Out.

Then came the blue-collar anthems: first Already Gone in February 1999, then Passenger in August. It was the knockout blow. Again, Powderfinger had shored up its Triple J base before delivering the goods to commercial radio.

With sales now closing on 400,000 copies, *Internationalist* proved Piticco's point: Powderfinger was the number-one choice of middle Australia. Even Celebrity Head, which rather unfairly aimed a bazooka at the smallest of targets – the song was originally named after a local street-paper journalist – underlined the point: Powderfinger were the people's band first and critical darlings last.

By October 1999 Powderfinger was the most successful band in the country. They scooped the ARIA awards, taking out Best Album and Best Group; in May 2000 Passenger was awarded the prestigious Song of the Year award by the Australian Performing Rights Association. Commercially, the band was miles ahead of Regurgitator, Spiderbait and even silverchair – although the latter boasted a stronger overseas profile, something *Internationalist*'s title had obliquely addressed.

While The Day You Come had been produced by Lachlan Goold at Sing Sing Studios in Melbourne, the rest of the album was recorded by an American, Nick DiDia, previously the engineer for Pearl Jam producer Brendan O'Brien. DiDia quickly slotted into the Powderfinger network, coaxing powerful performances from the band while adding a smart but not overly glossy finish. Having worked on the band's last three albums, DiDia is Powderfinger's unofficial seventh member.

Paul Piticco: Well, unless something changes, he's the band's producer. We've always tried to have kind of a family mentality to how we do things, and Nick's definitely got that . . . I mean, everybody likes everybody, and it feels good, it makes it feel like there's more to it than making money out of Powderfinger's art.

Powderfinger's stability was their greatest asset. The band ran itself as a democracy, leading to plenty of arguments, but the value placed on each member's input was genuine: publishing royalties were split evenly between the five performers. Of course, one could also argue that Powderfinger were successful enough to afford such a luxury, but that ignores the eight years the group laboured before Pick You Up transformed them into a platinum commodity.

Some bands peak early. Almost all the great ones, however, take several years to hit their stride. As Powderfinger approached their fourth album, the old-fashioned virtue of giving artists the necessary time to develop rang louder than ever. The band's old friend, John Zucco, was given the plum job of overseeing A&R for the project.

> **John Zucco:** I had the title, but I wouldn't want to claim any credit there, because those guys know what they're doing. If nothing else they have remarkably good instincts, they've always been able to back their judgment, and I think that's one of the reasons why they've been able to keep moving up a couple of notches with everything they do.

The band had maintained its momentum with stellar contributions to two film soundtracks, recording These Days for the Australian crime thriller *Two Hands* and My Kind Of Scene for the much bigger budget *Mission: Impossible 2*. The latter was a coup for the group, giving Powderfinger their first major American exposure when the soundtrack went platinum (one million sales) Stateside. Both songs would be reprised on *Odyssey Number Five*, recorded in April 2000 at Sing Sing.

If *Internationalist* had been cautiously received two years earlier, despite its initial number one placing, there would be no such reservations this time. In Piticco's words, *Odyssey Number Five* 'just went stupid' upon its domestic release in September 2000. Within three months, the album had shifted a phenomenal 350,000 copies. (The album is now officially *eight times* platinum in Australia, with sales over 560,000.)

And this time even the critics had no doubts. The punters were right – from front to back, *Odyssey* was an outstanding album. Playing entirely to the band's strengths – mid-tempo rockers and fire-starter ballads – the songs oozed emotion, with Fanning's rawest set of lyrics married to superbly realised tension-and-release arrangements. Moreover, for the first time it felt like a proper album, with the band creating an overall mood rather than simply cutting and pasting its best dozen tracks.

> **Bernard Fanning:** We wanted to do a shorter album, because then we probably had a better chance of marrying the songs together. So that was something that we were conscious of when we started writing for it; it was definitely the most contrived in the sense that we knew what we were aiming for before we started.

My Happiness was the first single. Built on a chugging acoustic rhythm and oscillating lead, it was not a difficult choice, even given the quality of the surrounding material. Coming after My Kind Of Scene, it was the song that would be used to push the band into the American consciousness. In Australia, however, the band was confident – and powerful – enough to follow My Happiness with the caustic Like A Dog. This time there was no denying which politician was in Fanning's sights.

> **Ian Haug:** That didn't get played on Triple M, because they thought too many voters for John Howard would get offended, both within the station and on the airwaves, probably. It's good to make people think about things, rather than telling someone the way things should be. And Bernard's very good at doing that lyrically. He's become less and less cryptic as our career's advanced though!

It hardly mattered. Triple J was welcome to Like A Dog. Commercial radio had the rest of the album to play with.

With the worldwide release of *Odyssey Number Five* by Universal, Powderfinger set off on their first major tour of the US in February 2001, performing My Happiness on David Letterman's *The Late Show* for their American television debut. And somewhere along the way, things went according to the script of *This Is Spinal Tap*, where Artie Fufkin – the hapless local record company spruiker – promises the band massive radio exposure, yet is unable to entice buyers to the band's in-store appearance.

> **Paul Piticco:** The song just didn't react with the public. It was the number one most added song on radio, in the Top 10 most played songs for a couple of weeks, and it still didn't sell. It was sort of inexplicable.

Piticco, in fact, does a good job of explaining. Despite supporting British band Coldplay on tour – whose mellow *Parachutes* album had turned them into arena stars – Powderfinger's sensitive-guy rock had been surpassed in America by jock-metal bands like Limp Bizkit. Possibly Powderfinger's music fell in between: too heavy for one demographic, too vulnerable for another. When the band mounted their own headlining tour in May, they were confronted with the reality of trying to crack the US market without a hit.

> **Bernard Fanning:** I know it's the oldest cliché in the book, but it's true, and that's why Jackson Browne wrote that album *Running On Empty*. We went on tour in America on a bus twice, and I understood where he was coming from, where you drive into places you've got no relationship with, and you don't even like performing there.

The band maintained its image as the quintessential blokes of Australian rock. Several articles suggested the members were too content admiring the view from the verandas of their new homes in Brisbane to be bothered moving within more elevated company. Asked whether they had received any feedback for My Kind Of Scene from *Mission: Impossible 2* star, producer and fan Tom Cruise, Darren Middleton joked that Cruise had left a message on his answering machine, 'but I haven't got back to him'.[4] Perhaps the music wasn't the only thing the Americans didn't get.

But the group were not about to die wondering.

Bernard Fanning: The key thing for a band like us in America is to go and play live, because we're not going to really impress people with our personal appearances or our interviews. Everyone was amazed that we would actually go and talk to the punters after the shows.

Paul Piticco: I don't think it's about fluking a radio hit; I think it's about doing the work. We're a working rock band – make great album, find person at record company who also thinks it's a great album, have them put the record out, and go and tour on it.

Powderfinger, above all else, had the balance right. They were ambitious enough to work for their success without ever letting the prizes – or the pitfalls – get in the way of the process. They also stayed hungry: if anything, the band's 2003 album *Vulture Street* was even better than *Odyssey Number Five*, looser and more upbeat, but also more economical and buoyantly tuneful. With sales at home nearly matching its predecessor, there is little left for the band to do but take it to the world.

Besides, life in Brisbane is not quite what it once was, especially for Powderfinger's most recognisable member.

Bernard Fanning: Because we have a reputation for being friendly, people aren't reticent about approaching us, and me in particular. You can worry about that too much though. It's very rare for people to approach you and be aggressive and say 'You fucking suck'. They usually shout that from cars!

CHAPTER EIGHTEEN

today your love, tomorrow the world

If rock & roll was revitalised by Nirvana in 1991, it had become a sullen and unsmiling beast by 1995. The grunge explosion lingered like a bad hangover; the initial energy dissipated by a succession of frowning, introspective acts led by Pearl Jam and the Smashing Pumpkins.

While the UK looked to its storied pop history for inspiration, Australia produced its own variants on the Seattle sound in silverchair and Powderfinger. The local music industry, from bands to A&R representatives to journalists, had been infiltrated by the values of the indie-rock movement. As Craig Mathieson has documented in *The Sell-In*, the industry co-opted the scene, marketing the new bands – no matter how generic – as an alternative to the old.

No one wanted to be a star any more. It had become de rigueur for rock bands to be diffident, even apologetic about commercial success. Somehow the vitality and charisma of punk had become infected with the dreariest aspects of the folk movement, where street credibility ruled and selling out (regardless of how many records one actually sold) was the biggest sin. Pop had become a dirty word.

John Woodruff had watched many a musical trend come and go during a long and fruitful career managing the names that made Oz Rock: Cold Chisel, the Angels, Icehouse,

Diesel and the Baby Animals. But with those bands long
since overtaken by a younger, louder and snottier breed,
Woodruff had not had a hit for half a decade.

Now he had someone new: a baby-faced pop duo from
Brisbane going by the unlikely name of Savage Garden.
Woodruff had a nose for a hit – he had supervised the
creation of more than 70 albums, almost all of them
platinum – but as he shopped his latest find around, most
observers seemed to think he'd finally lost his marbles.

> **John Woodruff:** I thought I was heading for Scandinavia,
> because it sounded like Roxette to me. I went to LA, and I
> guess half of the companies sort of laughed, and the other
> half . . . Dreamworks had just started at that point, and the
> A&R guy there turned down I Want You halfway through
> the track – he didn't even get through the three minutes 28
> seconds of the song – and looked at me and went, 'Well, with
> respect, you haven't done your homework, have you?'

Darren Stanley Hayes was born in Logan City in 1972.
Logan is to Brisbane's southern outskirts much as Ipswich
is to the west; a separate municipality half an hour's drive
from the city. Like Ipswich, the working-class suburbs
around Logan suffer from a down-at-heel reputation, none
more so than Woodridge, where Hayes grew up. Yet he led
a mostly happy childhood, unaffected and unpretentious.

> **Darren Hayes:** When I think of growing up . . . There was a
> street called Paradise Road that I thought was the busiest
> in the world. Every Saturday I would cross Paradise Road to
> walk down to the local shopping mall. I would go to this record
> store called Woody's, and look through all the vinyl I couldn't
> afford to buy . . . It was a very sheltered and a very innocent
> upbringing. It wasn't until I hit 17, 18 that I realised there was a
> stigma attached to where I lived, and that I was growing up in
> a neighbourhood that was kind of rough.

In the early '80s Hayes was swept away by the magic of pop music, sitting by a radio cassette deck with a blank tape at the ready, waiting to hit the record button when Michael Jackson's Thriller began its bass-driven strut through the tiny speakers. *Thriller* was the modern link to the few hand-me-down Motown records Hayes owned and loved. As the '80s progressed, his tastes broadened, taking in everything from Duran Duran to the Smiths and U2.

The difference between Hayes and any other suburban teenager was his seriousness in his quest to emulate the success of his idols. Such ambitions, however, were completely out of sync with his surroundings. A regular lead in school musicals, Hayes was determined to go to the performing arts school at Kelvin Grove, but guidance counsellors urged him to pursue a steadier career. Their belief that Hayes was university material was unusual in itself.

> **Darren Hayes:** Very rarely did anyone [from my school] even go on to university then, it was kind of a new thing then to go and get a tertiary entrance score or anything like that . . . So being in the debating team, or doing speech and drama, singing or acting – God forbid you wanted to be a pop star, you just never mentioned that.

Hayes did go to university, but not to Kelvin Grove. Instead, like Bernard Fanning before him, he started studying journalism at the University of Queensland. Later he began an education degree. When his dreams of stage and screen failed to materialise, Hayes grew frustrated, feeling he had sold himself out. But Hayes didn't play an instrument; didn't even know anyone in a band. Nor could he relate to the exploding indie scene on his doorstep: his first love was the mainstream '80s pop of his teenage years, and no one was playing it any more.

In 1993 Hayes realised he was making excuses for himself. After being challenged by a girl who told him

straight – if he wanted to be a pop star, what was he
doing boring himself at university? – Hayes picked up a
copy of street paper *Time Off.* Turning to the classifieds
section, he called the number on the first 'singer wanted'
advertisement he saw, placed by a band called Red Edge.
The number belonged to Daniel Jones.

> **Darren Hayes:** I spoke to Daniel on the phone and we just
> clicked. And I almost talked myself out of the audition – after
> 20 minutes I said, 'You know what, maybe this isn't a good
> idea, because I don't know if I'm into the music you're into.'
> He kept listing a lot of Australian artists like Noiseworks, and
> the only Australian band that really turned me on was INXS.
> And Club Hoy, which was an acoustic act that I used to love.
> But I turned up and sang, and I was so nervous I sounded like
> shit . . . Everybody in the room except Daniel passed on me.
> I think the two of us just knew there was a connection there.

Daniel Jones was born in 1973 in Essex, England. After
his family's migration to Australia, Jones grew up in the
semi-rural suburb of Shailer Park, also in Logan. Leaving
school at 15 to concentrate on music, he formed Red Edge
with his older brother Oliver. Although primarily a covers
outfit, the brothers were being courted by publishing
agency Warner Chappell. The original songs, according to
Hayes, strove for an Australian pub rock sound, a direction
reflected by the band's taste in covers: 'I was from the
school of Duran Duran and Michael Jackson, trying to
sing Khe Sanh.'

Hayes nevertheless stuck with Red Edge for 18 months,
finally quitting after one rendition of Khe Sanh too many in
Alice Springs. But his rapport with Daniel Jones remained
strong: even as he left, Hayes expressed his desire to keep
working with the talented multi-instrumentalist. Jones was
also keen, and he loaned Hayes a keyboard and sequencing
manual. Hayes, uncomfortable with the technology and
perhaps still unsure if he had whatever it took in him,

never opened it. Eventually Jones took the initiative.

> **Darren Hayes:** He called me up and said, 'Do you want to come over and write a song?' I went over to his house and got on the keyboard and I showed him this house riff. And he said, 'Are you sure you want to make music like that?' And I said, 'Well, what was your idea?' And he played this beautiful, moody progression that became A Thousand Words, which ended up on the first album.

A band manager's life is a never-ending stream of demo tapes and CDs, each one a snapshot of someone else's dreams. John Woodruff was used to looking after rock bands, so this particular tape – a glitter-covered cassette from a band calling itself Dante – stood out immediately for its sheer incongruousness: 'I thought, well, I'm going to have to listen to this one.' The first track on the five-song tape was To The Moon And Back.

> **John Woodruff:** It was pretty much as it ended up on the album. Obviously a bit rougher, because it came from a home studio, but that same vocal, same arrangement. That was enough for me. Much as we were in the middle of the grunge era and I managed rock bands, it was pretty undeniable. So I got on a plane and I was in Brisbane the next morning.

Darren Hayes and Daniel Jones had been writing songs for over a year when they met Woodruff in a Brisbane hotel room in early 1996. While Jones was working in a printing factory – accounting for the sparkling cassettes – Hayes had finally dropped out of university, taking a job in a video store. His family was horrified. But so strong was the musical chemistry between the pair, they were convinced nothing was beyond their grasp, even as the rejection letters piled up. Woodruff was sold.

John Woodruff: I thought they were brilliant. I thought
the discussions that we had together were some of the
most honest and frank – albeit somewhat naive from their
perspective – that I'd ever had with a new artist. That was what
got me, even more so than the music. I was still debating that
with myself, because the closest thing to a pop band that I'd
ever looked after before was Icehouse.

Woodruff shopped the demo around: 'It wasn't that
I got a bad reaction, it was that I got no reaction.' He
decided to sign Savage Garden – renamed after Anne
Rice's *The Vampire Chronicles* – to his own start-up label
JWM Productions and publishing company, Roughcut.
At around the same time he played the demo to producer
Charles Fisher. Fisher had worked on a diverse array of
Australian albums by artists yet to find their way in the
studio, from Radio Birdman through to 1927.

John Woodruff: Charles was good with people who had no
studio experience [because] he believed that if you taught
them how to make a record and they were as talented as you
thought, they'd give you back a brilliant recording. But that
takes serious time, because it means you've got to record
every track a number of times.

Savage Garden took eight months to make. It was a
costly exercise: Woodruff relocated the duo to Sydney for
the duration, and studio musicians needed to be hired to
fill out the sound. Most of the money was spent on the
mix by Los Angeles hit-maker Chris Lord-Alge. Woodruff
refinanced his house to complete the project, but by then
he had Village Roadshow interested in doing a licensing
deal to take care of the album's distribution. Roadshow's
advance helped cover Woodruff's outlay. He was also sure
that, in the end, he would get more than his money back.

John Woodruff: This was the first record that I'd ever owned at that point; I'd always signed the band away to other labels. But I knew what royalty structures looked like, it's just mathematics . . . It's not unknown to be able to get four or five dollars per record. So if it costs you $120,000 to make an album, that means you've only got to sell 25,000 and you've recouped. And I had no doubt we were going to sell 25,000 albums.

Savage Garden's first single, I Want You, was released in August. The song was utterly beguiling – the lyrics were delightful fluff, the melody was equal to the seductive promise of the title, and Darren Hayes' vocals were George Michael via Michael Jackson. 'It's part of the hardwire,' Hayes says. 'That's how I learned to express myself, how I learned to perform.'

The song climbed to number four on the charts; in December To The Moon And Back went all the way to number one. The song was Savage Garden's calling card – not even the ersatz acoustic guitar solo and synthesised string section could overwhelm the synth-pop heaven of the chorus. But the song that sent everything over the top was Truly Madly Deeply. As simple and natural as breathing, the lighter than air ballad showed the depth of songwriting mastery at work, even as it hugged the white line in the middle of the road.

John Woodruff: I remember saying, 'Well guys, Magical Kisses is not going to make it I'm afraid, that lyric is just not gonna do it for anyone.' And they went, OK, and changed it to Truly Madly Deeply. And I thought, well, it's a little better than Magical Kisses – I'll take it!

Savage Garden was not the first Brisbane band to export high-gloss teenage pop from Brisbane. In the late '80s, Indecent Obsession had several hit singles after signing to

Ian 'Molly' Meldrum's label Melodian. The band achieved
more success overseas, especially in Asia and, notably,
South Africa, where Indecent Obsession made history as
the first western act to tour the country post-apartheid. Led
by the fey, blond-haired David Dixon, Indecent Obsession
were a boy band ahead of their time.

Savage Garden's timing, however, was perfect. In the
UK the Spice Girls had just broken through the Britpop
phenomenon to reclaim the giant slice of the pop market
reserved for early teenagers. It didn't hurt, of course, that
Darren Hayes and Daniel Jones were as striking as the
songs they created. Hayes' almond-shaped blue eyes and
delicate features were as boyishly innocent as his persona.
Jones was taller, with streaked blond hair and a lean face
that broke easily into a smile.

While videos for I Want You and To The Moon And Back
clogged early morning video shows, Woodruff took off for
the United States. Scandinavia, it turned out, could wait:
for every A&R executive who thought their label was too
cool for Savage Garden, another one badly wanted – even
needed – Savage Garden. When Arista's Clive Davis and
Columbia's Donny Ienner squared off over the band, the
game was well and truly on.

It must have been a particularly galling loss for Clive
Davis when Columbia won the battle for Savage Garden's
signatures. Within months of the album's release in March
1997, Savage Garden's Australian success was multiplying at
an exponential rate. I Want You and To The Moon And Back
broke the US top 10, while Truly Madly Deeply vaulted to
number one, enjoying a record-breaking stay of 134 weeks
on the Billboard chart.

In Australia the band was up there with children's
entertainers the Wiggles: one year after its release, *Savage
Garden* had sold more than 750,000 albums in their home
country alone. The album spent a historic 12 weeks at
number one. In October the band swept the ARIAs, taking
out eight awards, including a gong for Best Independent

Release. With guitar-based indie rock slowly being ground under corporate wheels, it was a telling irony.

Hayes and Jones were also on the road for the first time. Accompanied by a full touring band, the duo had entirely bypassed the traditional live circuit, going from the studio to entertainment centres and stadiums, all with a set created by the designers of U2's *Popmart* tour. It was an extraordinary fulfilment of two boyhood dreams.

> **Darren Hayes:** We were never apologetic. At the time it was part of indie credibility that you had to pretend that everything was all an accident. But it's not . . . We were very honest about the fact that we were extremely ambitious, extremely positive thinkers – dream it, be it.

> **John Woodruff:** If you want to compete in a worldwide marketplace, the people that you're competing with, they don't think about anything else, they're possessed. And Darren in particular has always seen his competition as being Michael Jackson, Madonna, George Michael, Bowie [and] U2.

Even the relatively cautious Jones had never placed boundaries on what Savage Garden might achieve.

> We didn't think that it wouldn't work, because we had to think it would. It's like a kid not having fear . . . A kid will do something absolutely stupid, because he has no idea what fear is. We didn't know how to fail.[1]

It was a rare insight from Jones, who was already taking a back seat in promotional duties. Jones liked making music, not talking about it, and while he enjoyed performing, travel wearied him. He was essentially a homebody. 'He was very much about the family,' Woodruff says. Hayes, too, increasingly sensed Jones' reluctance: 'I always felt guilty that I was dragging him along for the ride.'

Hayes was battling his own demons. Although

infinitely more comfortable in the spotlight than Jones, his private life was collapsing under the strain. When a tabloid journalist broke the news that Hayes was married, press reaction varied between disbelief and derision, as if the fact that Hayes had managed to keep his wife of three years out of the public eye was evidence he himself was in the closet. The couple's split in late 1998 only fanned speculation about Hayes' sexuality. While Jones simply melted away into the anonymity of Brisbane's bayside suburbs, the naturally gregarious singer felt he was slowly suffocating.

> **Darren Hayes:** We were thrust head-first onto this roller coaster . . . I mean, we're talking 20 million albums sold in the space of four years. We played in basically every single country in the world. We became millionaires several times over, became celebrities. The ability to walk around Brisbane was taken away from me – I couldn't walk around Brisbane and feel comfortable in my own skin.

Hayes dealt with the situation like a true pop star. He moved to New York.

Much of Savage Garden's second album *Affirmation* was written across continents with the aid of a hard disk recording system. Jones would send his songwriting partner zip disks of information, allowing Hayes to record guide vocals and melodies over the top. Hayes would then do rough mixes which he sent back to Jones by post. The first song to be written this way was The Animal Song, a glorious romp that showed the duo had lost none of their childlike enthusiasm and infectiousness.

As the album started to take shape, however, the mood changed. Hayes began to pour out his heart and hurt, writing increasingly literal accounts of loss and grief. The Lover After Me and I Don't Know You Anymore saw him sifting through the rubble of his marital separation with heart-tugging honesty. Not that the subject matter was all first-person navel-gazing: on the ghostly Two Beds And A Coffee Machine, Hayes sang of a woman packing her kids in the car and leaving her violent spouse in the dead of night. It was a long way from the froth and bubble of I Want You.

Hayes and Jones longed to bring an edge to the darker material, and expressed interest in working with William Orbit, who had just produced Madonna's *Ray Of Light*. Don Ienner, however, wasn't about to let his biggest new act reinvent themselves for critical favours. He introduced them to Walter Afanasieff, whose résumé boasted Mariah Carey and Boyz II Men. Afanasieff's Wallyworld studios in San Francisco were more suggestive of a theme park than a workplace, and the man himself was calm and reassuring. Hayes, stressed and unhappy in New York, was easily swayed.

As the recording unfolded, those around the band grew concerned. The Animal Song had already been released as a single, and the title song Affirmation was cut from the same cloth – a musical update on Max Ehrmann's famous *Desiderata*. Both songs highlighted Savage Garden's sincerity and warmth. But the rest of the album was unbalanced. Those lured by the single would be in for a rude shock. What the album really needed, everyone agreed, was another Truly Madly Deeply. An insulted Hayes and Jones dug their heels in.

Woodruff had seen what his charges were capable of when they were pushed.

John Woodruff: They told me, we can't do that – that was then, this is now, all the stuff you would expect. And my attitude back to them was, look, we'll sell three million copies of this record, and that's great. But if you give me a positive love song . . . 'Well, we can't!' OK then, fine, we'll sell three million. And about an hour later they came down from the

guesthouse on the studio property, and Daniel turned to me
and said, 'Here's your song for morons.'

The song was I Knew I Loved You. 'And I said, 'Oh. Yeah,
OK. That'll do. Thanks!' Woodruff laughs. The song would
take Truly Madly Deeply's place as the longest charting
song in Billboard's history.

Savage Garden was already on borrowed time when
Affirmation was released in November 1999. Daniel Jones
had decided he'd had enough.

John Woodruff: I sort of respected that decision, because
I've always said to other bands, if you don't want to do this, if
you don't want to be part of it, then don't do it . . . So the fact
that [Daniel] actually came to me and said he'd had enough I
thought was admirable, really. The fact that he said it right at
the point when we'd finished an album was unfortunate.

In the end Jones and Hayes agreed to carry on with a
planned world tour, after which they would take a two-year
break to reassess their future. The writing, however, was on
the wall. The burden placed on Hayes by Jones' immediate
and apparently permanent withdrawal from almost all
promotional duties was untenable: at worst, Jones' reputation
as the quiet one who wrote the music left Hayes looking like
a puppet.

Darren Hayes: I can't speak for Daniel, but I know that on
so many levels he just rejected so much of it. Travel was the
biggest thing that really got him down. He hated being away
from home, hated promotion. In the end he wouldn't do any
interviews, wouldn't do photo shoots, wouldn't even do videos
in the end. It was an incredible strain to put on a duo, because
I was doing everything.

While the band may have been in limbo, they were also at the pinnacle of their brief career. Approaching the end of what would be their final tour, the duo was approached to perform Affirmation at the closing ceremony of the Sydney 2000 Olympic Games.

Darren Hayes: That was probably the most important moment in my career, and not because of the prestige of it. For me on an entirely different level, it was the first time I'd ever really felt Australian, and proud to be Australian.

Two days before the show Hayes purchased a T-shirt bearing the Aboriginal flag from a local community store. He was a passionate believer in reconciliation between white and Aboriginal Australians, and the issue was alive then as never before: three months earlier, 120,000 Australians had walked the length of the Sydney Harbour Bridge in support of the cause. The Prime Minister, a permanent fixture at the games, was not among those supporters.

Although he wanted to wear his shirt on stage, Hayes knew there was a costume approval process, and he didn't want to get in trouble. At the ceremony he kept the shirt hidden under a jacket, arguing with himself, pacing around. Nervously, he flashed the shirt to Midnight Oil's Peter Garrett. Scheduled to play after Savage Garden, the Oils were guaranteed to make a statement and they did, famously playing Beds Are Burning in their black 'sorry' suits. Garrett grinned and gave Hayes the thumbs-up.

As he watched Christine Anu singing the Warumpi Band's Australian classic My Island Home, Hayes began to well up. He was going to do it. He had to do it. The call came. Hayes tore off his jacket. Two minders made to grab him, but it was far too late. Hayes was already on stage.

Darren Hayes: I knew I was the vanilla ice cream of Australian music, and that I had an opportunity to say something, to

mean something . . . I knew that we were going to appear after
the flag-bearing ceremony, and there would be one flag that
wasn't represented.

Savage Garden finished their touring commitments in
December 2000. Hayes felt as though his second marriage
was ending, and this time it wasn't mutual.[2] Unsure of his
future, he relocated to San Francisco in the new year to begin
work on a solo album with Walter Afanasieff. Jones, for his
part, was already making good his plans to continue his
musical career in a supporting role, writing and producing
songs for Brisbane band Aneiki under the umbrella of his
new label Meridien. But Savage Garden's split – if indeed it
was a split – remained under wraps.

In the end, Hayes' trusting nature got the better of him.
Speaking to the *Courier-Mail*'s Cameron Adams in October
prior to the release of his debut solo single Insatiable, Hayes
told the truth, believing Adams would hold onto his scoop
until an official statement was made. When Daniel Jones
woke up the next morning, the news was out. Some reports
even suggested Hayes had sacked Jones from his own band,
with Jones claiming he had never wanted to close the door
on recording with Hayes again.[3]

It was a messy, undignified end for Savage Garden who,
in every other respect, had never pretended to be anything
they weren't.

Darren Hayes: We never faked anything . . . For us to get up
again and make a third record just because it would sell more
than a Darren Hayes record, *that* would be selling out. I mean,
people can say what they want about pop music, but they
can't ever say we didn't mean it.

The simple truth was the two songwriters had grown
apart. Both have long since moved on: while Hayes launched
his second solo album in mid 2004, Jones continues to live

and work in Brisbane. Perhaps understandably, he has even less interest in talking about Savage Garden now than ever. And while in purely commercial terms Hayes and Jones rank among the most successful songwriting teams of all time, creatively the duo was a spent force.

Darren Hayes: For our first record we wrote 45 songs. For the second record we wrote exactly 13, and 12 of those were on the album and one was a B-side. Our chemistry and our passion to work together and our goals had shifted so much that it's a miracle that those 13 songs were written.

I honestly think we just wanted different things. At the time I didn't want it to end. It's been reported a thousand other ways, but it was not my idea that it ended. But now I can't imagine going back, and I have to commend Daniel for being brave about it.

The dream was over.

epilogue – no, your product

Sydney, 11 September 2001. The Saints – Ed Kuepper, Chris Bailey and Ivor Hay – are at Fox Studios, on stage together for the first time in more than 20 years, grinning as they bash through a half-remembered version of (I'm) Stranded to celebrate their induction into the ARIA Hall of Fame. Hours later, unfolding events in New York will see them bumped from the front pages of the next day's newspapers. Some bands never get their timing right.

Clinton Walker nervously introduces the group to accept their statuettes. Kuepper mumbles diffidently; Chris Bailey – ever the diplomat – thanks ARIA for the butt plugs. The event is being pre-recorded for the main awards telecast in October, where fellow inductees INXS will command nearly 15 minutes of airtime. The Saints get about 15 seconds. It's the barest of acknowledgments, but enough to raise the prospect of the long estranged Kuepper and Bailey working together again.

> **Ed Kuepper:** Chris was interested in me playing guitar in his version of the Saints, but not interested in working with me beyond that. I understood where he was coming from. I thought well, OK, if I'm back in the band I'm obviously going to be directing things, [but] he was really not interested in entertaining a working relationship along the lines of what we used to have.

Chris Bailey: It was like peeling away 30 years; the relationships between the three of us were exactly the same! I'd actually discussed it with Ivor about 10 years ago, we were chatting about Ed for some reason. And [we thought] it was really weird how, when you hang out with Ed, you have to go back to being the guy you were at 14 and have the same relationship you had back then.

Bailey's resentment is understandable. The singer complains that, while he took the name, his former songwriting partner has 'probably got more mileage than I have out of the Saints in a lot of respects'. While Bailey's most recent recordings under the Saints banner have fallen through the cracks, the original brand is stronger than ever: *All Times Through Paradise*, a box set of the first three albums with remastering supervised by Kuepper, is the last word on one of the truly seminal bands of the '70s.

It is a similar story for the Go-Betweens who, Velvet Underground-like, were always destined to be bigger after their demise. The original six albums have all been reissued in lavish double-CD editions, along with a best-of set *Bellavista Terrace* and a patched together 'lost' album of demos from the band's early years. David Nichols' biography of the band has been reissued internationally by the estimable Verse Chorus Press.

More importantly, the Go-Betweens are a recording entity again, with Robert Forster and Grant McLennan backed by Adele Pickvance on bass and former COW and Custard drummer Glenn Thompson. The line-up first played the Zoo in December 1995, warming up for a one-off show in Paris on the invitation of French magazine *Les Inrockuptibles*, which had just named *16 Lovers Lane* the third best album of the '80s (following the Pixies' *Doolittle* and the Smiths' *The Queen Is Dead*).

Robert Forster: It was a really nice big old Parisian theatre, and there were about 800 people there. People had come over from England, and we'd play a song and we'd just have to count in the next song over the applause, because people just weren't stopping. And we walked off stage and people were screaming and throwing things at us, and we came back for four encores. It was pure Hollywood.

Forster and McLennan continued to play sporadically as a duo, doing a run of shows to promote the worldwide release of *Bellavista Terrace* in 1999. By 2000, both songwriters had resettled in Brisbane.

Robert Forster: [*Bellavista Terrace*] was coming out so I said, 'Let's just do an acoustic tour,' Grant and I, we'd do interviews on the road and then at night we'd play a show in a club. And pretty soon into that we were having a great time . . . It was Grant's idea, he came to me and said, 'I think we should make a record,' and I said, 'Yeah, great.' I hadn't put out an album since 1996, since *Warm Nights*, so I had seven or eight really good songs.

The Friends Of Rachel Worth (recorded with Sleater-Kinney drummer Janet Weiss) marked a strong, if somewhat tentative return for the Go-Betweens: often the album felt more like two solo albums cut and pasted together than a genuine collaboration. But there was no denying its successor, the sparkling *Bright Yellow Bright Orange*, released to a rapturous reception in 2003. With the third post-reformation album *Oceans Apart* hailed as a masterpiece upon its release in 2005, the Go-Betweens are more viable than ever.

Of the '90s bands, the two most successful ensembles have continued down their respective paths – one a superhighway, the other a sidetrack. Powderfinger have toured extensively throughout Europe and the UK, selling out shows everywhere on the back of *Vulture Street*'s release by the V2 label. The band's extraordinary Australian success may yet be translated to a large-scale international audience.

When the Livid Festival grew legs in 2002, travelling to Sydney and Melbourne, Powderfinger headlined over Oasis. For Peter Walsh, the symbolism was obvious.

Peter Walsh: The original reason Livid started no longer exists. Brisbane doesn't have to prove anything anymore. The whole thing now has come full circle – that we could go from having to bring local bands back here to exporting the event interstate, with a home-grown band headlining, the statement was too good not to make.

Regurgitator, conversely, are commercially and artistically back on the borderline. In September 2004, the band holed up for three weeks in a transparent mobile studio in Melbourne's Federation Square as the stars of a reality television program for Channel V called *Band In A Bubble*. Although the program was a hit, the resulting album *Mish Mash* was not, and the group's status is now in doubt.

Naturally, new bands have risen and fallen. Not From There, led by expatriate Austrian Heinz Riegler, burst through in 1998 with a stunning single Sich Offnen and a dissonant, intermittently compelling debut album, *Sand On Seven*. But the follow-up, *Latvian Lovers*, saw Not From There caught amidships: half electro-pop, half industrial rock, no one knew what to make of it. The band broke up soon after.

But by far the biggest success story belongs to George. Formed in 1996, the band's earnest hybrid of jazz, classical and rock seemed to strike a lost chord. Topped by the breathy vocals of Katie Noonan, George's debut album *Polyserena* entered the ARIA charts at pole position upon its release in February 2002, going platinum within weeks. The band's 2004 release *Unity* showed them outgrowing their early roots as – in co-leader Tyrone Noonan's description – a 'Jeff Buckley appreciation society'.[1]

Brisbane's music scene today is not so much a reflection of the city as an indicator of its changing fortunes. With the end of the Bjelke-Petersen era, an insular scene began to look outside for inspiration. Nowadays, when a Brisbane band touches on politics, they are more likely to be addressing the realities of life in John Howard's Australia (Powderfinger), or the American-led war in Iraq (George), or even the first world's exploitation of the third (Regurgitator).

Their endeavours are actively endorsed by the state. Peter Beattie – who currently enjoys a bigger majority than the National Party did when it had the help of the gerrymander – is known to hand copies of the latest Powderfinger and Go-Betweens releases to visiting dignitaries.

In August 2003 legal advisors for an ailing Joh Bjelke-Petersen submitted an ex-gratia compensation claim of over $350 million for loss of earnings, loss of reputation, legal bills and 'pain and suffering' caused by the Fitzgerald Inquiry. The claim was based on the technical premise that the inquiry had been improperly established.

Labor premier Peter Beattie treated the bid carefully. He had adopted an unofficial policy of rapprochement with Queensland's past; only days earlier, he had wheeled the 92-year-old Bjelke-Petersen around the redeveloped Lang Park, renamed Suncorp Stadium. His old foe was in the degenerative stages of Parkinson's disease; for that, if nothing else, Beattie accorded Bjelke-Petersen respect.

Bjelke-Petersen's compensation claim was followed two weeks later by another, this time from his former police commissioner. Terry Lewis – paroled in 1998 after serving half his 14-year prison sentence for official corruption – never accepted his jury's verdict. His attempt to rewrite history was immediately rebuffed: it was, in author Ross Fitzgerald's words, an insult to the intelligence as much as it was to the citizens of Queensland.[2]

After two months, Bjelke-Petersen's claim was also rejected. The crown solicitor advised the government that not only were the Fitzgerald Inquiry's legal credentials beyond question, Bjelke-Petersen had been lucky to escape a retrial on perjury and corruption charges. Undaunted, the former premier's advisors took their claim to Buckingham Palace. They had learned little from the past: not for the first time, Her Majesty declined to intervene in Queensland's affairs.

As Bjelke-Petersen's health declined, another old campaigner continued to cling to life. Improbably, Triple Zed is in better health now than it has been in 20 years. By the late '90s, equity in the station's Fortitude Valley headquarters gave it sufficient leverage to purchase a one-third stake in Broadcast Park on Mt Coot-tha, a joint venture shared with classical broadcaster 4MBS and Christian network, Family Radio. A 12-kilowatt transmitter and a tower reaching over Mt Coot-tha's tree line enabled Triple Zed's signal to be beamed clearly throughout Brisbane for the first time.

Slowly, the station began to adopt a more pragmatic approach to its future. After years of bitter infighting and inaction, the collective slowly died away. Triple Zed's manager and promotions coordinator are both paid for their efforts, and while the quality of the station's output still varies wildly, it has successfully applied for government funding for a range of employment training programs. The station's old siege mentality is gone: a belated adjustment, one might say, to no longer living in a state of siege.

Brisbane today is a very different place from what it was even a decade ago. Not even its harshest critics could accuse it of being a big country town, but neither is it an international city on the scale of Sydney or Melbourne. Not yet.

Jim Soorley – whose 12-year administration did much to transform the city's visage – left office pushing for the construction of a horrendously expensive tunnel under the Brisbane River; now, a new lord mayor, Campbell Newman, is promising to build five of them. He may yet be serious. By the middle of the century, Brisbane is predicted to be a vast urban sprawl of over 5 million people, linking the Gold and Sunshine Coasts.

Stoked by a growing population, a protracted boom in the property market has placed intense pressure on Brisbane's few remaining landmarks. After hosting the reformed Blondie one last time, Festival Hall was pulled down in August 2003 to make way for another block of luxury apartments. For some, the demolition of the old boxing pavilion turned music venue was all too familiar: while Festival Hall's architectural significance was hardly on par with Cloudland, its rich social history was undeniable.

As the population has filtered back from the suburbs to the inner city, venue operators have been faced with growing noise complaints from residents, even around the traditional nightclub strip of Ann and Brunswick Street in Fortitude Valley. Recognising the resource on its doorstep, in 2001 the Brisbane City Council commissioned an independent study into how best to protect and promote the city's music culture.[3]

Otherwise, Brisbane is, well, relaxed and comfortable. The culture has changed. Grant McLennan, who returned to Brisbane in the mid '90s, found himself as impressed as he had been so many years before, after leaving Cairns to come to boarding school.

Grant McLennan: You could actually get a handle on the scene here. You didn't have to sneak around anymore; there was almost a bit of an infrastructure happening. There were art galleries. There were people talking about writing. There was even a writers' festival! And it's a beautiful town, as well. I love river towns, I always have.

Writers have indeed played a role in the renewal of the city's self-image. While Andrew McGahan's *Praise* and *Last Drinks* captured the paranoia and disturbance of the Bjelke-Petersen years, Nick Earls' suburban love stories – especially

Zigzag Street – pinpointed a lighter, cheerfully self-deprecating consciousness. The two novelists contrasted in much the same way as the Saints and Go-Betweens before them; Earls even named one of his books, *Bachelor Kisses*, after a Go-Betweens song.

> **Nick Earls:** I think writing was always going to be it for me, but [the Go-Betweens' third album] *Spring Hill Fair* was the signal that you could come from Brisbane and still have an impact. It's interesting that it wasn't a novelist; it's interesting that it wasn't David Malouf, and I'm not sure why it wasn't. Perhaps because he was of my parents' generation.

By 2001 recognition for Earls' novels was so high that the author starred in a council television campaign that sold Brisbane back to Brisvegans. This wasn't just a warm, comfortable, laid-back city. No, it was a creative, exciting, happening place. The weather wasn't just beautiful one day and perfect the next. Frankly, it was hot out there. Now you could go to a gallery, go to a restaurant, go see a band, play in one yourself.

No one was about to stop you trying.

notes

Introduction – Know Your Product
1. See R McLeod, 'Young Identities',
   http://www.breakmyface.com/bands/youngidentities.html
2. I McFarlane, *The Encyclopedia Of Australian Rock And Pop*, Sydney,
   Allen & Unwin 1999, p. 706.
3. A McGahan, *Last Drinks*, Sydney, Allen & Unwin 2000, p. 73.
4. Quoted in A Stafford, 'Dream Believer', *Rolling Stone* (Australia),
   May 1997, pp. 23–24.

Chapter 1. A Million People Staying Low
1. P Burgess, quoted in S Harris, Political Football: The Springbok
   Tour of Australia 1971, Melbourne, Gold Star 1972, p. 13. This
   notorious incident occurred during the Springboks' 3 August match
   in Toowoomba, on the Darling Downs. A 21-year-old student
   demonstrator, Brian Tovey, had his nose broken in the unprovoked
   assault by a rugby union fan. Despite the assault occurring directly
   in front of numerous police and the identity of the assailant being
   known, no charges were ever laid.
2. P Charlton, *State Of Mind: Why Queensland Is Different*, Sydney,
   Methuen-Haynes 1983, p. 16.
3. Charlton, p. 75, and H Lunn, *Behind The Banana Curtain*, Brisbane,
   University of Queensland Press 1980, pp. 121–123.
4. Charlton, pp. 138–139.
5. ibid., p. 139.
6. A McGahan, *Last Drinks*, Sydney, Allen & Unwin 2000, pp. 143–144.
7. H Lunn, *Joh: The Life And Political Adventures Of Johannes Bjelke-
   Petersen*, Brisbane, University of Queensland Press 1978, pp. 14–15,
   24–25.
8. ibid. p. 27.

9. R Fitzgerald, *From 1915 To The Early 1980s: A History Of Queensland*, Brisbane, University of Queensland Press 1984, p. 245.
10. E Whitton, *The Hillbilly Dictator: Australia's Police State* (Revised Edition), Sydney, ABC Books 1993, p. 10.
11. Fitzgerald, p. 261.
12. Lunn, *Joh*, p. 255.
13. Harris, p. 135.
14. Lunn, *Joh*, p. 93.
15. ibid., p. 94.

Chapter 2. Guerrilla Radio

1. See 'FM In Australia: The Background, The Future', *Radio Times*, vol 1.1, December 1975, p. 6.
2. J Tebbutt, 'Constructing Broadcasting For The Public', in H Wilson (ed) *Australian Communications And The Public Sphere: Essays In Memory Of Bill Bonney*, Melbourne, Macmillan 1995, p. 130.
3. ibid., pp. 128–129.
4. Edited transcript of John Woods' opening speech to mark the birth of (then) 4ZZ, 8 December 1975. This speech, plus an extract from its parallel three years later on 15 December 1978, was replayed on 4ZZZ (along with the Who's Won't Get Fooled Again) on 20 November 2001, as a tribute to Woods after his death from leukaemia.
5. 'News And Information', *Radio Times*, vol 1.1, December 1975, p. 4.
6. R Fitzgerald, *From 1915 To The Early 1980s: A History Of Queensland*, Brisbane, University of Queensland Press 1984, p. 571.
7. ibid. pp. 571–572.
8. 'In Depth', *Radio Times*, March 1976, pp. 12–13.
9. '4ZZZ High Power', *Radio Times*, vol 1.6, May 1976, p. 11.
10. Brisbane Women's Media Group, 'Triple Z: Maintaining Credibility or, Did Homogenised Radio Turn Sour?', *Hecate*, vol 3.1, February 1977, pp. 110, 113.
11. 11. G Williams, *Generation Zed: No Other Radio Like This*, Brisbane, Kingswood 2000, p. 76.
12. 'Top Ten', *Radio Times*, January 1977, p. 13.
13. 'Music', *Radio Times*, vol 1.1, December 1975, p. 5.
14. Anon, Letter to the editor (with reply by Michael Finucan), *Radio Times*, October 1977, pp. 8–9.
15. 'Pick Of The Platters Of '77', *Radio Times*, January 1978, p. 9.

Chapter 3. The Most Primitive Band in the World

1. C Walker, *Stranded: The Secret History Of Australian Independent Music*, Sydney, Pan Macmillan 1996, pp. 9–10. Additional biographical detail on the Saints was drawn from this source.
2. ibid. pp. 11–12.

3. ibid. p. 19.
4. D Kimball, 'The Saints: The Most Primitive Band In The World', 2000. URL: http://saints.binke.com.au/bio-2.html. This site was also an additional source of biographical information.
5. J Ingham, *Sounds*, 16 October 1976, p. 37.
6. Walker, p. 22.
7. V Johnson, *Radio Birdman*, Melbourne, Sheldon Booth 1990, pp. 93–94.
8. Kimball, URL: http://saints.binke.com.au/bio-4.html.
9. I McFarlane, 'Memories Are Made Of This': liner notes for *The Saints: Wild About You 1976–1978*, Raven 2000.
10. ibid. McFarlane lists the track sequence on the master tape box dated 25/10/77 as follows: (side one) Orstralia; Lost And Found; Perfect Day; Run Down; A Minor Aversion; Private Affair; (side two) No, Your Product; New Centre Of The Universe; River Deep, Mountain High; Untitled; Misunderstood; Do The Robot. These sessions have been released on the *All Times Through Paradise* box set.
11. C Walker, 'Ed Kuepper: Exile From Main Street', *Rolling Stone* 468 (Australia), March 1992, p. 58.

Chapter 4. The Striped Sunlight Sound
1. D Nichols, *The Go-Betweens*, Sydney, Allen & Unwin 1997, p. 24.
2. Forster discusses his taste in cover versions in Nichols, pp. 21–22.
3. Nichols, pp. 36–37.
4. These are now available on CD as *78 'til 79: The Lost Album* and include both Able Label singles as well as the two recordings made for Beserkley.
5. Nichols, p. 88.

Chapter 5. Task Force versus the Brisbane Punks
1. R Fitzgerald, *From 1915 To The Early 1980s: A History Of Queensland*, Brisbane, University of Queensland Press 1984, p. 572.
2. Former police constable Michael Egan gave this quote after resigning from the force following a demonstration in March 1979. This and figures for numbers of arrests and charges are both cited in Fitzgerald, pp. 573 and 575.
3. Fitzgerald, pp. 583–584.
4. This is of course not the same band as the Sydney group formed in the 1980s.
5. C Walker, *Pulp*, No. 1, 1977, p. 9.
6. Walker, *Pulp*, Nos. 3 and 4, 1978, p. 4.
7. Information on Murphy's Marauders and the Task Force courtesy of J S Reid, pers. comm., January 2002. See also interview with the Brisbane Devotee (aka Reid) in the *Cane Toad Times*, 'Australia's

Future?' issue, 1979, pp. 7–10.

8. Reid, January 2002.
9. Clinton Walker reported on this gig in *Pulp*: 'What the paper failed to mention, however, was the kids bashed by cops, the cops posing as punks in paint-splattered shirts and busting anyone for swearing in conversation, and the kids who were harassed by cops as they tried to go home as instructed. "We'll stop any punk rock in Brisbane," one cop was heard to utter.' Reprinted in *Stranded: The Secret History Of Australian Independent Music*, Sydney, Pan Macmillan 1996, pp. 39–40.
10. Rob Cameron, 'Pub Rock Revived', *Semper*, 7 June 1978, p. 33.
11. See for example Richard McGregor's review of *Lethal Weapons* in the Australian issue of *Rolling Stone*, 27 July 1978; also Viola Sharp in *Semper*, 24 May 1978, p. 35; Richard Guilliatt, 'Sign To Suicide Or Suicide To Sign?', *RAM*, 2 June 1978, p. 9.
12. While the labels on the original single mark the B-side as 1977 and the A-side as 1978, Razar's Marty Burke claims Warren Lamond told him (in a drunken moment) that 1977 was a ruse, designed to indicate the Leftovers had beaten their peers into the studio, if not onto plastic.
13. Read more about the Leftovers' brief but eventful career in the excellent liner notes of *The Fucken Leftovers Hate You*, released on CD by the Dropkick label in 2003. The slipcase features a heartfelt memoir by associate David Holliday (who helped fund the band's single), as well as reprinting several articles and letters.

Chapter 6. Swept Away

1. D Nichols, *The Go-Betweens*, Sydney, Allen & Unwin 1997, p. 57. A photograph of one of these shows is featured in the book's photographic insert.
2. Dennis Cantwell's father, who was working in real estate at the time, did some work scouting locations for the program.

Chapter 7. Last of the Leather Age

1. A letter from Shepherd to the fan club was reprinted in Vivien Johnson's biography *Radio Birdman*, Melbourne, Sheldon Booth 1990, p. 79.
2. B Shepherd, liner notes to *Fun Things* EP, Pennimann 2000.
3. ibid.
4. The reality is slightly more complicated than Peno remembers. A Stand Alone was among four songs recorded for the band's sole, unreleased studio recording in mid 1980, while Igloo, according to Medew, was written immediately afterwards. The three other tracks: Real Gone; Time Moves Fast; It's So Hard. This recording has been bootlegged, appearing on European compilations of the

Screaming Tribesmen.
5. In 2003 the EP was remixed by Murray Shepherd for a new
   compilation, *The Savage Beat Of The Screaming Tribesmen*, and now
   packs a wallop to rival the Fun Things.
6. D Laing, CD liner notes to *Do The Pop! The Australian Garage Rock
   Sound 1976–87*, Shock 2002, p. 17.
7. Just Skin, Lost, This Reason and Through My Heart all began life
   as End songs before their appearance on a series of Died Pretty
   albums, Through My Heart as late as 1993's *Trace*.

Chapter 8. Everybody Moves
1. Quoted in T Creswell, 'Taking the Low Road to the Top', *Rolling
   Stone* 472 (Australia), July 1992, p. 77.
2. Quote attributed to Ian Sinnamon, then the head of the Department
   of Architecture at the University of Queensland. Source: Elaine van
   Kempen, http://www.nationaltrustqld.org/cgi-bin1/memories.pl.
3. G McLennan, quoted in liner notes for CD reissue of *Send Me A
   Lullaby*, Circus 2002.
4. C Walker, *Stranded: The Secret History Of Australian Independent
   Music*, Sydney, Pan Macmillan 1996, p. 105.
5. R Fitzgerald, *From 1915 To The Early 1980s: A History Of Queensland*,
   Brisbane, University of Queensland Press 1984, pp. 584–587. Hinze's
   even more draconian draft legislation enabled not just police but
   private security firms to search and detain suspected anti-games
   protesters without a warrant, and conferred upon them immunity
   from prosecution for any assault or wrongful imprisonment.
   Rather than explicitly rule such action in or out, the resulting
   Commonwealth Games Act, whether by accident or design, was
   sufficiently vague for no one to be really sure.
6. G Williams, *Generation Zed: No Other Radio Like This*, Brisbane,
   Kingswood 2000, p. 28.
7. J Biafra, *Maximumrocknroll*, No. 10, 1983. Reprinted online:
   http://homepages.nyu.edu/~cch223/australia/info/dktourreport.html.
8. Aurukun is an Aboriginal settlement on the west coast of Cape York
   Peninsula, far north Queensland. Title of the land had been given over
   to Comalco for mining purposes, a company in which the premier's
   family and many of his ministers held shares. See E Whitton, *The
   Hillbilly Dictator: Australia's Police State*, Sydney, ABC Books 1989,
   pp. 19–20.

Chapter 9. Brisbane Blacks
1. R Fitzgerald, *From 1915 To The Early 1980s: A History Of Queensland*,
   Brisbane, University of Queensland Press 1984, p. 586.
2. L Woodward, 'Aboriginal uproar as Tomkins is at it again',
   Australian, 15 October 1982, p. 11.

3. Fitzgerald, pp. 528–529.
4. C Walker, *Buried Country*, Sydney, Pluto Press 2000, pp. 14, 262.
5. ibid. p. 263.
6. See M Aird, *Brisbane Blacks*, Southport, Keeaira Press 2001, p. 82.
7. Perhaps a conservative estimate: Ross Watson gave a figure of 250 calls for an eight-hour program to Garry Williams (see *Generation Zed*, p. 55), but in an interview with Judi McCrossin this was revised down to between 120 and 150 per day.
8. Now the Australian Broadcasting Tribunal.

Chapter 10. Too Much Acid

1. E Whitton, *The Hillbilly Dictator: Australia's Police State*, Sydney, ABC Books 1989, p. 92.
2. ibid. p. 107. Whitton details the breakdown of Lewis' corrupt monies as follows: $2221 a week in bribes; $3923 from illegal gaming bosses Vittorio Conte and Geraldo Bellino and $5307 from prostitution identities Anne-Marie Tilley and Hector Hapeta. Having already been refused a knighthood by the Queen in 1982, Lewis' diaries show several meetings with Bjelke-Petersen confidant Sir Edward Lyons 're honours' before finally receiving a recommendation from the premier in August 1985.
3. ibid. pp. 114–115, 162–163.

Chapter 11. SS Brigade

1. A McGahan, *Last Drinks*, Sydney, Allen & Unwin 2000, p. 173.
2. Dickie recounts this story in *The Road To Fitzgerald And Beyond*, Brisbane, University of Queensland Press 1988, pp. 157–161. After watching the move take place, Dickie was followed by police as he cycled home; days later, the house at which he was staying received several threatening phone calls, along with an apparent bullet hole in the front window after a police vehicle had been observed outside the house.
3. E Whitton, *The Hillbilly Dictator: Australia's Police State*, Sydney, ABC Books 1989, pp. 121, 124.
4. ibid. pp. 150–151.
5. ibid. p. 130; see also Dickie, pp. 193–194.
6. Bjelke-Petersen received support from his Aboriginal Affairs minister (and now independent MP for the federal seat of Kennedy) Bob Katter Jr, who banned condoms from Aboriginal community stores with the immortal line, 'Condoms are despicable things that won't prevent the spread of AIDS but will encourage the community to have sex with gay abandon.' See Dickie, p. 190.
7. McGahan, p. 1.
8. This letter was reprinted on the back page of *Semper*, No. 1, 1989 under the title 'Union Logic', along with Litster Mann and

Ffrench's blacked-out legal advice to the union executive and Victoria Brazil's leaked plans for Triple Zed's eviction.

9. D Porter, 'Radio station 4ZZZ on campus', file note, 21 February 1989, p. 1.

10. ibid. pp. 2–3. Porter writes in part: 'Within an hour of that meeting the director-general of education rang the vice-chancellor, at the request of the minister, urging the vice-chancellor to provide the student union with the written confirmation requested by Ms Brazil. The vice-chancellor spoke to the director-general the following day and explained the background and that a further meeting was to be held later that day.'

11. ibid. p. 1. Porter also writes 'the university would support the student union in any move to evict 4ZZZ through court action'.

12. S Chen, 'Victoria rules the campus', *Sun*, 13 January 1989, p. 19.

13. One of the union's more contentious contributions to college life was a special bus service running from the campus colleges to the Royal Exchange and Regatta Hotels in Toowong. See J Phillips, 'Victoria Brazil states her claim', *Courier-Mail*, Monitor, 13 May 1989, pp. 1, 4.

Chapter 12. Cyclone Hits Expo

1. Biafra and Alternative Tentacles were charged under Californian law with distributing 'harmful matter to minors' after including a poster by Swiss artist HR Giger (famous for designing the creatures used in the *Alien* films) in the Dead Kennedys' *Frankenchrist* album. The case was dismissed when the jury failed to reach a verdict. Biafra had been a vocal campaigner against the so-called moral majority and, in particular, the activities of the notorious Parents' Music Resource Centre. Led by the bouffant-haired Tipper Gore, wife of future presidential candidate Al Gore, the PMRC led the crusade against 'pornographic' music that eventually led to the introduction of the widespread 'parental advisory' system of record labelling. In his singling out of the Dead Kennedys for attention, and by claiming to be acting as a 'concerned parent', Pasterkamp's cues and rhetoric were clearly derived from that used by the PMRC.

2. J Burke, 'Cassette rocks hearing', *Sun*, 15 May 1989, p. 7.

3. D Fardon, Decision By Bench: [Constable]   *Katarina Ruzh Bosnjak Versus Frank Warwick Vere*. Magistrates Court, Brisbane, 16 May 1989, pp. 158–163.

4. P Dickie, *The Road To Fitzgerald And Beyond*, Brisbane, University of Queensland Press 1988, p. 280.

5. See E Whitton, *The Hillbilly Dictator: Australia's Police State*, Sydney, ABC Books 1989, pp. 183–185 for a full account of this legendary exchange.

6. G Roberts, 'Nat poll promise: a "porno" rock ban', *Sydney Morning*

Herald, 10 November 1989, p. 3. Cooper also wildly predicted a gay Mardi Gras on the Gold Coast should Labor come to office; one of his ministers, Bob Katter Jr, later promised to walk 'backwards to Bourke' if there were any gays in his Charters Towers electorate.

Chapter 13. Rock Against Work!

1. J Marx, 'Parables For Wooden Ears' (review), *Rolling Stone* 499 (Australia), August 1994, p. 90.
2. Quoting Marx again, from the above review: ' "Tail", for example, is tangled and inert and teeters precariously on the brink of disappearing up its own arsehole . . .'

Chapter 14. Spring Hill Fair

1. *Time Off*, by then Australia's longest-running street paper, was established in 1980. After an internal split, *Rave* was created in 1991. The dance-oriented publication *Scene* followed in 1993.
2. Cricket had in fact become something of a common bond in the Brisbane scene. Many of the musicians and local industry figures were obsessive followers of the flannel game, with unsung local band Chopper Division founding the Brisband Cricket Competition. Former *Time Off* editor Simon McKenzie was (literally) the 11th member of the Webfinger XI, comprising members of Powderfinger and Webster: 'You had [producer] Magoo umpiring while Bernard Fanning bowled his outswingers (with some genuine pace I might add) against Peter Walsh. That was the sort of people who were playing. You might actually get an audience for that these days.'
3. A third Hansen sister, Mary, was a long-serving member of British band Stereolab until her untimely death in a road accident in 2002, aged 36.
4. Bob Ellis relates this encounter in his story for *J-Mag*, 1994–1995, p. 43.

Chapter 15. Black Ticket Day

1. G Williams, *Generation Zed: No Radio Station Like This*, Brisbane, Kingswood Press, 2000, p. 39.
2. ibid. pp. 62–63.
3. P Barclay, 'Queensland: 10 Years After Fitzgerald', Radio National, 16 May 1999, reprinted online: http://www.abc.net.au/rn/talks/bbing/stories/s26032.htm
4. J Birmingham, 'It's Raining Cops', *Rolling Stone* 533 (Australia), March 1997, p. 40 (reprinted in the anthology *Off One's Tits*, Vintage, Sydney 2002). Triple Zed put forward this allegation as evidence that the actions by police that night were premeditated. If the riot gear belonged only to the five PSRT initially assigned to cover the event, however, this cannot be sustained.

5. Criminal Justice Commission, *Police Behaviour At A Triple Zed Market Day: Report Of An Investigation*, Brisbane, 1997, p. xii.
6. ibid. p. viii.
7. M Hele, 'Military police accused over festival brawl', *Courier-Mail*, 21 October 1996, p. 2.
8. Cooper stated at his press conference: 'We will work together and make sure that we have the arrangements with senior police and the management of 4ZZZ to work together to make sure the next one works well', quoted by J Baird in 4ZZZ (Media Release), 'Cooper assures future of 4ZZZ Market Days', 21 October 1996.
9. Criminal Justice Commission, p. xiv. See also pp. viii–xi, xiii–xiv.

Chapter 16. The Human Jukebox
1. Now the Powerhouse Centre for Live Arts.
2. C Mathieson, *The Sell-In*, Sydney, Allen & Unwin 2000, p. 196.
3. A Stafford, 'New Faces: Kiley Gaffney', *Rolling Stone* 526 (Australia), September 1996, p. 36.
4. This version was eventually released as I Like Your Old Remix Better Than Your New Remix on *Unit*'s fourth single (!/Modern Life).
5. A Humphreys, 'Unit' (review), *Rolling Stone* 544 (Australia), January 1998, p. 99.

Chapter 17. New Suburban Fables
1. The Day You Come was nominated for Song of the Year at the 1996 ARIA awards; it also came in at #6 on Triple J's Hottest 100 listener's poll for that year.
2. A Stafford, 'Ben Lee vs the World', *Rolling Stone* 560 (Australia), April 1999, pp. 38–39, 110. After calling Lee a 'precocious little cunt' in Sydney weekly *Revolver*, Lee hit back at Fanning in an interview with the author. Rather than retract his remarks, Fanning instead toned them down to 'smart-arse little wanker'.
3. Oxley was the former seat of former federal Labor leader Bill Hayden, who held the seat from 1961 to 1988 before becoming governor-general. While Fanning may have been lyrically coy in regards to Hanson, the same could not be said of local band Escape From Toytown, whose song The Fish And Chip Bitch From Ipswich was a characteristically blunt denunciation. The song topped Triple Zed's Hot 100 poll for 1996.
4. In R Yates, 'Trusty Old Jackets', *Massive*, September 2000, at http://www.ozmusic-central.com.au/powderfinger/text/articl31.htm

Chapter 18. Today Your Love, Tomorrow the World
1. A Stafford, 'Dream Believers', *Rolling Stone* 535 (Australia), May

1997, pp. 23–24.
2. See I Shedden, 'Darren Hayes: Miami sound machine', *Weekend Australian*, Review, 9–10 October 2002, pp. 4–6.
3. See for example D Scatena, 'Pop duo ends on sour note', *Daily Telegraph*, 6 October 2001, p. 3 and 'Solo the loneliest number', p. 23.

Epilogue – No, Your Product

1. In K Munro, 'George', *Rolling Stone* 576 (Australia), July 2000, p. 30.
2. L Willis, 'Joh Bjelke-Petersen and Terry Lewis seeking compensation for Fitzgerald Inquiry', *PM*, 19 August 2003, reprinted online: http://www.abc.net.au/pm/content/2003/s927935.htm
3. See T Flew et al., *Music Industry Development And Brisbane's Future As A Creative City*, Brisbane, BCC/QUT, 2001.

playlist

Earlier editions of *Pig City* featured a highly selective discography/soundtrack that guided readers through as much of the music described in the book as possible. This was done chapter by chapter, attempting to put the recordings into context. It also allowed me to mention a number of artists that did not otherwise make their way into the body of the book.

For the 2014 edition, as the streaming era began to overtake CDs, the soundtrack was dropped. This was arguably a mistake, but it was impossible to keep up with titles as they went in and out of print or were superseded by new compilations and releases; the information dated virtually from the moment of publication.

We now live in the age of the playlist and, notwithstanding my own reservations about streaming, Spotify represents the most accessible way for newcomers to *Pig City* to listen to the music that inspired me to write it in the first place. So this is primarily aimed at readers who may be hearing this music for the first time.

This playlist hews more closely than the original edition to the artists under direct discussion. Of course, not everything is on Spotify, and you'll have to go to YouTube to track down some other essential earlier items from the era. It cuts straight to the Saints, picking up from the book's subtitle and leaving out the prehistory in chapters one and two.

As I wrote at the time: 'This list of recordings is a reflection of my biases, obsessions and prejudices and, of course, a starting point only.' The beauty of a playlist is that you can add (and subtract) as you please, especially as other songs are uploaded – with the necessary disclaimer that, in the digital age, everything is ephemeral and nothing is fixed.

Chapter 3 – The Most Primitive Band in the World

Spotify: The first three Saints albums are all essential. These songs are a quick primer charting their progression from the (I'm) Stranded single (1976) through to the more measured but equally devastating rock-and-soul punch of *Prehistoric Sounds*. Know Your Product is the bridge between the two; pity no one was ready for it at the time.

Brisbane (Security City) is a solo Ed Kuepper composition, while Simple Love is the lead cut from the *Paralytic Tonight Dublin Tomorrow* EP – the first Chris Bailey–led release under the Saints' name, illustrating the divergence of direction between the two writers. Follow both paths at your own discretion from there, including Kuepper's work with the Laughing Clowns.

- The Saints – (I'm) Stranded (1976)
- The Saints – This Perfect Day (stand-alone single version, 1977)
- The Saints – Know Your Product (1978)
- The Saints – Swing For The Crime (1978)
- The Saints – Brisbane (Security City) (1978)
- The Saints – Simple Love (1980)

YouTube: Check the band's ferocious live set from Paddington Town Hall, 1977, culminating in the blistering version of Nights In Venice.

Chapter 4 – The Striped Sunlight Sound

Spotify: The first two Go-Betweens singles, plus the A-side of I Need Two Heads, their sole single for Postcard Records in 1980, were all composed by Robert Forster, before Lindy Morrison's debut on drums.

- The Go-Betweens – Karen (1978)
- The Go-Betweens – Lee Remick (1978)
- The Go-Betweens – People Say (1979)
- The Go-Betweens – Don't Let Him Come Back (1979)
- The Go-Betweens – I Need Two Heads (1980)

Chapter 5 – Task Force versus the Brisbane Punks

Spotify: British band the Stranglers make a cameo here for a song that directly referenced Bjelke-Petersen's police state, after an infamous date at the Queen's Hotel on 27 February 1979.

- The Stranglers – Nuclear Device (The Wizard Of Aus) (1979)

Otherwise, none of the local uber-punk acts discussed in this chapter have made it to Spotify, and the original singles all command three- to four-figure sums among collectors. You can, at least, try before you buy on YouTube:

- The Survivors – Undecided (1977 demo – a ballistic cover of the Masters Apprentices song)
- The Survivors – Baby Come Back 7" (1978)
- Razar – Stamp Out Disco B/W Task Force (Undercover Cops) (1978)
- The (Fucken) Leftovers – Cigarettes And Alcohol 7" (1979)

From this extremely febrile era, see also:

- Just Urbain – Just Urbain 7" (1979)
- Young Identities – New Trends EP (1980)
- The Upsets – Back To Afghanistan (1980)

Chapter 6 – Swept Away

Spotify: The Riptides' full catalogue is now available to stream, as is the Apartments. Peter Milton Walsh is, in this writer's opinion, the finest Australian songwriter most Australians have never heard of.

- The Riptides – Sunset Strip (1978)
- The Riptides – Tomorrow's Tears (1980)
- The Riptides – Hearts And Flowers (1982)
- The Apartments – Help (1979)
- The Apartments – Mr Somewhere (1985)
- The Riptides – Swept Away (1987 – from the live album *Resurface*, recorded in Brisbane)

Chapter 7 – Last of the Leather Age

Spotify: All credit to the LCMR label, keepers of the flame for many a lost Brisbane artist, for officially releasing a four-track EP of demos by the 31st in 2017. This EP included the original version of A Stand Alone, recorded as a demo in 1981 with Ron Peno on vocals. The Screaming Tribesmen released the definitive take in 1984. At time of writing, only the 1987 recording of Igloo is available to stream.

I'm cheating a bit by including Damien Lovelock's cover of The End's Ghostown, another song about Brisbane written for the End by Brett Myers. Myers later formed Died Pretty with Peno in Sydney.

- The 31st – A Stand Alone (1981)
- The Screaming Tribesmen – A Stand Alone (1984)
- The Screaming Tribesmen – Igloo (1987, originally released in 1983)

- The Screaming Tribesmen – Date With A Vampyre (1985)
- Damien Lovelock – Ghostown (1988)

You'll need to search YouTube for the following:

- *The Fun Things* EP (1980) – one of the most prized (and priciest) Australian punk collectables!
- The End – My Confession 7" (1981)
- *The Screaming Tribesmen* EP (1982, but better heard on the CD compilation *The Savage Beat Of The Screaming Tribesmen*, released in 2003)
- The Screaming Tribesmen – Igloo (original single, 1983)

Chapter 8 – Everybody Moves
Spotify: The playlisted songs here capture the sound of the Go-Betweens moving from pop through post-punk and back again, with Grant McLennan emerging as a songwriting force. Pig City is of course the song from which this book took its name. While not from Brisbane, Midnight Oil's Dreamworld is a direct rebuke to both Queensland's white-shoe brigade and demolition cowboys the Deen Brothers; the song references Cloudland, which the band played many times.

- The Go-Betweens – Your Turn, My Turn (1981)
- The Go-Betweens – By Chance (1983)
- The Go-Betweens – Cattle And Cane (1983)
- The Parameters – Pig City (1984)
- Midnight Oil – Dreamworld (1987)

Chapter 9 – Brisbane Blacks
Spotify: The extraordinary catalogue of Kev Carmody is available to stream, as are a handful of songs by Dennis

Conlon and the Magpies, aka Mop and the Dropouts. Only songs from Carmody's debut album *Pillars Of Society* feature on this playlist, being recorded during the period covered by this chapter. His is one of the great Australian songbooks.

- Mop and the Dropouts – Brisbane Blacks (1982)
- Kev Carmody – Pillars Of Society (1988)
- Kev Carmody – Black Deaths In Custody (1988)
- Kev Carmody – Thou Shalt Not Steal (1988)

Chapter 10 – Too Much Acid

Spotify: The work of John F Kennedy is on Spotify under a variety of names, including John Kennedy and early singles under the name JFK and the Cuban Crisis. Brisbane '82 wasn't actually recorded until 1999, but best captures the era of which he speaks.

- John Kennedy – Brisbane '82 (1999)
- Ups and Downs – The Living Kind (1986)
- Boxcar – Freemason (1988)

While no recordings by Tex Deadly and the Dums Dums made it to vinyl, a couple of cassette-only tracks have surfaced on YouTube, including Crazy (originally released on the 1983 cassette compilation *Leaving Home For The Party On The Roof*) and the obviously Cramps-inspired Voodoo Doll. *Shocker*, the sole album by Pineapples from the Dawn of Time, is on YouTube. Listen to the whole damn thing.

Chapter 11 – SS Brigade

The chapter title was taken from a rare 1982 hardcore single by Public Execution (1982). A compilation of archival material, including this single, was released in 2013 and, at time of writing, was available to stream via Bandcamp.

Chapter 12 – Cyclone Hits Expo

Spotify: The first Livid Festival was an all-Brisbane affair, and brought the Saints (sans Ed Kuepper) and the Go-Betweens back to celebrate the city's musical history. This roughly coincided with their greatest commercial successes (relatively speaking):

- The Saints – Just Like Fire Would (1986)
- The Go-Betweens – Streets Of Your Town (1988)

It would be remiss not to include the Dead Kennedys' Too Drunk To Fuck – not only for the song being the subject of the Rocking Horse Records' obscenity trial, but for the San Francisco band's earlier experience in Brisbane when they played Festival Hall in 1983.

- The Dead Kennedys – Too Drunk To Fuck (1981)

The title song for this chapter was by Choo Dikka Dikka, recorded live on 4ZZZ and officially released only on the CD compilation *Behind The Banana Curtain*. It can be streamed via YouTube only.

Chapter 13 – Rock Against Work!

Spotify: The playlisted songs represent a quick survey of the early work of the artists featured in this chapter:

- Screamfeeder – Tower (1992; single first recorded under the name the Madmen, 1989)
- Dreamkillers – Father Can You Help Me (1992)
- Powderfinger – Reap What You Sow (1993)
- Screamfeeder – Wrote You Off (1993)
- Screamfeeder – Around A Pole (1993)
- Pangaea – Power Of Three (1994)
- Regurgitator – I Like It Like That (1995)

Chapter 14 – Spring Hill Fair

Spotify: These songs cover Custard from 1992 to 1998, digressing to Dave McCormack, Glenn Thompson and Bob Moore's collaboration with Robert Forster (on Forster's album *Calling From A Country Phone*). Custard's cover of Jonathan Richman's Since She Started To Ride is indicative of where both McCormack and Forster were coming from at the time.

- Custard – Melody (1994)
- Custard – Bedford (1992)
- Robert Forster – Falling Star (1993)
- Custard – Since She Started To Ride (1995)
- Custard – Apartment (1995)
- Custard – Girls Like That (Don't Go For Guys Like Us) (1998)

Chapter 16 – The Human Jukebox

Spotify: On the playlist are a selection of songs from Regurgitator's first three albums on the Warner-owned EastWest label:

- Regurgitator – I Sucked A Lot Of Cock To Get Where I Am (1996)
- Regurgitator – Music Is Sport (1996)
- Regurgitator – I Like Your Old Stuff Better Than Your New Stuff (1997)
- Regurgitator –! (The Song Formerly Known As) (1997)
- Regurgitator – I Will Lick Your Arsehole (1997)
- Regurgitator – I Wanna Be A Nudist (1999)

Chapter 17 – New Suburban Fables

Spotify: No deep cuts here – just Powderfinger's biggest singles when they were the dominant Australian rock band of their era.

- Powderfinger – Pick You Up (1996)
- Powderfinger – The Day You Come (1998)
- Powderfinger – Passenger (1998)
- Powderfinger – These Days (2000)
- Powderfinger – My Happiness (2000)
- Powderfinger – (Baby I've Got You) On My Mind (2003)

Chapter 18 – Today Your Love, Tomorrow The World
Spotify: Likewise Savage Garden (this band didn't really do deep cuts).

- Savage Garden – I Want You (1996)
- Savage Garden – To The Moon And Back (1996)
- Savage Garden – Truly Madly Deeply (1997)
- Savage Garden – Affirmation (1999)
- Savage Garden – I Knew I Loved You (1999)

Epilogue – No, Your Product
Spotify: Returning to where we started, with tracks from the Go-Betweens' reformation in 2000–2006, and two cuts from the Saints' reunion at the Pig City concert, held by Queensland Music Festival at the University of Queensland on 14 July 2007 (released in 2009).

The final track is by Scott Kannberg, better known as Spiral Stairs, from US band Pavement. This is not a cover of the Parameters' song, but his own composition, written while he was living in the northern suburbs of Brisbane. Someone loaned him a copy of the book ...

- The Go-Betweens – The Clock (2000)
- The Go-Betweens – Surfing Magazines (2000)
- The Go-Betweens – Finding You (2005)
- The Go-Betweens – Here Comes A City (2005)
- The Saints – The Chameleon (2009)

- The Saints – The Prisoner (2009)
- Spiral Stairs – Pig City (2017)

Scan this code to access the *Pig City* playlist on Spotify.

bibliography

Books

Aird, M. *Brisbane Blacks*, Southport, Queensland, Keeaira Press, 2001.

Birmingham, J. *Off One's Tits*, Sydney, Vintage, 2002.

Blunt, B. *Blunt: A Biased History Of Australian Rock*, Melbourne, Prowling Tiger Press, 2001.

Carolli, L et al. (eds). *Radio Timewarp: Ten Years Of Independent Radio In Brisbane*, Brisbane, Creative Broadcasters, 1985.

Charlton, P. *State Of Mind: Why Queensland Is Different*, Sydney, Methuen Haynes, 1983.

Coaldrake, P. *Working The System: Government In Queensland*, Brisbane, University of Queensland Press, 1989.

Craik, J, Bailey, JJ and Moran, A (eds). *Public Voices, Private Interests: Australia's Media Policy*, Sydney, Allen & Unwin, 1995.

Dickie, P. *The Road To Fitzgerald And Beyond*, Brisbane, University of Queensland Press, 1989.

Doyle, J (ed). *Sounds Like A Jilted Generation: 4ZZZ–FM 1975–1995*, Brisbane, Creative Broadcasters, 1995.

Fitzgerald, R. *From 1915 To The Early 1980s: A History of Queensland*, Brisbane, University of Queensland Press, 1984.

Harris, S. *Political Football: The Springbok Tour Of Australia 1971*, Melbourne, Gold Star, 1972.

Hayward, P (ed). *From Pop To Punk To Postmodernism: Popular Music And Australian Culture From The 1960s To The 1990s*, Sydney, Allen & Unwin, 1992.

Lunn, H. *Joh: The Life And Political Adventures Of Johannes Bjelke-Petersen*, Brisbane, University of Queensland Press, 1978.

Lunn, H. *Behind The Banana Curtain*, Brisbane, University of Queensland Press, 1980.

Johnson, V. *Radio Birdman*, Melbourne, Sheldon Booth, 1990.

McBride, F and Taylor, H. *Brisbane: One Hundred Stories*, Brisbane, Brisbane City Council, 1997.

McFarlane, I. *The Encyclopedia Of Australian Rock And Pop*, Sydney, Allen & Unwin, 1999.

McGahan, A. *Last Drinks*, Sydney, Allen & Unwin, 2000.

Mathieson, C. *The Sell-In: How The Music Business Seduced Alternative Rock*, Sydney, Allen & Unwin, 2000.

Nichols, D. *The Go-Betweens*, Sydney, Allen & Unwin, 1997.

Reynolds, P. *Lock, Stock And Barrel: A Political Biography Of Mike Ahern*, Brisbane, University of Queensland Press, 2002.

Savage, J. *England's Dreaming: The Sex Pistols And Punk Rock*, London, Faber & Faber, 1991.

Spencer, C, Nowara, Z and McHenry, P (eds). *Who's Who Of Australian Rock: Complete Discography Of Every Group* (Fifth Edition), Melbourne, Five Mile Press, 2002.

Walker, C (ed). *The Next Thing: Contemporary Australian Rock*, Sydney, Kangaroo Press, 1984.

Walker, C. *Stranded: The Secret History Of Australian Independent Music 1977–1991*, Sydney, Macmillan, 1996.

Walker, C. *Buried Country: The Story Of Aboriginal Country Music*, Sydney, Pluto Press, 2000.

Wear, R. *Johannes Bjelke-Petersen: The Lord's Premier*, Brisbane, University of Queensland Press, 2002.

Whitton, E. *The Hillbilly Dictator: Australia's Police State*, Sydney, ABC Books, 1989.

Williams, G. *Generation Zed: No Other Radio Like This*, Brisbane, Kingswood, 2000.

Wilson, H (ed). *Australian Communications And The Public Sphere: Essays In Memory Of Bill Bonney*, Melbourne, Macmillan, 1989.

Articles and essays

Anon. Letter to the editor (including reply by Michael Finucan), *Radio Times*, October 1977, pp. 8–9.

Baird, J. (media release) 'Cooper assures future of 4ZZZ Market Days', Creative Broadcasters, 21 October 1996.

Baird, J. (media release) '4ZZZ condemns army whitewash of Military Police assaults on Market Day crowd', Creative Broadcasters, 8 December 1996.

Baker, G. A. 'Australian police raid record store: Guns n' Roses, Dead Kennedys albums nabbed', *Billboard*, 4 March 1989, p. 72.

Beatson, J. 'The 4ZZFM Story (Part 1)', *Radio Times*, vol 1.2, January 1976, p. 4.

Beatson, J. 'The 4ZZFM Story (Part 2)', *Radio Times*, vol 1.4, March 1976, p. 16.

Beatson, J. 'The 4ZZFM Story (Part 3)', *Radio Times*, vol 1.5, April 1976, p. 8.

Birmingham, J. 'It's Raining Cops', *Rolling Stone* 533 (Australia), March 1997, pp. 38–40, 42.

Blake, E. 'Just Desserts? Custard', *Rolling Stone* 540 (Australia), October 1997, pp. 90–92, 94, 96, 128.

Blake, E. 'Kiley Gaffney's Fluffy Rock', *Rolling Stone* 539 (Australia), September 1997, p. 26.

Blake, E. 'Regurgitator: Back to the Future', *Rolling Stone* 544 (Australia), January 1998, pp. 50–55.

Bradley, A. 'Survivors', *Juke*, 15 October 1977, p. 16.

Brazil, V. 'President's Report', *Semper*, March 1989, pp. 33–34.

Brisbane Women's Media Group. 'Triple Z: 'Maintaining Credibility or, Did Homogenised Radio Turn Sour?', *Hecate*, vol 3.1, February 1977, pp. 108–114.

Burke, J. 'Cassette rocks hearing', *Sun*, 15 May 1989, p. 7.

Burke, J. 'Clergyman undeterred by record verdict', *Sun*, 17 May 1989, p. 3.

Bye, C. 'The bitter battle for Brisbane', *Australian*, 31 May 1989, p. 20.

Carney, S. 'Drift/Calling From A Country Phone' (review), *Rolling Stone* 484 (Australia), June 1993, p. 83.

Cameron, R. 'Pub Rock Revived', *Semper*, 7 June 1978, p. 33.

Chen, S. 'Victoria rules the campus', *Sun*, 13 January 1989, p. 19.

Cheverton, J. 'Hello Victoria . . . You're Sacked', *Semper*, No. 3, 1989, p. 37.

Cheverton, J. 'Oh No, Not Another Occupation', *Semper*, No. 2, 1989, p. 8.

Cheverton, J. 'Union Control Out of Control', *Semper*, No. 1, 1989, pp. 4–6.

Counihan, M. ' "Giving a Chance to the Youthful Muse": Radio, Records & the First Australian Music Quota', *Media Information Australia*, No. 64, May 1992, pp. 6–16.

Creswell, T. 'Taking the Low Road to the Top', *Rolling Stone* 472 (Australia), July 1992, pp. 76–77, 94.

Criminal Justice Commission, *Police Behaviour At A Triple Zed Market Day: Report Of An Investigation*, Brisbane, 1997.

Ellis, B. 'Wahooti Fandango? Don't You Worry About That!', *J-Mag*, 1994/1995, pp. 42–46.

Fardon, D. Decision By Bench: *[Constable] Katarina Ruzh Bosnjak Versus Frank Warwick Vere*. Magistrates Court, Brisbane, 16 May 1989, pp. 158–163.

Finucan, M. 'Venue Violence', *Radio Times*, October 1978, p. 7.

Fitzpatrick, K. 'The Blitz Column', *Courier-Mail*, 23 February 1989, p. 33.

Flew, T et. al., *Music Industry Development And Brisbane's Future As A Creative City*, Brisbane, BCC/QUT, 2001.

Gardiner, R. 'Brisbane', *RAM*, 4 November 1977, p. 34.

Gardiner, R. 'Survivors Grow Their Own', *RAM*, 24 February 1978, p. 8.

Gardiner, R. 'Brisbane', *RAM*, 24 March 1978, p. 36.

Gardiner, R. 'Brisbane', *RAM*, 5 May 1978, p. 33.

Grimson, T. 'Powderfinger Break the Barrier', *Rolling Stone* 531 (Australia), January 1997, p. 22, 24.

Guilliatt, R. 'Sign to Suicide or Suicide to Sign?', *RAM*, 2 June 1978, p. 9.

Hall, M. 'Regurgitator', *Rolling Stone* 534 (Australia), April 1997, pp. 62–65.

Hall, M. 'Hot Return: Powderfinger', *Rolling Stone* 580 (Australia), November 2000, pp. 56–60.

Hawker, P. 'Picasso & Me', *Rolling Stone* 482 (Australia), April 1993, p. 24.

Hele, M. 'Military police accused over festival brawl', *Courier-Mail*, 21 October 1996, p. 2.

Hill, B. 'Here's a public chance for defining obscenity', *Age*, 18 March 1982, p. 10.

Humphreys, A. 'Unit' (review), *Rolling Stone* 544 (Australia), January 1998, p. 99.

Hutson, D and Sawford, G. *Out Of The Unknown: Brisbane Bands 1976–1988*, Brisbane: Time Off Publications, 1988.

Johnston, C. 'Burn Out Your Name' (review), *Juice* 8, October 1993, p. 106.

Jones, A. 'Drongos, Yobbos and Derros, Yes. But are Ockers Rockers??', *New Musical Express*, 22 December 1979, pp. 32–33, 77.

Kats, G and Treason, J. 'Who's That Knocking at the Door?', *Soft Option*, Nos. 7/8, December/January 1984, pp. 43–46.

Knowles, D. '21 years gone but still not forgotten', *Sunday Mail*, 9 November 2003, p. 32.

McFarlane, I. 'It's Better to be a Saint than a Sap! The Saints', *Prehistoric Sounds*, vol 1.1, 1994, pp. 2–13.

McFarlane, I. 'The Sound and the Fury! Fun Things', *Prehistoric Sounds*, vol 1.3, 1995, pp. 41–47.

McFarlane, I. 'The Beasts of Bourbon: The Wild, the Willing and the Inner-City Blues', *Prehistoric Sounds*, No. 4, 1996, pp. 2–15.

McFarlane, I. 'Died Pretty: Towers of Strength', *Prehistoric Sounds*, No. 4, 1996, pp. 16–25.

McFarlane, I. 'Pissed On Another Planet: The History of Aussie Punk 1976–83', *Prehistoric Sounds*, No. 4, 1996, pp. 38–50.

McGregor, R. 'Lethal Weapons' (review), *Rolling Stone* (Australia), 27 July 1978.

McKenzie, S. 'Lollapalooza to Livid', *Rolling Stone* 501 (Australia), October 1994, p. 27.

McKenzie, S. 'The Spring Hill Clubhouse', *Rolling Stone* 527 (Australia),

October 1996, pp. 33–34.

Marx, J. 'Parables For Wooden Ears' (review), *Rolling Stone* 499 (Australia), August 1994, p. 90.

Mathieson, C. 'International Arrivals', *Rolling Stone* 554 (Australia), November 1998, pp. 74–76, 78, 81.

Mathieson, C. 'No Pain, No Gain', *Rolling Stone* 568 (Australia), December 1999, pp. 84–87.

Mathieson, C. 'To the Moon & Back', *Rolling Stone* 549 (Australia), June 1998, pp. 72–75, 110–111.

Molitorisz, S. 'Under the Influence', *Rolling Stone* 534 (Australia), April 1997, pp. 29–30.

Munro, K. 'George', *Rolling Stone* 576 (Australia), July 2000, p. 30.

Orr, J and Wockner, C. 'Evicted staff seize studio', *Courier-Mail*, 15 December 1989, p. 1.

Owen, R. 'Moralists want records to be heard, not obscene', *Weekend Australian*, 18–19 February 1989, p. 20.

Phillips, J. 'Vital issues behind the campus capers', *Courier-Mail*, 19 September 1989, p. 9.

Porter, D. 'Radio station 4ZZZ on campus', file note, 21 February 1989.

Potts, J. 'Music on Public Radio', *Media Information Australia*, No. 64, May 1992, pp. 17–23.

Roberts, G. 'Cooper links ALP to drugs', *Sydney Morning Herald*, 9 November 1989, p. 5.

Roberts, G. 'I can't stop gay games, says Premier', *Sydney Morning Herald*, 19 November 1989, p. 5.

Roberts, G. 'Magistrate says the magic word and charges dropped', *Sydney Morning Herald*, 17 May 1989, p. 3.

Roberts, G. 'Nat poll promise: a "porno" rock ban', *Sydney Morning Herald*, 10 November 1989, p. 3.

Roberts, G. 'Qld's morality police aiming at new records', *Sydney Morning Herald*, 1 March 1989, p. 2.

Sawford, G. 'New Faces: A Guide to the New Brisbane Music Scene', *Rolling Stone* 501 (Australia), October 1994, pp. 26–27.

Scatena, D. 'Pop duo ends on sour note', *Daily Telegraph*, 6 October 2001, p. 3.

Scatena, D. 'Solo the loneliest number', *Daily Telegraph*, 6 October 2001, p. 23.

Schloss, G. 'Four-letter word no longer offensive: SM', *Courier-Mail*, 17 May 1989, p. 1.

Sharp, V. 'Lethal Weapons', *Semper*, 24 May 1978, p. 35

Shedden, I. 'Darren Hayes: Miami sound machine', *Weekend Australian*, Review, 9–10 March 2002, pp. 4–6.

Short, J. 'New barrier to imported records', *Australian Financial Review*, 28 July 1977, pp. 1, 8.

Stafford, A. 'Ben Lee vs the World', *Rolling Stone* 560 (Australia), April

1999, pp. 38–39, 110.

Stafford, A. 'Gurge Overkill', *Rolling Stone* 516 (Australia), December 1995, p. 34.

Stafford, A. 'New Faces: A Guide to New Brisbane Bands', *Rolling Stone* 512 (Australia), August 1995, pp. 31–32.

Stafford, A. 'New Faces: Kiley Gaffney', *Rolling Stone* 526 (Australia), September 1996, p. 36.

Stafford, A. 'New Vibrations: The Beach Boys Haunt Screamfeeder', *Rolling Stone* 511 (Australia), July 1995, p. 25.

Stafford, A. 'Redneck Wonderland', *Rolling Stone* 552 (Australia), September 1998, pp. 46–48, 51.

Stafford, A. 'The Human Jukebox', *Rolling Stone* 524 (Australia), July 1996, pp. 24, 26–27.

Street, J. '(Dis)Located? Rhetoric, Politics, Meaning and the Locality' in Straw, W et al. (eds), *Popular Music: Style And Identity*, International Association for the Study of Popular Music, Seventh International Conference Proceedings, Montreal: Centre for Research on Canadian Cultural Industries and Institutions, 1995, pp. 255–263.

Thompson, M. 'Some Issues for Community Radio at the Turn of the Century', *Media International Australia*, No. 91, May 1999, pp. 23–31.

Toohey, P. 'There is Justice in Queensland', *RAM*, 14 June 1989, p. 3.

Vickers, R. 'The Grudge: New Wave', *The Rat*, No. 2, 1977, p. 6.

Walker, C. 'Leftovers', *Pulp*, No. 1, 1977, p. 10.

Walker, C. 'Survivors', *Pulp*, No. 1, 1977, p. 14.

Walker, C. 'Leftovers', *Pulp*, Nos. 3 & 4, 1978, p. 4.

Walker, C. 'The Exchange Hotel; Atcherly House', *Semper*, 15 March 1978, p. 25.

Walker, C. 'The Survivors', *Semper*, 12 April 1978, p. 23.

Walker, C. 'Ed Kuepper: Exile From Main Street', *Rolling Stone* 468 (Australia), March 1992, pp. 57–59, 96.

Walker, J. 'Brisbane: The Late Developer', *Weekend Australian Magazine*, 6–7 September 2003, pp. 22–29.

Ware, M. 'Criminal Record', *Planet*, vol 9.2, 1989, pp. 5–6.

Woodward, L. 'Aboriginal uproar as Tomkins is at it again', *The Australian*, 15 October 1982, p. 11.

Wooldridge, S. 'Wahooti Fandango' (review), *Rolling Stone* 499 (Australia), August 1994, p. 88.

Unattributed articles

'The Aliens', *The Rat*, No. 5, 1978, p. 11.

'The Brisbane Devotee', *Cane Toad Times*, 'Australia's Future?' issue, 1979, pp. 7–10.

'Censorship: More Weirdo Stuff from Queensland', *Gazette Of Law And Journalism*, No. 11, June 1989, p. 7.

'Criminal Records', *RAM*, 8 March 1989, p. 3.

Editorial, *Semper*, No. 5 1989, p. 2.

'FM in Australia: The Background, The Future', *Radio Times*, vol 1.1, December 1975, p. 6.

'4ZZZ High Power', *Radio Times*, vol 1.6, May 1976, p. 11.

'In Depth', *Radio Times*, March 1976, pp. 12–13.

'In Depth', *Radio Times*, October 1976, p. 8.

'Just a matter of taste', editorial, *Courier-Mail*, 20 May 1989, p. 29.

'Land Rights', *Radio Times*, vol 1.1, December 1975, p. 8.

'Music', *Radio Times*, vol 1.1, December 1975, p. 5.

'New venue looks like surviving', *Telegraph*, 29 May 1978, p. 14.

'News and Information', *Radio Times*, vol 1.1, December 1975, p. 4.

'Pick of the Platters of '77', *Radio Times*, January 1978, p. 9.

'Programme Notes: Educational Series', *Radio Times*, vol 1.4, March 1976, pp. 10–11.

'Razar', *The Rat*, No. 5, 1978, p. 11–12.

'Razar', *Fad*, 1978, p. 11.

'Seized records are 'common stock', *Courier-Mail*, 15 February 1989, p. 4.

'Student leader ignores petition for resignation', *Courier-Mail*, 20 April 1989, p. 14.

'Timor', *Radio Times*, vol 1.1, December 1975, p. 8.

'Top Ten', *Radio Times*, January 1977, p. 13.

'University students arrested', *Courier-Mail*, 13 April 1989, p. 3.

'Wow, Sirs! Wowsers . . .', *Radio Times*, May 1977, p. 11.

Websites

Not all of the following may still be in their cited locations online.

Barclay, P. 'Queensland: 10 years after Fitzgerald', Radio National, 16 May 1999, URL: http://www.abc.net.au/rn/talks/bbing/stories/s26032. htm

Dunn, P. 'Camp Luna Park/Cloudland Ballroom: Brisbane, QLD during WW2', URL: http://home.st.net.au/~dunn/locations/camplunapark. htm.

Kimball, D. 'The Saints: The Most Primitive Band in the World', URL: http://saints.binke.com.au/

King, M and Bell, J. Brispop.com, URL: http://www.brispop.com.au/

Knight, A. 'Won't Get Fooled Again', Brisbane Institute, URL: http://www.brisinst.org.au/resources/knight_zzz.html

Macpherson, D. 'Early Punk Brisbands (1977–82)', URL: http://homepage.powerup.com.au/~toxico/brisband.htm

McLeod, R. 'Young Identities', and David Holliday, 'Just Urbain'. Both on Ryan Richardson's Break My Face site, devoted to late '70s/early '80s punk collectables. Follow the links from www.breakmyface. com

Van Kempen, E. 'Vanishing Queensland: Reader Contributions – Cloudland', URL: http://www.nationaltrustqld.org/cgi-bin1/memories.pl

Willis, L. 'Joh Bjelke-Petersen and Terry Lewis seeking compensation for Fitzgerald Inquiry', *PM*, 19 August 2003, reprinted online: http://www.abc.net.au/pm/content/2003/s927935.htm

Other articles and web pages:

'Cloudland Ballroom', URL: http://www.geocities.com/milesago2001/cloudland.htm

Interview with Brad Shepherd, i94 bar, URL: http://www.i94bar.com/ints/bradshepherd.html

Interview with Ed Wreckage on Dropkick Records site, URL: http://www.dropkick.com.au/ (follow link to the Leftovers)

Powderfinger, URL: www.powderfinger.com

Powderfinger Central, URL: http://www.ozmusic-central.com.au/powderfinger/central.htm

The Saints Directory, URL: http://www.xs4all.nl/~cjbailey/directory.htm – Chris Bailey's official Saints site.

Recording notes

Burke, M. Liner notes for re-release of *Shutdown Countdown* EP, vinyl 7", 2001. (Technically this was not a reissue: remaining copies of the original EMI custom-pressed EP, between 80–100, were rounded up and released with the picture sleeve intended for its original release in 1979.)

Forster, R. Liner notes for the Go-Betweens' *78 'til 79: The Lost Album*, Jetset Records CD, catalogue no. TWA019CD, 1999.

Holliday, D. Liner notes for the Leftovers' *The Fucken Leftovers Hate You*, Dropkick Records CD, catalogue no. BEHIND006, 2003. (The liner notes for this album also contained a wealth of other reprinted articles and letters.)

Lee, S. Liner notes for the Go-Betweens' reissued *Send Me A Lullaby*, Circus Records CD, catalogue no. FYL009, 2002.

Male, A. Liner notes for the Go-Betweens' reissued *Before Hollywood*, Circus Records CD, catalogue no. FYL010, 2002.

McFarlane, I. 'Memories Are Made of This', liner notes for the Saints' *Wild About You 1976–1978*, Raven CD, catalogue no. RVCD–107, 2000.

Shepherd, B. Liner notes for the reissued *Fun Things* EP, vinyl 7", Pennimann Records, 2000.

Walker, C. Liner notes for the Saints' *Scarce Saints: Hymns Of Oblivion 1977–1984*, Raven CD, catalogue no. RVCD–04, 1989.

Unattributed:
Liner notes for Various Artists, *At The Führer's Request* . . . vinyl LP, Rubber Records 001, 1985. Later amended to *At The Solicitor's Request* . . . under legal duress. See discography for further details.
Liner notes for Various Artists, *Behind The Banana Curtain 1975–2000*, Warner Music CD, catalogue no. 8573861182, 2000.

permissions

Song credits
p. 1 'Lee Remick' © Forster/McLennan (licensed by Festival/Mushroom
Publishing, obo Complete Music); p. 68 'Nights In Venice' 1977 © Kuepper/
Bailey (Mushroom Music Publishing) p. 75 'Brisbane (Security City)'
© Kuepper (Mushroom Music Publishing) p. 81 'Karen' © Forster/McLennan
(licensed by Festival/Mushroom Publishing, obo Complete Music); p. 94 'Don't
Let Him Come Back' © Forster/McLennan (licensed by Festival/Mushroom
Publishing, obo Complete Music); p. 104 'Task Force (Undercover Cops)' © Burke/
Razar (Control); p. 119 'Help' © Walsh (Control); p. 123 'Mr Somewhere' © Walsh
(Complete Music); p. 146 'Cattle And Cane' © Forster/McLennan (licensed by
Festival/Mushroom Publishing, obo Complete Music); pp. 152–3 'Pig City' © Kneipp
(Control); p. 160 'Brisbane Blacks' © Conlon (Control); p. 164 'Thou Shalt Not Steal'
© Carmody (Song Cycles); p. 166 'Black Deaths In Custody' © Carmody (Song
Cycles); p. 174 'Brisbane '82' © Kennedy (Control); p. 174 'SEQEB Scabs' © de
Hesse (Control); p. 176 'Too Much Acid' © Pineapples from the Dawn of Time
(Shoddy Productions); p. 205 'Cyclone Hits Expo' © Choo Dikka Dikka (Control);
p. 238 'Melody' © McCormack (Universal); p. 246 'I Want To Be Quiet' © Forster
(licensed by Festival/Mushroom Publishing, obo Complete Music); p. 255 'Fantastic
Plastic' © McCormack (Universal); p. 281 'Music Is Sport' © Yeomans (EMI Music
Publishing); p. 285 'I Will Lick Your Arsehole' © Yeomans (EMI Music Publishing).

Text credits
Permission to quote from Andrew McGahan's *Last Drinks* kindly granted by Allen
& Unwin. Permission to quote from Clinton Walker's *Stranded* kindly granted by
Pan Macmillan.

acknowledgments

Pig City began as the thesis component of an MA in Creative Writing undertaken at the Faculty of Creative Industries, Queensland University of Technology. My thanks go to the staff and students of the faculty, in particular those in the schools of journalism, media studies and creative writing. Special thanks to my supervisors, Donna Lee Brien and Jason Sternberg, and to Joanne Shepherd, who helped steady my course during the inevitable rocky periods.

Thanks to everybody at University of Queensland Press, especially Laurie Muller and Madonna Duffy, who bravely punted on this project when it was in its infancy. (Madonna's ongoing support for this book – including this new edition – spans its entire two-decade run.) Nick Earls, with typical generosity, helped talk them into it. Julia Stiles was a sensitive and thorough editor. Judi McCrossin and Ewan Burnett at Burberry Productions gave me a handy gig undertaking research for a drama series based on the adventures of Triple Zed, research that was also essential to this project.

Additional thanks for this 20th anniversary edition go to Tony Giacca, who reworked his original cover design, to Eamon Sandwith, and to the many other artists who have honoured *Pig City* by speaking so kindly of its impact on them.

Jeff Cheverton, Tony Kneipp and Greg Williamson all entrusted me with personal scrapbooks full of material I would otherwise have spent hundreds of hours searching for. Jane Grigg helped track down several elusive contacts. Tony Kneipp graciously allowed me the use of the title *Pig City* itself. Thanks are also due to the staff past and present at Skinny's and Rocking Horse Records, especially Warwick Vere, Cheryl Bliss, Phil Smith, Tam Patton and Richard Hunt.

Last and most of all, I extend my gratitude to all those who gave freely of their time to be interviewed, not only for their generosity, but for their enormous artistic and cultural contributions that have made Brisbane a better place to live. They are the collective inspiration behind this book, and I can only hope I've done their achievements appropriate justice.

This book is dedicated to Simon McKenzie and Craig Wilson, my Rock & Roll Friends, and to my mother, Sue (1947–2023).

index